Elizabeth: One of Many
1940-74

ALSO BY BISHOP & FULLER

Co-Creation: Fifty Years in the Making
Mythic Plays: from Inanna to Frankenstein
Rash Acts: Thirty Snapshots for the Stage
Seven Fabulist Comedies
Realists
Galahad's Fool
Blind Walls
Akedah: the Binding
Masks
Frankenstein: DVD
The Tempest: DVD
Descent of the Goddess Inanna: DVD

Available at
www.independenteye.org
or
www.damnedfool.com

Elizabeth Fuller

Elizabeth: One of Many

A Memoir of Discovery: 1940-74

WordWorkers Press
Sebastopol, CA

Elizabeth: One of Many
1940-74

© 2022 Elizabeth Fuller

All rights reserved. This work is fully protected under the copyright laws of the United States of America and all other countries of the Copyright Union.

No part of this publication may be reproduced in any form without prior consent of the copyright holders, except in the case of brief quotes embodied in critical articles and reviews.

Printed in the United States of America.

For information:
indepeye@gmail.com

For purchases:
www.damnedfool.com

ISBN: 978-0-9997287-9-6
LCCN: 2022902045

CONTENTS

Preface — 1
Her Name Is Elizabeth — 5
Seven Sisters — 15
Sail On! — 26
Imaginary Numbers — 38
Kicked Out — 56
Home Again — 68
Well, Let's Do It — 80
Fraud — 94
Music — 104
Rehab — 112
Learning the Craft — 128
Grits — 141
Milwaukee — 162
Coping — 174
Theatre X — 188
Fits and Starts — 203
New Life — 211
Sink or Swim — 231

PREFACE

In February of 2020, I turned eighty. It felt really good to be eighty, flat-out 100% eighty, not "almost eighty," as I had been claiming for a while. It's a lovely number. Round and balanced and substantial, like me. I'm a short solid blue-eyed blonde; I've kept the hair California-colored, medium-length, and like to wear it loose when it's fluffy. My legs are good from the gym, ditto butt, but there's definitely a little belly. I'm working on that, so at least it's fairly round and high. Ditto breasts. My face looks pretty much as it did when I was fifty.

"Elizabeth, you're not eighty, you're shitting me!"

"Wanna see my driver's license?"

We partied the whole weekend, and it was right up there on the scale of peak experiences, the perfect punctuation mark to the past twenty years in California. Our son Eli came up from San Francisco, and daughter Johanna flew in from her long-time home in Italy, with a recipe list and an agenda: "Mama, I'm doing the cooking. Get over it." She arrived on Tuesday, shopped with me on Wednesday, cooked all day Thursday and Friday, and staged it all to completion on Saturday and Sunday. More than forty people came to our Sebastopol home over the two days. This was my day, and here came the folks who would make it real.

Conrad kept watch on the front door to prevent our two house cats from becoming roadkill. Most everyone brought a card, so there was a gorgeous array on the fireplace hearth. Our huge walnut dining table was covered with goodies, and Jo's food was a Dutch painting, a portrait of abundance. Because the invitation was described as a drop-in any time between noon and nine, most times there were anywhere from six to ten folks gathered, so it was possible to embrace and talk to everyone.

Ah, the people—a road-map to my life. A dawn caress from Conrad, my mate for nearly sixty years: "Happy birthday, my sweet." An exhausted furious hug from our daughter at the airport: "Goddamn! Two hours in line. Hello Mama, Papa!" A Sunday morning call from our son, en route: "Where are you? I thought we were meeting at HardCore!" And Flora, beloved artist, colleague and friend since 1966, who flew in from Milwaukee on Friday: "Johanna! It's been—how many years has it been?"

The gang of five, husband and wife, son, daughter, friend, heartstrings measuring the years of connection (sixty, forty-seven, forty-five, fifty-four) with this eighty-year-old. Never mind that the freezer had chosen the crucial moment to go on strike; it had been building up to it for two weeks, either freezing the vodka solid or flirting with thawing everything. The repair guy replaced one part but had to special-order the main control panel, which would take a week, so we bought blocks of ice, cooked up a storm, hauled out the wine, and started welcoming the people who appeared from the many layers of my life.

The layers? We've been students, teachers, parents, writer/performers, radio producers, puppet-makers, modern pagans dancing naked around bonfires, and remaining devoted to each other for nearly sixty years while having some wonderful lovers. We met at Northwestern, lived briefly in Evanston, moved to California for Conrad's PhD, taught in South Carolina, moved to Milwaukee, toured over most of the Midwest with Theatre X,

Preface

surprising ourselves by getting pregnant just as the teaching nest-egg ran out. We split off to form The Independent Eye, lived in Chicago while having another baby, then moved to Lancaster PA while touring the country and renovating our own theatre. When both kids were out of school, we ran a theatre in Philadelphia for seven years, then finally moved back to California, the sweet town of Sebastopol, our own house, and this party.

And these people. Performers: I played Flora's daughter in our adaptation of *Hecuba* at the University of South Carolina in 1967; in 1969 we persuaded her to come join our company in Milwaukee. Our friends Michael and Valerie have made a remarkable life creating and touring puppetry globally, supporting themselves with their shows while loving each other madly and raising a son. Anthony was Caliban in our *Tempest* and showed up fresh from paragliding: "Hey, anybody wanna learn to fly?" And the most essential folk in theatre, the audiences: Lou was there when *Dream House* was at an arts center: "Girl, I will never forget when your clown took off all her clothes."

Many beloveds from our years of polyamory: three friends were chatting in the living-room when a tall good-looking man appeared at the front door. "Hey, guys, it's my New York lover!"

Fellow writers. Fellow pagans. Fellow artists. Fellow humans. And far-off friends wrote some extravagant emails:

> *Elemental, yes you are. Root and stem of joy and sorrow. Bud and bloom of please and satisfy, blue flame of spirit ascendant...*
>
> *You just keep growing, morphing, and getting more beautiful...*

I never imagined I would grow up to be someone described this way. I have been a compulsive liar, a shoplifter, a forger, a sexual pirate, and now and then a suicidal wreck. At the same time I'm a professional actress who can do electrical wiring, sound design, set construction, and double-entry bookkeeping; I have two grown kids; I've composed over fifty musical scores for theatre;

and I still please my man in bed. I'm embarrassed to include those quotes, but I should take my daughter's advice: "Just get over it."

In 2010 when Conrad and I wrote a joint fifty-year memoir, it was a new way of seeing our life together, and I loved the view. Ten years have passed, and I want to do the same thing for myself. I have been many people, and some of them are hard to face. I want to take each one by the hand, look her in the eye, acknowledge her, maybe read her the riot act, and then embrace the whole bunch.

Revisiting some of these scenes has been pretty sweaty, but this is not an entry in the poor-me sweepstakes. I know plenty of women who have been through much worse, I've played some epic transgressors on stage, and I've learned something from every story. Battling depression and dissociation has been a life-long challenge, but this is not a memoir about recovery. It's about discovery.

1.
Her Name Is Elizabeth

From a carton of my adoptive mother's old letters and diaries, it was clear that our relationship got off to a rocky start. On a cold February 24th in 1940 Homer and Mary Davison scraped the ice off the windshield of their new gray Chevy, put their Swedish house-helper Olive in the back seat, alongside a roast turkey and a baby basket, and started the 800-mile drive from Indiana to Brooklyn. They made slow time on the icy roads and stopped overnight in Pennsylvania.

The girl who would be theirs had been born nine days ago, and their attorney told them to be at Riverdale Hospital on the 26th to collect their baby. Mary's long-time friends Doris and Mac lived in a residential hotel near Times Square where they would spend Sunday night; the turkey was a dinner gift. Olive was given a movie ticket to see Raymond Massey in *Abe Lincoln in Illinois* at Radio City Music Hall, allowing the friends a chance to share excitement about the new daughter.

Early Monday morning Homer and Mary went a few blocks up Eighth Avenue to the attorney's office, got their paperwork, and headed for Brooklyn with Olive. It was a tense half-hour; sleet had cleared up overnight, but it was very cold, and traffic on the Brooklyn Bridge was slow. The highways were still icy, so they'd bought Olive a ticket to take the baby home by plane and get picked up at the South Bend airport by family friends. Homer's lobbying job required him to be in Washington DC that same day, so the plan was to find the hospital, get the baby, and drive to the airport in time for Olive's 3:05 flight. The new parents would go straight to Washington; on Tuesday Mary would start driving alone back to Indiana.

She had lived in Manhatttan in her drama school days, so for her this was familiar territory, but for Olive it was another world. The long dark of the Lincoln Tunnel had frightened her, but today the arches of the Brooklyn Bridge made up for it: "Mrs. Dah-vi-son, why are they building churches on the bridge?" She never imagined there would be so many green parks in a big city, and she was startled to see crowds of Blacks in Bedford-Stuyvesant's neighborhood of Victorian houses. As they drove into East New York, things got shabbier, and Riverdale Hospital was not impressive: a long squat two-story brick structure that looked like a high school. Street parking was easy.

They left Olive in the car, grabbed their paperwork and baby basket. Their lawyer had called ahead, and they were expected. After presenting their papers, they were taken to a room and asked to wait; Mary sat in the only chair. Before long a nurse wheeled in a little metal trolley topped by a quilted basinette, looked at their papers, and left. "Take your time, and check in with the front desk when you're ready to leave." The baby in the box was asleep, covered by a light blanket. Homer and Mary looked at each other, then at the baby. A long moment of silence, and Homer checked his watch. "We'd better get ready to go." They had brought a hooded wrapper, but Mary had never faced dressing an infant before: the first of many challenges to come. She succeeded in getting the tiny arms and legs wrapped up, but it took so long that they were nearly late for the plane.

They ran to the car, got Mary settled with the baby in her arms, and allowed the shivering Olive a quick peek before Homer started the car. A crosstown rush, and forty-five minutes later, they were at the airport. New York Municipal Airport (not renamed LaGuardia until 1953) had just opened three months ago, and they'd been startled to find it surrounded by stretches of mud and sand. The car joined the departure lines and crawled to the foot of the semi-circular drive that led up to the terminal entrance. They pulled as close as possible to the big glass doors and nestled the baby in the basket: "Here, Olive, take the baby and run, the plane's just about to take off!" No one had thought to provide a bottle of milk.

Homer and Mary watched as the young woman with the heavy coat, suitcase, and wicker basket hustled through the doors and disappeared. They had been with their daughter for less than an hour. The cab behind them leaned on its horn; they drove down the ramp and headed for Washington DC. Mary stayed with Homer that night in his DC hotel, then started back to Valparaiso, driving slick roads alone through the foggy Alleghenies and on through West Virginia, Ohio, and southern Indiana. The journey took her three days; she would be on her own for eleven weeks before Homer came home.

Back on February 15th at Riverdale Hospital, after her 6-pound 11-ounce baby was born, there was no record of the birth mother's first conscious experience. It might have been the cheerful voice of a nurse:

"Oh hello, Sweetie, you're awake. How do you feel?"
"Boy or girl?"
"Now, now, you know you're not supposed to…"
"Boy or girl?"
"Girl."
"When can I see her?"
"I'm sorry."

The hospital had an Unconditional Surrender of Parental Rights, allowing no physical contact, but soon a clerk came to the room with clipboard, forms, and a pen.

"What are you going to name her?"

"I can do that?"

"Yes you can. It will go on the original birth certificate. No one can see it, but it will still be there. Do you need time to think, or do you already know?"

"Elizabeth. Her name is Elizabeth."

It would be seventy-eight years before that baby discovered she'd been given her mother's own name. My amended birth certificate substituted the names my mother had chosen. *Linda* was for the pretty daughter of a friend, and *Ellen* was Mary's mother's name. My mother was charmed that by spelling "*Ellen*" differently, she could make the end of the middle name run into the beginning of the last name and repeat "*Linda*." *Linda Ellin Davison*, that was me.

The baby's eleven-day stay in the Brooklyn hospital had been in a room full of bassinets, and she was held only by the nurses responsible for feeding and changing her. Out of the birth canal, into a padded box, fed by a schedule, then suddenly taken for a cold bumpy ride through the streets of Brooklyn and Queens—boarding the plane, feeling the roar of the props, getting "airplane ear" at stops in Buffalo and Detroit, and finally getting off at South Bend, Indiana. Was the journey a nightmare?

∼

I had the dream recurrently until well into my twenties. Over and over, I would be walking a dirt road into the woods behind my childhood home, where I saw the same thing: a little conical hut on stilts, and overhead a huge dragonfly with searchlight eyes. I'd wake up and wonder why that image so terrified me. Years later, I was on a trip to pick up someone at a small airport. It was dusk, the control tower had a conical roof, the aircraft's landing lights completed the picture, and I suddenly saw my nightmare. I broke out in a sweat, my heart hammering. At eleven days old, hungry and terrified, I'd arrived after dark at a cold windy airport and was carried through the sleet to a car. I researched that Indiana airport and found a vintage photograph. There it was: my nightmare in black and white.

∼

Who were my new father and mother?

In 1899, Homer Davison was born ouside Marshall, a little farm town in central Illinois. He never lost his country roots, though his family later moved to the state capital, Springfield. A student at the University of Illinois, he spent his summers working on livestock and grain farms. His major was animal husbandry, and after he graduated in 1921, he was hired by the Chicago Live Stock Exchange.

He had a big frame, over six feet and a solid build. A strong and ambitious man, his essential nature was sweet and caring. At the age of twenty-five he became a Vice President at the American Meat Institute, the Chicago-based trade association for meatpackers and livestock producers; his major job was lobbying. As the momentum of war built, his ability as a lobbyist attracted attention, and he spent more and more time in Washington DC. He worked his way up to be President of the AMI from 1957 to his retirement in 1963. His career was in business, but his true joy was in the farm-country world of the earthy and tangible.

He married in 1928, bought a northern Indiana farmhouse and 85 acres in 1935, and joined the ranks of Chicago commuters. He kept all kinds of animals on the land, butchered hogs himself, and built a smokehouse for the hams. His business connections made it possible for him to bring home a side of prime beef and cut it down for the freezer. He put in a vegetable garden, and his pride was the sweet corn that didn't get picked till the kettle was boiling.

Hunting was a passion; he loved his succession of bird dogs, and every fall he took a couple of weeks to hunt pheasant, grouse, and woodcock from the base camp of his wife's little cottage in Cadillac, Michigan. Woodworking was another hobby, and his basement shop had good equipment—table saw, lathe, drill press, band saw—and racks of fragrant lumber. Most of his projects were furniture, but sometimes his imagination seized bigger projects. When he got a certain look, eyeing a wall of the house, it was inevitable that sledgehammers came into play, a new foundation was laid, stud walls reared their heads, and a new room would appear.

His greatest passion was Mary. Their love was intense, though sex was problematic for them both. He had adored his mother and never forgave his father for cheating on her again and again; and it didn't help that his college fraternity had a traditional initiation ritual, a trip to a Black whorehouse. On their wedding night he wept: he had hurt her.

His business had him away from home for months at a time, and he wrote often. Some fragments from letters:

March 4 — I'm going to try and get away the end of this week…
March 14 — I've made a reservation to come home on Easter…
April 16 — Dearest, I don't know when I can get home…
April 19 — I am figuring on getting home next Friday…
April 24 — I'm leaving Friday night. I think I will have to come back in a week or so.

∼

Elna Maria Magnuson was born in 1892 in Menominee, Michigan, and inherited her Norwegian mother's fair coloring and her Swedish father's jaw and chin. Her mother had come to the USA as a child and landed as an orphan: both parents died on the voyage. The seven little girls were fostered out among different Norwegian families, and when Ellen Olive Johnson was seventeen, she married a thirty-year-old Swede. She had Elna when she was eighteen and a son three years later. The marriage was harsh, and Ellen became unstable: once the children stood outside a locked bedroom door beating their little fists against it and crying, "Mama, Mama, don't!" She had yelled through the door that she was killing herself.

In 1905 Ellen got a divorce and sent her daughter to boarding school. Elna went on to Augustana College and drama school: the American Academy of Dramatic Arts in New York. After graduation, she got her first engagement: only a bit part but on Broadway. After war and the flu pandemic disrupted her progress in theatre, she switched to comedy, changed her name to Mary Manson, and had a ten-year career in vaudeville performing all over the country. A natural comedienne, she was earning good money in a colorful profession. Her father had torn her mother to pieces, the men she worked with were either cheating or gay, and she swore she'd never marry. Then she met the man who changed her mind, and, in her diary's words, she "*discontinued theatre.*"

When they met, she was touring with Harry J. Conley's company, booked into a good slot in the "LeMaire's Affairs" revue at the Woods Theatre in the Chicago Loop. Vaudeville was the TV of the time, a circuit of theatres all over the country with ever-changing bills of entertainment managed by two big bookers, Keith-Albee in the East and Orpheum in the west. Chicago was roaring in 1927, and young executives drank and clubbed a lot, with a taste for the louche. Prohibition was a joke. Mobsters rubbed elbows with the white-collar set, and so did entertainers.

One Tuesday after work, the young executive went to the Woods Theatre, a short six blocks north of his high-rise office building. He saw the hearty comic actress and was smitten. It took him a dedicated year of courtship, but in 1928 they married into a lifelong love bond. She gave up the theatre career that had made her an independent woman. In her 1930 journal she wrote: "*I want a baby. Please.*" She was nearly forty years old; she had told Homer she was thirty-two.

At first the loss of the stage wasn't so bad; she was in love and she had a vital urban life in Chicago with a circle of good friends. The Depression hit, but it didn't cramp their style. He had an executive job in the Chicago Loop. They had a woman to cook and clean. She took piano lessons, French lessons, and even studied painting with a well-known artist. They ate steaks. Chicago was good to them.

In 1935, Homer made his dreams of country living a reality. Friends had bought a place near Valparaiso and urged them to think about moving. They visited often, liked what they saw, bought land and a farmhouse nearby, and moved in on September 14th. He wrote a note to her, which she kept in her diary:

> *I'm awfully happy tonight, do you know it? I always wanted to live on a farm. I'm going to live out here always, I know it.*

In the first years, they often made trips to Chicago, had dinner parties at their new house, and some of their Chicago friends moved to the area. But no baby was forthcoming. Once it was clear that pregnancy would not happen, they began to investigate adoption. A well-respected agency turned them down, likely because of age, so they turned to the grey market and found a pregnant young woman who would surrender her baby to persons unknown. They had her checked out: a good student at UW/Madison, literate, musical, white, Episcopalian. An attorney from a New York firm was retained to handle the details, the girl was sent east. He had an executive job in the Chicago Loop, and all they had to do was wait. When the time came, the baby came.

The newborn was reliant on a woman who had no idea how to be a mother: by now nearly 48 years old, no experience with children, in charge of a creature in a big house in the country. Mary's beloved husband, the center of her life for eleven years, wasn't there when the baby cried at midnight. He wasn't there to talk his loving baby-talk when she got her hands dirty changing diapers. She tried to bond with a baby at a time of desperate loneliness.

Her Name Is Elizabeth

I always knew I was adopted. I was told, "We really wanted you." But it never occurred to me that I grew in a woman's belly. Somehow I imagined—long after I knew how babies were born—that I got delivered in a box. Boxes could get sent back.

Being adopted carried with it an obligation. I was accused of not loving enough: "Maybe I should just divorce you. You don't know how to love. You want me to do that?" I didn't know anything about other families, I just knew that I was uniquely defective, I was adopted.

Breaking a child's will was prominent in published advice on child-rearing in the Thirties and Forties, and it was pretty grim. Rigid schedules for feeding and toilet-training backed it up. Crying? Don't let them do it. My mother had never been around small children and had no friends who had them. Her years of desire for a baby gave her plenty of time to read up on raising a child, and most of what I experienced was prescribed in behaviorist books.

"Sit! Stay! Don't move unless I tell you." That wasn't to the dog, it was to me, two years old, the time when kids discover that they have a will and give parents stories to tell about the Terrible Twos. "No, sit down or I'll smack you, I mean it!" Dogs can learn, and so could I. Baby Linda became obedient, and when I made a mistake, I lied: anything to avoid rousing anger. "Did you wet your pants?" "I faw down in a puddle." I lied often.

Misbehaving had consequences. In our house, there was a narrow corridor between the main entry hall and the kitchen. Above the counter on one side were cabinets with mixing bowls, utility plates, cups, and glasses. Below the counter were cabinets down to the floor, eye level for me as a toddler, and one day I had lots of fun hauling out the pots and pans. They made a wonderful noise as I stacked them into towers, banged them on each other, and made a rowdy clatter. I was told not to, did it again, and was told louder. When I did it again, my mother crammed me into the now-empty cabinet, slammed the door shut, and left me wadded up in the dark until I stopped crying. I never went near the pots again.

"What's the matter with you? What's the *matter* with you?" She actually expected an answer. I'd cry; I was terrified and couldn't help it. "Stop crying, stop it right now!" With her dog-training methods, she was trying to raise me right, doing the best she knew. I was gifted: I learned fast.

"Finish your dinner. You've got five minutes."

"Not hungry!"

"Do as you're told or you'll get a spanking." I think that was the only time I ever got spanked. I was so humiliated that I actually got sick, ran a fever, and got put to bed. No more spanking.

When my mother was feeling good, her smooth round face was funny and happy. I could never predict when it would transform into the essence of rage, blazing full force. It would happen in an instant: she became another being. A big blonde woman whose ivory-skinned face could turn bright red, her years of being on stage had given her a powerful voice and a razor-sharp tongue. She scared the hell out of me.

There are no splints for a broken will.

2.

Seven Sisters

In 1975 I was creating a character enmeshed in a situation of child abuse, and I needed to do some research to give me a framework. My actor's instincts were coming up with things that felt right, but I didn't know anything about abuse as a social issue, so I got recommendations from people in the field and started reading. At first, I was reacting to somebody else's nightmare. I could read the horrific descriptions of physical abuse as something outside my own experience and be profoundly disturbed, but I'd file it mentally as necessary material. Then I encountered stories of emotional abuse, the shaming and denigration that wound deeply but leave no visible scars, and my mind froze. These stories weren't somebody else's nightmare, I knew them myself. This is how I grew up.

I'd always been sure my problems were my own fault, the result of my unique inadequacy. Stepping to the other side of the mirror and seeing that I wasn't alone was a shock. I immediately recoiled and rejected the thought. No, I was given everything, I wasn't abused. How can I say that about my mother?

I had to work it through and ask Conrad to help me. This was an important play we were creating together, and I couldn't afford to ignore what I could bring from my own past. We talked, I read more cases, I replayed old scenes in my mind, and when it gradually got through to me, I was overwhelmed with the unfairness. It took work to let honest anger have its place, but when it did something useful came with it. Once I planted my feet on solid ground and let the rage rip, I found a new strength.

Later I found a door to forgiveness and even empathy. It was years in coming, and by the time I might have had guts enough to try to talk honestly with my mother, alcohol and dementia had shut the door. In writing this, I revisit both my pain and hers. Fault is an irrelevant concept. Neither of us was choreographer of our dance.

～

For me, survival meant guessing what role I was expected to play and then doing my best to play it. At two, I'd been taught all forty-eight state capitals by rote: "Ohio?" "Cumblumpus." "Kansas?" "Peeka." "Florida?" "Tassy." It made no sense to me, but I got praise when I was correct and a scolding when I goofed. Eventually I got all the syllables right, and when they took me along to friends' parties, it became a game. People took turns giving me states' names, and laughed and applauded at my answers. "What a brain! You're only two? Aren't you a smart little thing!" I started early with learning my lines.

By four, I'd taught myself to read and soon had a new role in party games. "Here, Linda, take this book and just open it somewhere. What does it say?" No chance to learn my lines in advance, but the grown-ups loved the mistakes. The worst I remember was the story of Cupid and Psyche. I made a wild guess at Psyche—"Pea-sick"—that brought down the house. I nearly peed my pants. If I'd been one of those adults, I would have laughed too. They clapped and meant it as praise, but it felt like raw mockery.

When I was five, I got a brother. From what I overheard, my dad spoke as if he were buying another hunting dog. He and a friend had each wanted to adopt a boy. Something pointed them toward Oklahoma, and they went down together to check the possibilities. They found two baby boys and more or less tossed a coin to see who got which. So that's how you did it: you went to the baby store and got a baby.

When the baby came home, they had our family doctor check out their choice, and they took me along. Dr. Poncher stripped the baby, inspected, poked and thumped, then listened with his stethoscope. "Well, you've got a good one here. Healthy, good heart and lungs, strong bones." "You're sure about the heart? The other one had a blue-baby problem." "Nope, good baby here." I assumed a defective one could be sent back.

My brother Chris was everything I wasn't. He was happy, gregarious, playful and loud, with beautiful brown eyes. Eventually he tired of people cooing, "Where did you get those big brown eyes?" "They came with my head."

I craved solitude and silence and didn't adapt well. Later I saw how readily he could get out of scrapes just by being who he was, and I felt gypped, but he had the awful burden of having my brain held over him like a hammer. The worst thing about that was that he had a good time anyway.

We never succeeded in becoming siblings, which I regret deeply. We never grew into a joint story, and so he is not present in these pages. His story was his own, and it is not mine to tell.

I have holes in my memory. When I was brought home, a high school girl from down the road had been hired to be a helper. Alice was in charge of things like cuddling and feeding and changing diapers and such. I have not the slightest memory of her, even though she was there past my first birthday: when my parents took me to New York in 1941 to get my adoption finalized, they took Alice along. A few months later, my mother wrote in her diary:

I hope you and Alice continue to know each other when you grow older. She is so lovely and dear and good. And you love her ever so much more than you love any of us now. But we hope to deserve more love from you as you grow.

At age eighty, when I read that diary, I wept. *And you love her ever so much more than you love any of us now.* It must have hurt to write that. I can now hear pain as well as anger when she'd yell, "You don't love me! You don't know how to love!"

But I did: Alice, she said I loved you. Thank you for your gentle sweetness. How is it that I don't remember you at all? The girl who held and cuddled and fed me? And when did you leave? I have no idea.

∽

I really like that little kid, the one I was for a while. My moon-loving pagan self is grateful that I was blessed with a strong early love of the earth, the dirt, the freedom to wander in the woods and fields. Once I started down the cattle chute of "genius" and "prodigy" things got gnarly, and being told over and over that I had no heart had its effect. But as long as I could get out in the woods and get dirt under my nails, I had my own world.

The little kid had two faces. There was Woods Girl and House Girl. Woods Girl took every chance to ramble and be in the dirt. On the hill south of our house, the sandy soil was loose and warm, and I loved digging downward-sloping, arm-sized tunnels. Once I was inspired to bury a treasure. I pooped and scooped it in and felt really proud of my gift.

When I was Woods Girl, I was happy in my body. The milkweed pods didn't care whether I wore glasses—they gave me their silky poof to blow into the wind. My apple tree didn't read my report cards, she just let me snuggle. Woods Girl loved seeds. There was a huge bush of trumpet-vine near the house. I loved to crawl underneath, pluck a flower, and sip its drop of nectar. When the pods dried, I could scoop out the feathery seeds. They were dark amber, with a small black center and a crisp transparent halo like a priest's hat. I would gather enough to bury my hands and feel the incomparable beauty of their slithery shapes. The pleasure was so keen it made me want to sing.

As a small child I was strong, agile, and a fearless explorer. We had an old barn that was full of unexplained lumber and tools and spiderwebs puffy with dust. Half the ground floor was parking for our two cars, and one corner in the back had been converted into a smokehouse for hams. But there was an upstairs, and I loved to prowl around up there—it felt so exotic. Why I never fell through the ceiling I don't know.

What did get me was the pile of old garden equipment by the front entrance. I tripped and fell into the gaggle of forks and handles, winding up with the sharp tine of a pitchfork sticking through my calf. I don't remember the pain, I just detached myself and went to show my mother. She freaked out enough for both of us.

"Go outside and play" didn't come with a lot of don'ts. We had a vegetable garden on the west side of the barn, and I'd yank a carrot up, brush it off, and chomp. My father raised a few chickens, but not every year; when the chicken-house was vacant, it smelled funky, but it was all mine, my secret cabin in the woods. Those woods were all mine too. Wild, no paths other than those made by roaming animals; not many brambles, mostly cool fragrant shade, with evergreens to make it smell like wine. There was one stretch of fence between woods and a bare field, but it had a stile: little magic stairs out in the middle of nothing.

I had the whole twelve volumes of *My Book House*, and in some of those stories there were people who could see and talk to fairies. I was sure it was real, and I wanted so much to do that. Part of my compulsion to go wandering out into the fields and the woods was the deep conviction that there was a special place somewhere that nobody knew about. If I could discover it, I would find the fairies or at least something that could recognize me as one of their own.

I did find a place like that, a little boggy forest pond with an enormous fallen tree trunk spanning it like a bridge. It was covered with emerald moss, and I could lie face-down and inhale its magic. Every plant and wildflower in that place felt like part of me, a private special kinship. In my naivete I was sure I was the only human who had ever been there, and when the neighbor's boy said he knew all about it, I cried.

The best refuge of all was a gnarly little apple tree south of the house on a sandy hill. I was a good climber and could get up into a place where the branches began to spread. There was a hole in the tree, and a tiny jewel-like tree frog lived in there. We became good friends. That tree accepted me; I felt safe and embraced. If I hadn't been able to roam the countryside, I would never have made it. I took my solitude into the warm arms of my fields and forests and found kin. I didn't know it was healing me, but it kept me alive.

∽

House Girl had problems with her body. Private parts and toilet training were triggers. Once I was told to stay on the potty until I actually did something; when it took too long, my mother stuck a sliver of soap up my butt to hasten things. It hurt. It's a miracle I ever learned how good it feels to do a good hearty dump.

At the age of eight I fell off my bike and broke a front tooth. When I came crying into the house for comfort, my mother yelled, "How could you do that? It's a permanent tooth so it's just going to have to stay that way." I learned to stop smiling after that. My long hair, which I loved, was too hard to take care of. Finally she grabbed my ponytail, cut it off, and had the hairdresser give me a stinky perm.

My body had lots of ways to be wrong. I had to get glasses when I was five. My flat feet required ugly orthotic shoes for years. My ankles weren't slender. My butt was too round. My teeth had an overbite, so I wore braces all through high school. Only as Woods Girl, perched on a limb in my apple tree, could I forget all that.

House Girl tried to toe the line. She recited the state capitals, she went to school, and once she understood what grades meant, she tried to forge a B into an A on her second-grade report card. She had only one major task: don't get your mother mad.

When Woods Girl was really little, she discovered that if she snuggled her hands in her crotch, it felt warm and good; it belonged to her, it was her own body. My first orgasm was when I was five. My parents had gone off to collect my new brother, and I was left with their nearby friends. I was put to bed in a side room, feeling more or less abandoned. I remembered my old private comfort and nobody was there to see me, so I curled up around my hands. A new instinct kicked in, I wiggled, and something happened: an astonishing surge of pleasure. I reveled in the afterglow for a minute until I remembered my mother's shaming, being pinned down, splayed, scrubbed with cold cream and kleenex. "Why are you red there? Are you playing with yourself?" In an instant I was overcome with shame, and it was scalding.

Nevertheless, the miracle was mine, my secret comfort, and I used it often, though my need to hide it distorted my sexuality well into adulthood.

∽

That's the debit side of my mother's ledger. There were gifts on the credit side, and they were huge. I saw that a marriage could be a lifelong bond. Trust was absolute: when she took a tipsy nap in a costly hotel, left the bathtub running, and flooded the place, I was terrified of what my father might do. Her response? "I just want him to be here." I never saw her on stage—that ended years before I was born—but I could see the joy that filled her when she'd do a comic routine at a dinner party: performing was magic.

She was one of a kind and everyone loved her. She was volatile, unpredictable, deliciously funny, and no one in my parents' executive crowd was remotely like her. The fact that she often got drunk was hard to miss, but it just counted as one of her eccentricities. She'd honed her craft through ten years on the vaudeville stage, where you'd better be able to grab an audience or you'd land face down in the mud. And performance made her incandescent. Whether it was a simple Norwegian dialect sketch or a wild one-liner, she could land it.

Yet those years in the rough-and-tumble of vaudeville honed a razor edge. When she focused her rage on me, her verbal skills reduced me to instant snot and tears. Her abuse drew blood but left no marks. Nobody saw it, not even my father—or so I thought. Years later, on impulse I paid a visit to the home down the road from ours and talked to the boy I'd always seen as a klutz. In his adulthood, he was a staggeringly beautiful, centered man, and we had a candid conversation sitting below the grapevines that grew up his windmill. "We all knew what was happening to you but we didn't have any idea what to do about it. I'm so sorry." I was overwhelmed. I didn't make it up, it was real, and somebody saw it.

"There's the keeper of the tears..." It's the first line of a song I wrote long ago. My memory's oldest refrain is my mother yelling, "Stop crying!" That would usually be followed by "You're faking" or "You don't have anything to cry about." I didn't know how to stop crying, but it was clear that unless I did stop everything would escalate. I believe that the keeper of the tears was born of that dilemma. She became the one whose pain would always turn to tears, but she was separate from me. I could dissociate, step aside, and obey.

The song's second line was *"And there's the keeper of the anger..."* My mother was chronically overweight and hated it. She'd do one diet after another, make a list from all of them, eat it all, and get heavier. I became hyper-sensitized to her sounds at the dinner table, the chewing and swallowing and slurping, and I had to pretend not to hear. People eat, and there are noises associated with that, but for me they became something caustic, unbearable, a personal assault. I spent years at the dinner table in a state of suppressed rage. Of course there was no way to express this directly, so the anger turned inward. The keeper of the anger became the walled-off owner of those hot coals.

Then came *"There's the one who takes the fear and turns to stone…"* My mother's tantrums were often fueled by gin, and when the funny-smelling coffee cup showed up, I was in danger. At some point, having learned that crying was wrong and anger was unacceptable, going mute and invisible became workable. The one who takes the fear stepped up.

I didn't write that song, it just came full-blown into my mind when I was driving our daughter home from college. She'd been up all night packing and was sound asleep; in the silent car, my mind opened a window.

There's the keeper of the tears
And there's the keeper of the anger
There's the one who takes the fear and turns to stone.
There's the one who shuts the door
And says you cannot understand her
And she's scared to death she'll always be alone.
There's the keeper of the shame
And she's sure that she's to blame
And she hangs on to the pain like it's the answer.
There's the one with empty pockets
Who promises the moon
And there's the dancer.
Seven sisters, each one an only child
Crowded in a room where no one has the key—
—Find the questions
—Make the journey
—Dream the dream.

That was a painful and accurate description: *Crowded in a room where no one has the key.* The last three lines puzzled me until I understood that they were an assignment. Within the year I devised seven rituals of integration, one for each sister. I found the questions and made the journey. Then I began to dream the dream.

Right: Homer with baby
Below: Mary with baby

Right: Linda, 2, at piano
Below: Linda, 3, at mirror

Right: Linda, 5

3.

Sail On!

When I was six, I was enrolled in the local country school, a squat two-story brick building housing all twelve grades. In elementary school it was two grades to a room. Most of the kids were from the local farming community and were marking time until they could drop out. Assignments were printed on purple ditto, a flat-bed gel-system that made the classroom stink of alcohol. There were periodic health issues like lice and impetigo, and often students' heads were shaved and they wore stocking caps. It was a country school.

I was a problem, already knowing how to read and write. The school wanted to put me directly in the third grade, but my parents sensibly objected, and I was placed in second. Word spread rapidly that I could read. My second morning there, the kids decided to test me before the teacher came and pointed to a word that was still on the blackboard.

"Go on, read it if you're so smart!"

"German."

The little gaggle erupted in hoots. "How come you know that? That's who we beat in the war. Are you on their side? German! German! German!" When Miss Johnson came in, they all shut up.

Sail On!

Then the third grade teacher had a request. Could I come to the classroom next door and read from the third-grade reader? She brought me in, stood me up by the teacher's desk, and handed me their book. I read about a page, and then she told the class to get down under their desks in shame: this little kid could read better than they could. My popularity was off to a great start, and it was downhill from there.

I wasn't ready for this. I'd had almost no contact with other kids and had the social skills of a tree stump. I didn't know how to play, how to yell and rough-house, or how to shrug off mockery. In the eyes of these kids, I was a freak. Nobody else had coke-bottle glasses, and if they had flat feet they didn't have heavy corrective shoes. One year my mother got the idea it would be a great gift to have her old raccoon coat cut down to child-size, and the day I came to school in a fur coat was legend. Nobody else had private piano lessons. When I was made to perform at a talent show, they were vastly unimpressed, whispering, giggling, and pointing. But what was unforgivable was that I got good grades and my parents had money.

I routinely got shoved to the back of the cafeteria line at lunch, my class papers magically got scribbles on them, and my name was Four-Eyes. Recess time was hard to get through, except when we played Red Rover. When I was "sent over," all my repressed fury boiled up in me and I rushed that opposing line like a fullback. I busted it every time and was proud of my bruises.

I learned how to separate myself, and my freedom to roam after school gave me enough inner life to squeak through the early grades. Then in fifth grade, everybody took a standardized IQ test. I was somewhere in the stratosphere, and it got in the local papers. Meetings were arranged with my parents, and it was recommended that after sixth grade I be transferred into the Valparaiso city schools.

The idea of change was both scary and exciting. Unlike the township school with two grades to a room, there was a first-period homeroom in the morning and then a series of different rooms for different classes. And they had a library.

Everyone coming into the seventh grade came from somewhere else, so at first I was just part of the crowd. I did well in classes but didn't stand out. I volunteered to work in the library, and that became a haven. I learned the Dewey Decimal System right away and was a champion at shelving books. I didn't have to talk to anybody, and I could be myself.

But a big crash came with the Columbus Day assembly. A teacher had been told that I had a good memory and asked me to recite a poem, Joaquin Miller's *Columbus*. It was long and bloated, each verse ending *Sail on! Sail on! and on!* The kids were falling off their chairs with laughter. For the rest of that year and all the next, I was catcalled down the halls. "Sail on!"

The town's junior high school was a nine-mile trip one way. A man who lived near our home delivered furnace oil over the county, so my parents paid him to take me into town in the mornings. One day I had an algebra exam coming up, but the fuel-oil man had some problem and couldn't take me all the way. He drove me three miles down US 6 and dropped me off at a gas station on Highway 49, with six miles to go. He probably thought I could get a ride from someone heading into town, but I was too shy to ask and started to walk. I'd been on the road an hour when someone pulled over and offered a ride. Never mind all the stories about accepting rides from strangers: it was time for algebra class and I hopped in. Algebra was a favorite subject, with intoxicating riddles to unravel. I aced the exam.

While the students came from a variety of schools, all went on to Valparaiso High School. So the year-end assembly followed me. To my embarrassment and shame, I was called up six times for awards. After the third, people started to laugh. It should have been an empowerment, but it felt like "Pee-sick" all over again. Excellence was my ticket to survival and a source of humiliation.

Still, I wasn't in a backwater school now, and little by little I learned that excellence could be a kind of power. Nothing could make me popular, so I might as well go for what I was good at.

That included the piano. I'd started when I was five. In Chicago my mother had studied painting, French, and piano, and the piano teacher came out by train once a month for a home lesson. There was a good baby grand in the front room, and I was allowed to plunk the keys, told the names of the notes, and listened to my mother's lessons. Sitting on the couch, I heard a wrong note and piped up, "That's sposed to be F." What? The teacher played a note: what's that? "C." "How do you know?" "Sounds like C." I had perfect pitch. Soon I had my own lessons on these visits. It was a lifeline—for a time.

My immersion in piano quickly resulted in the annual agony of the spring recital. In Chicago, my teacher rented a room with a little stage and two pianos, twenty pupils on display, mostly girls. Everybody played a piece, starting with the youngest kids. The ride to Chicago was an eternity. "Don't you dare make a mistake! I would be so ashamed!"

I'd already walked the plank of reciting state capitals and cold-reading books aloud, so my first recital was just one more trial. I had a green cotton dress printed with teeny white flowers and was wearing my first pair of black patent leather Mary Janes. I hadn't been allowed to wear them outside the house before, and the soles were still smooth and slick. I slipped going up the stairs to the stage, and everybody gasped. It was OK, just my knee, not my fingers. I played without mistakes and was glad to go back to my chair and let my grumbly belly calm down. Toward the end of the recital, the big girls played some complicated music, very fast and sweet-sounding, and I decided I wanted to do that too.

It wasn't until junior high and the annual state music contests that the stakes got high. In my first winter of junior high school, I was urged to enter the district competitions. I got top ratings at the district level that year and the next, and once I was in high school I could go on to the state level where they actually gave little gold and silver medals. Those contests were like recitals on steroids, with the added horror of getting a written evaluation from the panel of judges; it was four years of trials and judgments, a system that shoved music into an iron cage for me. And it was public: the local newspaper published lists of the winners. Unfortunately, I won gold my first year and became locked into a ghastly competition with myself. At one point my mother threatened that if I came back with only a silver, she'd take an axe to the piano.

The bus trip to Indianapolis was three hours, and I always wondered if I'd get to a bathroom before my nerves made me explode. My hands would go icy cold and stiff, and I always feared there'd come a time when my fingers wouldn't work. The worst year was the one where, on top of everything, I had the cramps.

I was a flashy performer, all skill and no soul, but I was impressive. My last couple of contest pieces were Chopin's *Fantasie-Impromptu*, with its challenge of playing a right hand in four beats against a left hand in three, and then the fireworks of Ravel's *Jeux d'Eau*.

By the time I finished high school I had done a good job of constructing an approved identity. I had awards, medals, and was even allowed go on dates with the other National Merit Scholar—the first two in our school's history. The local newspaper wrote a feature about the whiz kids. And my resume was great, with a solid punch-line: I was valedictorian.

I had done everything I could to be perfect, and when I wasn't, I lied. I hid it, put it in a different part of my mind and locked the door. It was a devil's bargain. I had become an emotional slave and handed the end of the chain to my mother.

Sail On!

∼

It's hard to look at this now, to realize the depth and force of the brainwashing I inflicted on myself. I was a creature of radical contrasts: an instinctive sensualist, easily shamed. As a toddler, I had a soft blanket with a satin edge, and I found comfort in putting that in my mouth, chewing it, sucking on it. My mother ripped the satin off the blanket. Thank God I didn't suck my thumb.

I reworked myself to be married to the mind and divorced from the body. In fifth grade, I started to develop nipples and was terrified: I was sure I had cancer and was going to die. My left nipple had gotten puffy, and puberty was a word I'd never heard. Then the right one started to pop up. Mrs. Beach, the nicest teacher I'd had yet, found me crying in a remote corner down by the gym. "What's the matter, Linda? Did somebody hurt you?" Snuffle, silence, then whimpers, arms crossed. "It's not what you think; it happens to all the girls. Why don't you ask a girlfriend about it?" The whimpers became big braying sobs. "You don't think you have any friends?" Muffled howl. "Blow your nose and come upstairs. Let me get you a book from the library." It was an awful thing to be smart and supposedly know everything but be utterly ignorant about what everybody else knows. Of course I didn't dare take that book home.

My first period happened while I was riding horseback solo in the woods, and when I came home with stained panties my mother was really disgusted; her "Oh my God!" was nearly a scream. I was twelve years old, but she'd never mentioned the subject and there were no supplies in the house. "I'm going into town. Clean yourself up, throw those underpants in the trash, and use this wad of paper towel till I get back." For years after, I had terrible cramps every month.

Once puberty got going, I had nice little breasts, a very narrow waist, and a well-muscled butt, which annoyed my mother no end. All during high school, I had to wear a girdle.

Elizabeth: One of Many

I had only one friend in high school, and my total experience of "girl time" was limited to the days she came to our house and stayed overnight. She was the only person I knew who was remotely like me: a smart quiet girl with glasses who had a difficult mother and no boyfriend. Except for her, all through my school years I might as well have been from a different planet. That would explain a lot: I'd read all the science fiction in our town's library and could easily imagine it. I wasn't a plausible daughter to my mother. She was a big hearty comedienne and I couldn't take a joke. I loved hearing her funny stories at parties, and any fool could see how much she loved making people laugh, so why did my soul shrivel when laughter was directed at me? The four-year-old who brought the house down with "Pea-sick" felt laughter as humiliation. The seventh-grader who had to keep reciting when "Sail on" became a punch-line couldn't understand why it was funny. I got bailed out by Unk.

Unk. What can I say about Unk? His name was Helmer Carlson, but any friends of my parents were automatically dubbed Uncle and Aunt. He lived in Chicago and came to live with us after something blew up in his life; I think it involved his second wife. He was a wry funny man, all bones and loose pants and checkered flannel shirts. His face was craggy and narrow, with a little toothbrush moustache and a pointed nose, which reminded me of the prow of our canoe. He moved to our place when I was eleven.

My regular time with Unk was when, after the deal with the oil-truck man fell apart, he drove me to and from junior high school. And each year when my mother and father took off for Cadillac in hunting season or went to some meat-packer doings, Unk was head of the household and he was my breakfast responsibility.

It would go like this: I'm eleven, maybe twelve. It's October and my mother and father are away. My alarm goes off at 6:30, and it's still dark. I get up, get into my clothes, grab two eggs and four slices of bacon, and head across the frost-covered back yard to the door of the barn apartment where Unk lives. I let myself in, turn on the light, find the coffee in the cupboard. Fill the perk pot with water, put spoons of coffee in the basket, and set the unit on the burner. Get the frying pan out of the oven and spread the strips of bacon. Bread's in the cupboard, two slices in the toaster, get the butter out. This was a routine I knew, a comfort to think about nothing but that.

When the bacon's been turned a time or two, willing to lie flat, I call into the rooms, "Breakfast's coming!" When I hear an answering snort, it's OK to start the eggs. Bacon goes to one side onto a paper towel, eggs start sputtering in the fat, time to push the toast down. The percolator has had its hissy fit, time to turn the heat off. Bingo, everything's ready and Unk comes shuffling into the kitchen—long johns and flannel robe. I lay the food and coffee in place, get a big grin of thanks, grab my coat, and head back to the house. The air is cold, but I'm warm. I've just done something well.

Unk taught me to laugh. It wasn't easy. I was paranoid beyond belief and imagined that everything said was designed to humiliate me: a sort of masochistic narcissism. He badgered me with wisecracks and snipes that brought me to furious tears … and then finally got me to laugh. The alternative was axe murder.

"C'mon, little Four-Eyes, can't you take a joke?" I think he knew what he was doing, and I am eternally grateful to him. I didn't have the toxic history with him that I had with my mother, and he wasn't in the same category as my schoolmates. Maybe it was eased by the fact that he seemed to like me. Whatever, it worked. I finally cracked open and got it: not everything was about me.

He lived with us until I started my senior year. By then I could drive myself to school, and he wanted to retire to Florida. He moved there in 1956 and died of a heart attack five months later.

∽

Elizabeth: One of Many

Thinking about making breakfast for Unk reminds me that little of my learning happened in school. I have a bag of skills adding up to a PhD in survival, the bare necessities for thriving over a lifetime of independent theatre without a hefty income. I learned none of that in school.

Maybe I was born in the wrong century: I could have been a successful tinker. I can figure out how to fix stuff. Once when I was eleven or so, my folks went off to Michigan for hunting season and left me with Unk, and our dishwasher stopped working. I was alone in the kitchen and decided to check it out. The thinking went something like this:

It's a bunch of parts, and somebody put them together step by step, first to last. The last parts will be the ones I can see, so maybe I just work backwards. OK, first pull the plug. Whatever makes it go has to be down below the part that holds the dishes, behind this metal shell, but here are four big screws I can see. Yeah, now I can wiggle the case off. Look at all that! Get the flashlight!

Everything in there had a job to do, and something was goofing off. I found a timer, traced a series of valves, and found a cam that had come loose and fallen off. Its retaining clip was right next to it, so I put it back on its stem, clipped it in, plugged in the machine. It worked. The shell went back on and the job was done.

I was never taught to cook. I watched people who knew how and then tried stuff. When I was still pretty small, I was home alone (I got left alone a lot) and saw *The Joy of Cooking* open on the kitchen counter. I dragged a chair to the counter to climb up and look around for the canisters. My father liked lemon meringue pie, so I tried that. I remember only that I made a huge mess and came out with something you could eat with a spoon.

My father had a well-equipped woodworking shop in the basement. On weekends he would spend time down there, and he let me tag along. For safety's sake I was taught which things to leave strictly alone and how to work the ones I could use. My favorite was the drill press, I made weird little toys, and making scrap boards look like Swiss cheese was my idea of fun. He made tables and a big carved-wood trunk that we used for laundry. The first time he tried something with drawers, he got frustrated: those joints aren't easy. Then he saw what a true craftsman could do.

When I was eight, Congress passed the Displaced Persons Act, and my father sponsored an Estonian couple. An apartment got built on the far side of the barn/garage, and they lived there for three years. The husband did grounds work and used his carpentry skills to help finish the apartment, including built-in dresser drawers. He'd survived starvation in war-torn woods, evaded both Germans and Russians, married a widow with a child, and got his family to America. Hand-cutting a dovetail joint for a dresser drawer was a piece of cake. My father was flabbergasted: "He did it all by eye!" I got a new understanding of what doing things meant. As far as I knew, what mattered at school was the report card. *Doing things* was different. It filled me with satisfaction, and later I came to see how vital that was to the life I chose.

High school was like working a job. I got dropped off by Unk at 7:30 because Drama Club rehearsed before classes—I'd joined because it got me out of the house that much earlier. I did my classes all day, spent free time as a library volunteer, then walked down to the town library to plow through their science fiction shelves. I didn't check out the books; the point was to stay longer away from home. I'd arranged to get picked up at 4:30.

My sole duty was to get top grades, and I did that with fervor. I'd do anything for extra credit. Once I made a clay model of the Rosetta Stone for history class and stayed up all night punching in the teeny chicken-track hieroglyphs. I used my woodshop skills to make an elegant book for my biology leaf collection, with thin lauan covers and brass hinges. There was a weird kind of fun in this, and polishing my identity as geek freak wasn't without pleasure. As far as I knew, I'd go through life this way.

Elizabeth: One of Many

∼

The summer after my junior year I went to Interlochen National Music Camp and found my tribe. I wasn't a freak! It was like being an only child and suddenly finding a big loving family with brothers and sisters and eccentric maiden aunts. Here were people my own age who were musicians and dancers and artists. They worked together in concerts and plays and ballets, and they laughed a lot. Suddenly, I laughed a lot. I was housed in a cabin with fifteen other girls, and when after lights-out the bassoonist in her upper bunk honked her new reed like a goose, the whole cabin roared.

I'd never felt attractive, but here we were all comically alike. We wore incredibly dumpy uniforms. The girls brought their own white blouses, and the camp provided navy blue corduroy knickers. The most svelte figure in those things looked like a bratwurst.

It was heaven. The piano faculty pushed me out of the bravura stuff I'd been playing and sat me down to Bach. I played my flashy Ravel and Debussy pieces for the man who would be my teacher for eight weeks, and he said, "Very good, you have learned Jell-O very well. Now it's time for meat and potatoes." He assigned me a bunch of Bach and wouldn't take no for an answer. I thought it was awful, full of empty space, and it was anything but flashy. I hated it…

Until I learned to listen. At first I was resistant, but the Interlochen routine involved practice hours in private cabins, little chilly stone huts in the fragrant pine woods. Unlike practicing at home, I was alone. Nobody heard me. Being forced to learn something new in blessed privacy made something happen. I started listening to what I was doing, really hearing the music. It wasn't about flashy, it was about the sound, that starkly beautiful architecture. I came to understand the gorgeous construction of this music, to hear that austere massive beauty, to let it flow through me, to forget about showing off, and I fell in love. I had no idea music could be like this, so spare and so perfect. The E-minor three-part *Sinfonia* not only turned my head around, I found a space of grace and peace that was astonishing. I'd sit down to play it and I couldn't stop. It took me into an altered reality and left me shining.

And at Interlochen, my enthusiasm for "doing stuff" got a kick up. There were theatre classes. I signed up for stagecraft, and suddenly what I'd learned in my father's woodshop quickly made me the best and fastest at building canvas flats. Captain of the building team, that was me.

And showing feelings was OK. At home when I cried, my mother said, "You're faking." Here, at the final concert of the eight weeks, when the traditional closing piece (Howard Hanson's *Les Preludes*) began, all the campers burst into their own concert of tears. We were united by our joy at having been together and our grief at leaving.

Then I went back to high school.

4.
Imaginary Numbers

I was back home. I'd gotten top marks on my SAT test, and I had to start the college application process and burnish my credentials. Dead certain that I was headed for medical school, I talked to my counselor, who recommended the University of Michigan at Ann Arbor. My parents approved—close enough to home to keep tabs, far enough to be on my own—and my application was successful. More than successful: I would be in an honors program.

It was a strange year. It would be my sprint to the finish-line of a perfect college application and everything that had awakened during the summer had to be put on hold. The return to nerd-mode could be endured if I had a life-line at the end of it, so I lobbied hard to go to Interlochen again after graduation. It worked. I hid behind my glasses and braces, chose my classes carefully, and worked for perfect grades.

I had a huge crush on one of my teachers, and when he took the daring step of directing a student production of *Our Town* I wanted to audition. My parents said no, but I assisted in some of the rehearsals anyway. That play was unlike anything our Drama Club had done and I was as smitten with the play as I was with the director. It was a bright spot in a grim year.

And wonder of wonders, I finally got a boyfriend. The good-looking trombone player had also won a Merit Scholarship, and he asked me to the prom. My parents warned me about distractions but didn't say no. It was a new experience to be admired in a low-necked prom dress, enjoy some more casual dates and fall in love. I also stayed on track, became valedictorian, delivered a commencement speech without being catcalled, and went off again to the intoxication of Interlochen. This time I had someone with whom to share a sweet farewell.

Going into the college honors program, I was a solid investment. Languages? Straight A's in Latin and German, and I could fake my way through French without doing the homework until the last minute. Math was a game, and I could blaze through elaborate geometry proofs at the chalkboard, drawing with both hands. And, best of all, science. In eighth grade I had made ink drawings of every bone in the human body, neatly labeled, just as a private project. I won the Bausch & Lomb Science Award and got a big bronze plaque. Being valedictorian and winning a National Merit Scholarship were the final stamps of approval.

At 6:30 a.m, Sept. 12, 1957, I hugged my father good-bye as he headed off for his commute to the Chicago Loop. The Chrysler sedan would take me to Ann Arbor. When I got my driver's license, our Chevy "Woodie" had been my ride to high school, and I loved it. It had a great stick transmission, and I'd learned to rock my way out of any icy ditch. Brushing snow off the seat in winter was a small price to pay for independence, but it was a dilapidated beast with a leaky roof and holes in the floor. This was my mother's road trip, and it would be made in the dignified sedan.

My brother got on the school bus and we were free to go. It was harder saying goodbye to my cats than to any of the family, because I wasn't sure I would ever see the Blue Cat and her black tom again: my mother really had it in for them. But it was time, and off we went.

The car was crammed full of my stuff. I remembered another time my mother had loaded the car to the gills. We were driving the station wagon to take my father's newest hunting dog north to the trainer, and we spent the morning lugging and stowing supplies for the summer. About an hour out, my mother suddenly shouted, "My God, I forgot the dog!"

The first hour was a route I knew by heart. Every summer we'd go to Cadillac that way, but now, instead of going north through Saugatuck and Holland and Grand Rapids, we headed east to Kalamazoo and Ann Arbor, a four-hour drive. We kept going, with only a brief stop for sandwiches and coffee. It was a beautiful warm September day. The car was a year-old Chrysler New Yorker with automatic transmission and velvety seats, and it still smelled new—my chariot into the prologue to life as a practicing MD. I had no idea what was going to happen or that the same Chrysler New Yorker, three years later, would change my life again.

That first year of college, here's what the straight-A valedictorian did.

~

September '57, and Ann Arbor was beautiful. Warm sun and wide tree-lined streets greeted us, and it wasn't hard to find the way across town to the huge campus. My dorm was surrounded by the Observatory, Forest Hills Cemetery, Nichols Arboretum, and Palmer Field, an area known as The Hill. Alice Lloyd Hall was a long hike from where most of my classes would be, but I took it as a good omen that it was close to the Medical School. The oak trees were jumping with squirrels—red, black, and grey—and they fought each other constantly. Reds were the fiercest; a dorm mate later informed me that they tried to bite the balls off the greys.

We faced clogged traffic, cars packed solid, sweaty drivers jockeying for space to offload. We got my stuff up to the room, said good-bye, and there I was: seventeen, newly out of braces, thick glasses in pointy cats eye frames, the new nerd on the block.

Alice Lloyd was big. Four floors visible above the massive glass-walled lobby, polished stone, very modern, with dining halls and kitchen one floor below, and laundry and rec rooms a floor below that. And surprisingly comfortable rooms upstairs. I was in a triple room, the first to arrive. Nice room, but not exactly a warm nest: black tile floor, lime-ice walls, yellow curtains. After unpacking and stowing my things, I didn't know what to do, so I sat there and studied trigonometry for a while. Storm clouds were massing outside and the bare room got chilly. I dug out my favorite sweater, found pen and paper, wrote a letter to Pat, my best friend from Interlochen, and sat there alone. That began to feel silly, so I roamed the mammoth building a while, got lost, found a map, and went back to the room.

Finally a roommate arrived. Maureen was blonde, slender, and tall, with a lively sense of humor. We chatted our introductions and went down to the "picnic dinner" that had been moved indoors due to the pouring rain: hot dogs, potato chips, carrot sticks, celery, all in a cavernous windowless room full of huge tables. Then ten of us from the same wing went to a Big Sister's room, where we learned about house rules, clothing codes, quiet hours, signing in and out, penalties, and upcoming social programs. We got a tour of the building and flopped into bed.

The next day, Friday, felt a little like boot camp. Up at 6:45, we had breakfast in the same cozy basement and then were herded into the 3,500-seat assembly hall crammed with freshmen. Hill Auditorium was breathtaking. The seats were red plush, there were two balconies, and the orchestral stage was a huge ice-cream scoop, a quarter-sphere with six arches of lights spanning its ceiling from side to side. We listened to President Hatcher's welcome and then went on with the business of orientation, locating signs dividing us into assigned groups. Each group was lined up for I.D. photos, trooped to the health service for X-rays, and then liberated for a break.

I walked downtown, bought a teapot, kettle, cups, saucers, and spoons, and clanked my way over to a bookstore, where I was horrified at the cost of my textbooks. Thirty-two dollars later I lugged everything to a local bike store where I got a used bike, lock, and protective tarp. I managed to cram everything into the double baskets and pedaled my way uphill to the dorm. I was starting to get the campus geography straight. After dinner, I took a placement test in German and then went to my first "social event," a coed mixer at my dorm. I danced with a sophomore engineering student and wound up with a movie date. Hot stuff! After taking almost my entire high school career to get my first date, somebody danced with me and asked me out!

Saturday started with a math placement test, followed by another for English. And I had my first meeting with a dentist to repair the jagged front tooth I'd broken as a kid; the ten years without a smile were about to end. I met with my academic counselor and went through the pit-trader chaos of registration. It got me a schedule of English Comp, 2nd year German, Chemistry, Advanced Math, and Phys Ed: 15 hours, a typical first step toward med school. I wanted to get through undergrad in three years, and I was on my way.

The third roommate Nancy Jo arrived, and her dry humor was appealing. Nancy's major was Far Eastern Studies; she'd spent a year in Japan. The three of us started planning how to warm up our sterile room. "What can we do to this room to make it nice? There aren't any bedspreads; how much do bedspreads cost?" We had no clue, but we went shopping. Nancy Jo's year in Japan had given her a good eye; we found bedspreads that were an off-red that didn't scream *Dorm!* and a couple of nice Japanese prints for the walls. "Can we afford these?" "Let's just do it." It was the right choice; the room felt a lot better. "Let's celebrate." We had a tin of Constant Comment tea and a teapot. Nancy Jo and Maureen hit the vending machines in the basement: "Peppermints? Cookies?"

Imaginary Numbers

This was going to be OK. We wanted to have some personal money for impulse buying, so we all decided to volunteer for a bunch of paid psych experiments. As roommates, the three of us were off to a good start.

The dorm wasn't bad. The food wasn't home cooking, but it was plentiful. Living on The Hill was a pain when biking back, but it had a nice view. The dorm was adjacent to the Detroit Observatory: "Why Detroit? We're in Ann Arbor!" Being on the fourth floor, our window looked straight at its dome. Late one night I took a study break, brewing a cup of tea and reading a creepy science fiction story, and happened to look out the window. Instead of the smooth gray dome, I was staring down into a gaping black hole that was getting wider and wider. I panicked, then realized that observatories do open up to use their telescopes. I yelled at Nancy and Maureen. When they got to the window, the whole dome started rotating. We did a choral gasp and all broke out laughing.

The early days of adjusting to the dorm were endearing. *Endearing*: yes, that's the right word. These were trivial things but new to my experience. Adjusting to living with fifteen girls at Interlochen had been a start, but I had been dazzled to find kindred. Now I was on my own, still expected to do my job but not remotely experienced in how to live while doing that. These trivia were a big deal for me.

I liked my classes, although it was a big adjustment getting used to the level of work required. Not that I hadn't had homework in high school, but this was more demanding, and it didn't help that I had a huge bike commute from class to class. When the cold weather set in, the Asian flu ripped through the dorms; I had a light case, missing only one full day of classes, but the comfort of staying warm in bed made going out again harder. That was my first experience of cutting classes. It got easier.

Creative writing was a new experience, and I liked the edgy instructor, a grad assistant who was new to all this. He was young, skinny, nervous, very New York, and had a habit of pacing back and forth across the front of the room. It was funny watching the heads turn from side to side following him like a tennis match. I'd never tried to write before, but he liked what I wrote, which astonished me. In the first two months he read five stories aloud in class (anonymously), and four of them were mine. When I began to miss classes and blow off assignments, he allowed me to do make-up work, and my final piece was returned with the handwritten comment, "Bonne chance."

Chem started off with promise. I had trouble staying awake in lectures because they were covering the basics I'd already had in high school. I had to start drinking coffee at lunch to stay awake. But lab was great, lots of toys to play with; after a couple days of experiments the lab prof came up and said, "You ought to be an analytic chemist!"

German was a hard row to hoe. In high school I'd had the odd experience of feeling it to be almost a native language, besides having a mad crush on the teacher. Now it was boring: some desultory conversation and a focus on reading a couple of novels. It became a trivial exercise. I found myself objecting to a bad mark on a five-week test in translating the word *enge*: "Wie enge es wird nach Hause sein." I opted for *cozy*, rather than *restricted*. Maybe I was blocking my own experience of home life.

At first, math was my favorite. It was an elite class in analytic geometry; I'd never had trigonometry but talked my way around that prerequisite. Bad mistake. I was in the honors section taught by Dr. Raoul Bott, a renowned topologist whose German accent was a good copy of a Sid Caesar routine. Like everyone in the small class I held my breath as he would start to light a cigarette, forget about the match until it burned down to his fingertips, then drop it with a yelp. He'd often come to class with bits of toilet paper still stuck to his shaving mishaps. But he was a flat-out genius who loved his math with the gusto of a soccer fan. I liked him and was sure I could do this; math had always been second nature to me. The early weeks were OK; I even passed the exam designed to cull the losers, and my five-week grade report was an A. Then the course hit its stride, launched into the realm of imaginary numbers, and my brain froze. I was completely lost and didn't know how to cope: I had never faced this kind of failure before. Fear settled into the pit of my stomach, but dissociation was an old reflex, and the fear got pushed back.

Dissociation: it's a strange process, and it has never left me. Even now I catch myself slipping, "forgetting" some omission or mishap, relegating a difficult task to a walled-off place in my brain. The first episode I remember clearly was during high school. As I was packing music for the train ride to my Chicago piano lesson, my mother presented me with a plastic bag containing a hunk of round steak, a left-over from dinner. "Here, put this in, you'll love it for lunch." I knew it would be cold and rubbery and greasy, and I should have thrown it away at the train station. It would be gone, and I could just say nothing or claim to have eaten it. I didn't have the guts. Instead, I left it in my vinyl music case, where it proceeded to rot on the radiator behind my piano bench. The part of me that knew it was there was walled off and I did my daily piano practice oblivious to the smell. That's dissociation, junior grade. In my college days it became a sizeable problem, and during my first year of marriage it exploded into dangerous territory.

∼

Dating was a handy distraction, especially because I was so clueless at it. The first freshman mixer dates weren't winners, but then neither was I. If a date took me to a movie, it was expected that he would pay, and then I would grant whatever favors didn't "go too far." It wasn't a great thrill going to a movie, coming back to the commons room, and lurking in the shadowy corners while my date fumbled his hands up my skirt. Bad enough the anxiety of maybe being seen; worse, that no pleasure was involved.

Elizabeth: One of Many

My history of dating had been brief. I'd had one boyfriend at the end of my senior year, my fellow Merit Scholar, a match made in the wilds of academic competition. But Lee was not only smart, he was tall and blond, a really good trombone player, and I was over the moon to find myself wanted. In my fraught forays to the state music contests, the only bright spot had been doing piano accompaniment for his brass quartet. "Lee? He's so cool that Coke comes out of his spit valve." We had dates, then came home and tussled and wriggled: hot though innocent, and much more interesting than somebody fumbling on a dim dorm couch.

I could do solo with great results, but it never occurred to me that I could say, "Do that some more," or move a hand to a better position. My self-pleasuring was my scalding secret. As far as knowing what was possible with a guy, I was in the dark. I knew only that I had to protect my virginity, so it took meeting up with somebody who not only had some experience but wanted to please. I found one.

At the end of October I went to a grad student mixer, where I met some guys from the program in Hospital Administration. The one who struck sparks was Wolfgang—Wolf for short. He was 25 to my 17, but for me that was a plus. He was short and had a round cherub face that reminded me of George Gobel (a TV comedian I loved). Good dancer, funny, kept a conversation going—traits totally missing in my previous mixer dates—and when he was with me, he saw me. Given my obsession with a medical career, his field of study was a plus, but the best part was his sense of humor.

He asked me to the "Maize and Blue Note" dance for the next weekend, and the day after that we went on the Graduate Outing Club's three-hour hike. After getting back, we went to dinner at the Old German restaurant together (beef rouladen and German potato salad) and onward to see a movie, *Operation Mad Ball*. Sharing fits of laughter at Jack Lemmon and Ernie Kovacs was a bonding experience.

I abandoned the mixer game. It was a huge relief to find someone who found me attractive and interesting, to have a warm relationship that wasn't a clumsy battlefield. I could actually enjoy sexual attraction for its own sake. And I not only found an interesting partner, I found an extended circle of friends. Wolf had an apartment in Ypsilanti (about twenty minutes from campus) with two roommates, and their circle accepted me as a peer without making much ado about my age. They had brains, they had fun, they played bridge, and I became part of their family. It didn't hurt that I was a slam-dunk cook and got gifts from home like steaks and Cornish hens.

I spent a lot of time in the Ypsi apartment, and some of that time was alone with Wolf in his room. Little by little we became more intimate, but there was a line he would not cross. He knew I was a virgin, and he wasn't going to change that. He was good at pleasing me with his hands; it became an accepted thing that he would take care of himself the same way, and that was that. Eventually, by the end of the spring semester, we were talking about marriage someday. We stayed under the covers and never got naked.

I didn't share these details in my letters home, but in the fall I was babbling about the frequent dates, and my mother asked for particulars about this gent. On Nov. 19, I wrote a letter home:

The 'Wolf's' first name is Wolfgang! This is not a nickname; he was born in Berlin and came to the U.S. when he was five or six. After this school year, Wolf will take up his year of administrative residency at a hospital, probably in Cleveland. He likes music, but prefers the older classics to the newer composers. This is about all I can think of... Oh yes, he is not Jewish, not Catholic, not Lutheran.

When I read this recently, I winced. It took me a long time to see the ingrained, casual bigotry in my family. My father had grown up in southern Illinois and had a rotten racist attitude toward Blacks, though always expressed not with hatred but as just the norm. And one of my mother's closest friends had a lifelong Jewish lover, welcomed as her companion, yet my mother would think nothing of using phrases like "kike music." So I lied. Bullshit: Wolf was Jewish and my mother would never stomach that.

Soon I got a flame-thrower letter, reaming me out for having gone with Wolf to his apartment. I was amazed to find myself writing a letter that absolutely stood up for us. By this time I was part of a circle, not just a boyfriend but a "tribe." The letter was respectful but forthright and frank. I didn't know I had it in me.

I navigated the Thanksgiving and Christmas vacations carefully enough to be allowed to take part of the semester break at our summer house in Cadillac, housing my friends while they hit the ski slopes at Caberfae. About ten people, more women than men, everybody in sleeping bags. Then I spent a couple of days at home, Wolf driving me there and taking me back to Ann Arbor. Introductions were stiff but polite. I got routinely nagged about my dating Wolf but managed to avoid big fights. It was a good feeling that I'd survived one whole semester, and I breathed more easily once I got back to campus.

My anxieties about classes got wedged into the back of my brain. In late February when the fall grades came in, they weren't what I wanted, but they weren't bad.

English Composition	B
German 2nd Year	A
Inorganic Chem	A
Analytic Geom	C
Phys Ed	B

The elaborate construct I'd built on IQ and grades started to wobble. I was the valedictorian, the National Merit Scholar, the freshman in the elite honors program, so how come I wasn't getting all A's? My parents weren't happy. I wrote home:

Thanks for sending the fall grade report. That C in math won't harm my school standing; it's overall average that counts, and mine is very high in spite of the math grade. No, I didn't know about that until I got back; Professor Bott either got hard-hearted after sending postcards or else he goofed on recording grades on said cards.

Lies.

What hurt worst was that Analyt grade, because I knew I had been lucky to get even a C. I was never able to grasp the fundamental concept of imaginary numbers: the square root of minus one formed a scribble on a blank wall. I'd never before faced being unable to comprehend a concept, except perhaps my childhood experience in sorting the laundry. My brain defined me, and it wasn't up to the task. I couldn't drop the course, I needed the credit, but I had started cutting classes and it leaked over into other courses. My Composition instructor took pity and let me make up late work; I scraped through with a B.

My fabric of identity, my ticket to survival, was unraveling. I was beginning to be valued as an independent human being, and at the same time I was disintegrating, failing as a scholar and lying about it. I did a good job of propping up my image before the semester break, and my academic counselor approved a heavy schedule for the spring semester, 20 credit hours instead of 15, giving me the dubious honor of being the first freshman to have been allowed to take more than 18 hours. I came back to a freezing February facing three 8 a.m. chemistry lectures.

∼

The new semester offered a fresh start. Life went on. I got a surprise birthday party in my dorm room. I was in the hall bathroom brushing my teeth, getting ready to run out the door to a sorority rush event when Judy came screaming in: "Quick, Linda, come and help Maureen—quick!" I ran back to the room, foaming at the mouth and half-dressed. Every girl on the corridor was there, and on Maureen's desk was a beautiful chocolate cake with yellow candles and yellow frosting roses. It was a big cake, but there were twenty girls, and in ten minutes it was gone.

That was Saturday, and on Sunday I had another birthday celebration in Ypsi, cooking dinner for Wolf, his roommates Brad and George, and their girlfriends Ann and Jane. My parents had sent frozen Cornish hens packed in dry ice, enough for the six of us. I roasted them to a golden brown, fixed wild rice with mushrooms, Pepperidge Farm stuffing loaded with butter, sides of green peas and salad, and ice cream with strawberries for dessert. Brad gave me some balloons, George a mathematical puzzle, Ann a package of modeling clay, and Jane a box of extra-large gold stars that you paste on kids' foreheads when they do something exceptional. Sweet silly things. Wolf had already given me a set of Japanese prints on rice paper, translucent and glowing, and a tiny pair of gold earrings.

It was a birthday so different from the opulent childhood birthdays that would leave me with a sour-milk miasma of guilt. Christmas and birthdays had always meant running a gauntlet. I never knew how to be effusive enough to come across as grateful, and the obligation of thank-you notes was a grim challenge. No matter what I wrote, my words sounded fake to me. This time it was simple. I was loved.

I started cutting classes again and was sent to counseling. That led to a one-time appointment with a friendly shrink and a mandatory referral for a physical. They found a small cyst in my right breast. I couldn't get off the path from there, and surgical removal was scheduled. For work-up I'd need a pelvic exam, and I was terrified.

My orgasms were a secret shame. Masturbation was a word I didn't know. I was sure that nobody but me did anything nasty like that, and I'd die if anyone found out. In junior high when I had my tonsils out, I astonished the doctor by fighting like a wild animal against the anesthesia. I had read somewhere that being put under was like truth serum: if anybody asked me, I'd confess. They had to put me in restraints.

Now I was facing my first pelvic exam. I'd repressed my memory of childhood humiliation by my mother, and now I had to go through it again. Since then I'd never had to spread my legs for inspection, and here I was on a cold table, my feet in steel stirrups, a strange male doctor peering and poking. I dealt with it by floating up out of my body. The next day the cyst was removed, the biopsy was OK, I went back to classes and pretended that nothing had happened. I was ignorant of the concept of dissociation, but I'd become an expert in its practice.

I'd been dropped from freshman sorority rush, which was a relief. It didn't surprise my dorm mates or my friends in Ypsi: "Linder, you're just not the 'sorority girl' type." (Brad was from Boston.) Eventually I figured out that it was a compliment. Instead, I applied to an elite honors dorm, Martha Cook, and got accepted. The application had been reviewed before my godawful spring grade report came in, but they didn't reverse their acceptance. Maybe they thought I needed better surroundings, or maybe they believed in the tooth fairy.

By March there were red flags all over the place, but I managed to avoid seeing them. One part of me knew what was at stake: two girls in my dorm had flunked out after the first semester. Flunking was real. It happened, just not in my cozy world of Wolf and friends. I have no idea how I did such a good job hiding from myself.

I'd advanced from dissociation to depression. I'd never heard of either one, but I had advanced from one step to the next. Shoving uncomfortable events into a hidden closet was now amplified by new behavior. I was finding it impossible to get out of bed in the mornings and I couldn't concentrate. I was compulsively cutting classes. Taking the first step in making up missed work was something I couldn't face. I was coming apart.

My spring grades were a disaster. The only grade I earned was a C in German; everything else was a Withdraw or an Incomplete, except for flunking Phys Ed. I got my own report while still on campus, but it wouldn't be mailed to my parents until June. Bluffing like crazy, I wrote home:

Now that I have my little charts and schedules I will go to Prof. Angell, my counselor, and impress him with the mass of proof that I can graduate in three years and satisfy med school requirements.

I signed up for Speech 51 (Acting for Radio/TV/Theatre), arguing that a liberal arts component would look good when applying for med school; the rest was a bizarre set of choices: German, Physics, Zoology, History, and Choir. I went home for the summer.

I loved Wolf, I liked him, and he had been good to me. When he went off to his year's residence at a Cleveland hospital, we were sure that our attachment would survive the separation. It didn't. For starters, my mother ragged on me during the entire drive home, backed up by a woman friend who was sympathetic to her. By this time she knew Wolf was Jewish. "Jewish," "older," "taking advantage," and the killer blow, "You don't know what love is." The part of me that knew I could never stand up for myself stepped in and began to erase my feelings, put them in the distance. My letters became infrequent and impersonal, and when I went back to Ann Arbor, Wolf was in Cleveland for his residency. I'm sorry, Wolf.

I was living at home during the week, watching the mailbox for the grade report like a hawk while my father did his daily commute to Chicago. My mother stayed full time at our lakeside place in Cadillac, and my father and I drove up each Friday and came back late Sunday. I cooked dinner for the two of us, packed it in a basket, and we'd eat in the car and talk. I loved those four-hour drives. He had his special way of cooking pork chops, and I learned to broil beautiful thick ones perfectly. I'd pack a picnic with chops,

Imaginary Numbers

sliced ripe tomatoes from our garden, soft bread-sticks and a six-pack of Ballantine's Ale from the fridge. As the summer went on, he'd give me a Ballantine's too, and that crisp piney flavor is still sweet to my taste.

I'd tried and failed to find some kind of part-time hospital-related job in Cadillac but had other reasons to stay in Indiana. First, I was able to get a summer job with a nearby editing enterprise. I liked the owners, George and Dottie, it wouldn't hurt to make a little money, and it got me time away from my mother. And sooner or later the spring grade report would come to the Indiana address. I had to alter it.

I would walk home from work, run to our sky-blue mailbox, and shuffle through the mail. Sometimes my hands were shaking. The dread day arrived: I grabbed the envelope, ran into the house, and got started. My father wouldn't be home until six, my mother was in Michigan; I had time.

The spy novels I'd read had helpful descriptions of forgery techniques. I put on the tea-kettle and steamed the envelope open. Even knowing it would be bad, seeing the report in black and white was a shock, but I forced myself to see it as an art project. The course names, descriptions, and credits were all typed, but the grades had been hand-written in ink on the original. Xerox had just hit the market and this was a photocopy, so I was dealing with images printed on the surface, not ink soaked into paper.

The three "I" letters were off-center, crammed to the left to allow room for an actual grade when the Incomplete was made up; the W, C, and F were centered. My new letters would have to match. I got a pointed Exacto blade from my stash of art supplies, carefully scraped the surface of each "I" until its square was blank, smoothed the fibers gently with an eraser edge, and waited for my hands to stop cramping. After finding paper that looked like the same texture, I practiced using a fine-point art pen to build letter segments with tiny dots, blending them once they looked right.

The improved grade report looked convincing. The W and C had to stay, but the F easily became a B; I gave myself three other B's, glued the flap shut and put the envelope into the next day's mail. I wrote a note apologizing for getting no A's and was safe until fall. My successful job of forgery bought me a trouble-free summer. I spent time with my father and bonded more closely with George and Dottie. This sophisticated literate couple treated me like a real person; I wanted my life to feel like that. Anxiety got kicked down the road.

On weekends in Cadillac, I could get out of the house and do solo canoe trips on Lake Mitchell. One morning I paddled clear across the lake and explored a beautiful high-canopied pine forest, scuffling through a thick carpet of needles, even finding a few blueberries and wintergreen to nibble. Back in the canoe, I pushed off from the sand and cut through a large patch of reeds. It was full of black flies, and they swarmed on me, biting and stinging. It hurt like hell, but if I put the paddle down to swat them away I would get nowhere. It was either swat and stay put or move and get stung. If there was a life-lesson there, I was too busy sweating, paddling, and crying to pay attention.

～

I should have paid attention. As a kid I had lied a lot but it was sand-lot lying, evasions to cover for something I hadn't done or something I had done. Fibbing became second nature and when it worked, which was most of the time, it made life a lot easier.

The forgery I had done was big-league, but I blinded myself to that. The process itself had even been sort of fun, and I dealt with the inevitability of getting caught by what had become habitual: dissociation. It wasn't really me. A part of me knew that I couldn't get away with it forever, but I was an old hand at locking that part away with my other sisters. I'd just steered my canoe into the black flies, but it wasn't me. They were biting somebody else.

Imaginary Numbers

Linda, 12

Linda, 17, Senior Prom

Linda, 19

Helmer Carlson - "Unk"

5.

Kicked Out

I survived the summer and went back to Ann Arbor: a new year and a new start. My forged grade report was not questioned. As far as my parents knew, I was stable again, no A's but good solid B's. And me? I told myself it would all be OK. Three of those marks were incompletes, and when spring semester came around those courses would be offered again, and I would talk to my profs, make up work, and get final grades. The Keeper of the Fear had turned to stone.

My new honors dorm, Martha Cook, was a real piece of work: an elegant 1915 four-story brick building with a front entrance of massive wooden doors and mullioned glass, set in a peaked archway with a classically-draped statue atop the center. The rooftop was pierced by dormers, four round turreted towers anchored the corners, and the whole thing was impressive as hell. Once you went through those double doors, you were in a long two-story entry hall with a vaulted ceiling running the length of the building. With heavy velvet drapes, Tudor-style couches, armchairs, and carved sideboards, it could have been a period movie set. I was in heaven under false pretenses, but that thought got shoved aside.

My dorm room was small, but I bought a little set of wind chimes to hang over one of the windows, and my records and turntable fit neatly on a shelf under the tea table. A huge brandy snifter filled with hard candy sat on top next to the little white rice bowl used as an ashtray. I had only one roommate, and we got off to an amiable start. Back in May, I had met Betsy Higdon at a Martha Cook spring dance. She was a year ahead, a lively little brunette with a sharp sense of humor. "Betsy, your face looks familiar; what dorm were you in?" "Alice Lloyd. I was in the crowd for your surprise birthday party!" Oops. But she didn't take offense, and we hit it off.

I wrote home: *The room may seem small at first glance, but we are really comfortable in it. Things like the easy chair, the floor lamp, the solid old furniture, and the carpet make it downright luxurious after Alice Lloyd's cold austerity. Betsy smokes, but I don't mind.*

The course load for the year would be a killer, a double major of pre-med and speech. I had made a strategic case for the speech courses being a plus for medical school admission, but my choices—acting and directing for radio, TV, and theatre—were not just tactical. What I knew about theatre was that it had made my mother happy; what I knew about radio was that it had been a magic window during my isolated childhood and let me eavesdrop on other worlds. Chronic tonsillitis was a gift that often kept me home from school, and I'd wrap myself in a puffy comforter and listen for hours to the big short-wave radio upstairs in my folks' bedroom when I was supposed to be sleeping. Downstairs after dinner, I'd drape a blanket over the dining table and hide under there with Fred Allen, Jack Benny, and Baby Snooks. Now I was about to do it myself.

My mother had mocked my high school drama club activity, especially my voice. But Ann Arbor was the center of a network for radio drama and programs aimed at kids, and in the U of M studios I found a new reality. When I was downstairs in Angell

Hall behind a mic, only the guys in the control room could see me, and I was suddenly free. Once the heavy door whooshed shut, I could let a script take me anywhere. I found an instinct for funny voices, one that would let me do a kiddie show in very few takes, create unique personalities for each character, and keep track in real time. "Here, Linda, look this over. Sue had half the characters but she isn't here. I know you can do it by yourself. We'll start in fifteen minutes." I was in demand.

Registration for fall courses had taken three hours, lots of juggling to get courses and times I wanted, and at the end I ran across the gym to the speech table to sign up for acting, hoping to get the section taught by an instructor from Interlochen. Dr. Jack himself was behind the table; he grinned and growled, "You're going out for Gilbert & Sullivan, so keep Tuesday night free for the meeting." The fact that he remembered me made me catch my breath.

I went, signed up for both stage crew and chorus, and got an audition time. When Thursday afternoon came, I almost bailed, terrified that I'd humiliate myself trying to sing. I played it safe by doing something written for ugly old Lady Jane. I was sure I wouldn't make the chorus, but at least I'd survived. Later I wrote home: *I came home from the first crew meeting to find a girl waiting for me. 'Where were you for the rehearsal?' I'd been chosen! Me! Me who can't sing got into a twenty-girl chorus for which sixty or so tried out! We're even going on the road to Detroit and Toledo in early December! I'm excited!!!*

Radio was already a baited trap, but when I added G&S I signed my academic death warrant. There were tight-knit twin groups, onstage and backstage, I was part of both, and I preferred to be in the radio production rooms, not scrambling to make up work from my spring incompletes. I was kidding myself again.

There were lots of parties, and the booze flowed freely. I found a new self-image. I was certainly female and I relished the attention from the males, but I was also holding my own in the "guy" camp, wielding hammers and lugging flats and swearing with the best of them. In high school, I'd never been sexually attractive, and I had never thought of myself as physically competent. Suddenly I was a hot item. I was reminded of this decades later when an erotic buddy said he'd love to have a photo of me in nothing but high heels and a tool belt.

My mother had told me that I was unattractive, and as long as I believed that, it defined me. Now that it was no longer true, I lost my balance; without either will or center I was running full speed ahead. Performing was what sustained me through that year of lies, evasion, and stark fear. I loved the collaboration and comradeship, and the praise was intoxicating. So was sex.

I'd had a total of two boyfriends. I was sure that Lee only asked me to the senior prom because I was the other Merit Scholar. Getting kissed was a surprise, a sweet bonus. My relationship with Wolf had been a revelation, but it was focused on one person, comfortable and safe. Now unattached and full of the energy of performing, I was turning guys on, getting more assertive, and reveling in the chase.

My contact lenses had been uncomfortable all that year and I still wore those pin-eyed glasses, but now, with the advantage of a sink in the Martha Cook dorm room, I swore I'd put the lenses in and take them out as often as it took to get to all-day wearing. If I was going to remake my self-image, I'd have to put in the effort. I got rid of the glasses.

As a freshman I'd lightened my hair a little, but now that I could do hair color in my own room, I got blonder and blonder. After getting away from my mother, I had refused to let my hair get cut again, and now that it was long enough I could use big foam rollers and make it wavy. What a wonderful feeling to let it loose, shake my head, feel it brush my shoulders, and stretch like a cat. I'd missed my long hair so much, and now it was mine to grow again. I was free of my mother.

But how free? Every trip home was a test. Letters had to be written, phone calls made, and the calls became so toxic that the sound of the bell at the end of the hall made me break out in an instant sweat and fight diarrhea. My father was experiencing health crises, and my mother wanted intimate support at a time when it was hardest to muster.

I got some dates from both Gilbert & Sullivan and theatre classes. Terry was my acting partner in class and also did G&S props; he started walking me home from class. I found his attention flattering, but he didn't quite ring my bell. Theo was the manager of the G&S stage crew; he was stone gorgeous, 6'1", wavy golden-brown hair, and all the female crew members kept their eyes on him. I was the one he looked back at, and he definitely did ring my bell. One night when rehearsal ended early, I was waiting for Theo to meet me. Everyone had left except Dr. Jack and the music director Bob. "Waiting for your date, Lin? You don't have to worry, nobody would stand you up. Too cute." Bob pitched in: "I'll say! Three guys came up to me tonight and wanted to know the name of that blonde."

On a late-October Friday came the first of many crazy boozy G&S parties, all of which were at the apartment shared by Theo and his roommate Marshall, a super-techie who did lights and sound. Twenty people crammed into the living room and kitchen, and the music was overwhelming. Marshall had built his own hi-fi system and was by definition the DJ: Gregorian chants before the party got going, then Bartok's *Sonata for Two Pianos and Percussion*, followed by Stravinsky and then Dave Brubeck jazz—Marshall was one of a kind. I had been dating Theo and now was flirting with Marshall, drinking the Scotch that was offered, and taking pride in holding my liquor with the best of them. They were my tribe.

Theo had tickets for the big homecoming dance. Music by Les and Larry Elgart, it was in the elaborately decorated basketball court, and tickets had been sold to 1700 couples. We danced for three hours, then went to the Sugar Shack for a malt. When I wrote home about the evening, I didn't mention that we spent some time in his car before the malt; my heart nearly stopped when a powerful searchlight shot in the driver's window and caught me with my head buried in Theo's lap. The cop guffawed and told us to behave ourselves. "And don't let me catch you again, young lady. You should know better!"

Somewhere in the back of my mind I knew my debt would come due. I had three incompletes that would only become grades with repeat exams in the spring, but I was spinning in the double intoxication of partying and the world of performance that was becoming my core. Dissociation was my life raft; the constant ache in my belly could be ignored.

Radio got me going, and my scenes in acting class opened new territory. I did Elvira in *Blithe Spirit*, not a big scene but certainly different from my high school image; it was great fun being a sexy filmy ghost. Then, with two days' notice, a directing student wanted the soda-fountain scene from *Our Town*, and the class response was over the top. After Christmas I had another break-through and wrote home to brag:

The scene from 'Pajama Game' went up today. I am not much of a singer, and here I was, singing! I found a full, solid comedy voice somewhere, used it, and we knocked'em dead. Prof. Stasheff said that it was a very good thing to do, as it broke the typecasting that has been present in my work for their class.

Another letter three days later:

I am flying high today as a result of the final scene I did in directing class. It was a beaut from O'Neill's 'Beyond the Horizon.' When we were finished, there was a ten-second dead silence, then real applause; that silence was beautiful. Then Prof stood up and said, 'Just a minute, Linda, I want to say something. You ought to get a medal for this. I don't know what you're getting in 51, but

I'd sure give you an A+!' Then Dr. Jack said, *'Your acting ability has deepened and matured greatly this semester, and this was a beautiful, beautiful job.'*

The fall grade report came: an A in Acting, two withdraws (German and Physics) and four flunks (Zoology, History, Choir, and Phys Ed). I couldn't intercept it. When I went home for semester break, my mother screamed, "What were you doing? What were you doing?" My bewildered father sat in his leather armchair, stunned, while I turned into a boneless bag of tears and snot, weeping and groveling. We were in the beautiful cozy library with a wood fire burning, and we all were in hell. All my dissociated selves tried to say something coherent; whatever I said, lies or truth, it eventually worked. I was given another chance. I had the spring semester to try again, finish my incompletes, and do it right. I went back to Ann Arbor and wrote home with confidence:

This semester's classes have started off in good order, and I am determined to see that they continue that way. I have set myself a definite schedule and will stick to it without exception if it's the last thing I do! I must never, never let myself put anything off, even for an hour; if I do, I start all over again what happened last semester. My self-discipline went sliding, but I know that will never happen again.

Of all my letters home, this is the hardest one for me to read.

∽

In February I starred as Mary, Queen of Scots, in a half-hour radio show that would be submitted to a national competition. In March I was the lead in a one-act, *Trap Doors*, presented on the Lab Series, and it was so successful that we were asked to do a second performance. My next role in the Lab Series was in William Inge's *Glory in the Flower*. I was twenty, Jackie was forty but still naive and vivacious. It wasn't easy.

I was dating up a storm with multiple guys and had developed a strong letch for Theo's roommate, Marsh. I wrote a candid note home: *I like both Theo and Marsh, and what do I do now? If I go out with one, the other will sulk, and if I go out with neither, all three of us will sulk. Oh well, I guess it'll iron itself out in time.*

There were others, mostly from radio and theatre, and while I was mixing alcohol and risk, I was part of a tribe and held the line at keeping my technical virginity. From the perspective of today's standards, it sounds pretty silly, but I was dealing with a different time and a mother who thought sex was revolting. When I entered adolescence, I was endowed with a huge sex drive, and a colossal degree of fear was required to keep me chaste. I didn't have sexually active friends and didn't know diddly about how the game was played. Looking back, I owe an apology to a lot of guys I let come too close to the mark before saying no.

Then I made the mistake of accepting a double date proposed by a girl from my dorm. The guy was a spoiled high-wattage sophisticate, the Belgian-born son of an esteemed musician who was a guest on the music faculty; the kid had money and his own convertible. On the second date, we drank the vodka he carried in a silver flask. "It's OK, nobody can smell vodka on your breath. You won't get in trouble when you go back to the dorm." He parked with the top down up on Observatory Hill, and the evening got chilly. "Let's go back to my place and warm up before I take you home." A classic move, but the vodka had drowned my judgment. I was too impaired to know what happened, even though he gave me a review. "You really weren't much of a virgin. Did you ride horseback a lot?"

A few days later, a senior girl who lived down the hall asked me to come have a cup of tea. "Linda, are you all right?" "I'm coming down with a cold." "No, I mean, are you all right, after what happened?" "What are you talking about?" "That guy you went out with, he really has a reputation for stalking virgins and then boasting about it. He's been saying he had his way with you." "What? That's a lie. He sure tried, but he didn't get anywhere."

"Well, if you need somebody to talk to, I'm here." But I couldn't admit the truth to myself. It was one more thing to bury in the back of my mind.

Then I was cast in the chorus of the full University Theatre production of *Electra*. I didn't have a principal role, but the ensemble work was substantial. A month into rehearsals, spring break interrupted things and I went home. I talked too much about *Electra* and my mother exploded: "How dare you take time away from your studies! You have no business doing anything but making up for your failures. Pretending to be an actress won't get you anywhere. You have no looks, no heart, no voice, and no sense of humor."

And then came the day in May when Prof. Stasheff came up to me in the hall and said, "Tonight you shall put on a pretty dress and high-heeled shoes and be present at the Graduate Study Club at 7:30." I asked why and was told, "Never mind why. Just do as I tell you." That night, the Graduate Study Club been turned over to the Speech Department Honors Assembly, and I received that year's award for Radio-TV acting. The icing on the cake was the little article about it in the campus newspaper; I stuck the clipping in an envelope and sent it home without comment, but in my mind I yelled, "Gotcha!"

∽

What astonishes me now is how I could have been such a wreck and still keep putting up a front. Yes, I got that award, I had praise and good reviews, I was cast in good roles, and that painted a bright picture. It just wasn't a picture my family knew or valued. At home I was still playing my high school role, the brilliant girl who will get into med school in three years. In the face of failure after failure, I was still insisting that girl was me.

The popular definition of insanity? "Doing the same thing over and over again, but expecting different results." It was an accurate diagnosis. Again, I wrote home: *Finals will not be the wracking experience this semester that they have sometimes been, as these courses have frequent exams, necessitating constant review. This eases the final studying. This is a good thing, because I have two exams in one day, and one the next morning. Three three-hour finals in twenty-four hours might be a strain otherwise!*

My bluff didn't hold. Two C's, a D, an F, and an incomplete, along with an A in Stage Directing and a notice of flunking out.

When I came home in June of 1959, the grades hadn't arrived, and I was supposedly set to return in the fall; my room deposit for Martha Cook had been paid, and my stuff was in dorm storage. The axe had not yet fallen, but I was in too deep to get by with lies again. The verdict arrived. I had been kicked out and was back home where it all started. Nineteen years old and I was a child having nightmares again.

∼

Writing this from the vantage point of being eighty is an unsettling process. I was blessed to have a big cache of letters and diaries, as well as the implacable skills of a termite for burrowing into the woodwork. The challenge has been navigating the results, which time after time cast a flash-bulb clarity on the layers of reality I created with my lies. I didn't lie for advantage, I lied to survive, and then I had to hide the fact of lying from myself. It worked out—after all, I'm here writing this—but I honestly don't know how I steered through it.

It's not easy to reach out a hand across the years to my younger self, the girl who was claiming her birthright to sexuality and creativity. It's almost impossible for me to understand how I thought I could maintain this fiction. For a year and a half, I was split in three. One lived the life and reveled in it. One reported home about the fiction of my status. One crammed reality into a dark corner that hid the murk from everything except that painful corner of the gut. Still, it's hard to avoid a sneaky admiration for the skills of the amateur forger.

Reading the letters I wrote home during this time was at first so scalding that I couldn't cope; I put the box in the back of a closet. When I decided to start this memoir, I employed a start-up device: I created a document listing all the letters with only a date and a phrase for each. That created enough distance to allow me to read the actual letters. But I'm an actress. I can hear the sound of my fawning voice in the desperate lies, and I still squirm. Maybe by the time I have finished the final draft of this, I'll be able to listen.

Dear Mommy and Daddy,

This semester's classes have started off in good order, and I am determined to see that they continue that way. I have set myself a definite schedule and will stick to it without exception if it's the last thing I do! What I must do is never, never let myself put anything at all off, even for an hour; if I do, I start all over again what happened last semester. You see, I just got too good at putting things off for an hour, a day, a week, and eventually dismissing them entirely. So, I bound out of bed at seven every morning -- no more "five minutes more" -- wash and dress, review notes, etc., for fifteen minutes, eat breakfast, make my bed, then study until nine, when I leave for class. I purposely arranged it so I would have five nine o'clocks instead of three and two ten o'clocks; this way I can settle into the routine. I bawl myself out good and proper if I catch the old song-and-dance about "It's only a lecture and they don't take attendance: I can take the time to write a speech...", because I know now I'd never write the speech, just start the habit of cutting that lecture. My self-discipline went sliding last semester, but I know that will never happen again. ...

6.

Home Again

That final semester, spring of '59, was a non-stop workout in theatre and radio, and I was getting steady feedback about my growth as a performer. There were challenging scenes in class, terrific reviews for the William Inge one-act, and the department's award for acting. I was riding high-voltage energy and loving every minute. The high school obsession with medicine was left in the dust—this was right now and coming from my core. Something powerful had awakened in me. My mother's scathing criticisms? Overruled.

Back in December of '58, while I was still faking it as a sophomore, I proposed going to Interlochen again and sent in an application. When the fall semester collapsed on my head, I made a case for going anyway; I'd have to be somewhere, disgraced or not, and I swore I'd pay my own way. Dr. Jack, who taught there, said I would have the female leads in *The Old Maid* and *The Devil's Disciple*.

My application was approved. I was apprehensive about the span of time at home before Interlochen, but I had a convenient distraction. I was going to be a bridesmaid at Betsy's June wedding, a big whoop-de-doo in Kalamazoo. The bridesmaid's dress was a winner: a flattering apple-green satin, tight-waisted and full-skirted. Best of all, I'd stay three days with her family.

But first I had to navigate the white-water aftermath of my academic disgrace. It was doubly difficult because I had made such passionate promises after the fall semester. Eventually my father sat down for a heart-to-heart with him alone. "What do you really want to do? I'll support you for whatever you can do honestly, but you have to be forthright and say what you want. Never mind what you used to say, that's past. What's important to you now?"

"Theatre." There, I said it. I couldn't believe I had, but I did and the roof did not fall in. Northwestern University, whose theatre school had a great reputation, was in nearby Evanston. My father and I worked out a plan. I could go ahead with the summer at Interlochen, as long as I could pay my own way. When the summer was over, I would enroll for a non-degree year at Valparaiso University, the local four-year college, to prove that I could stick to academic discipline before more tuition went down the drain. I would live at home, an unnerving idea, but the deal was made.

Betsy's wedding was a colorful and delicious experience, and it wasn't long afterward that I arrived at Interlochen. My job applications hadn't panned out, but I found an alternative. I was invited to live in Dr. Jack's family house rent-free in exchange for helping with meals and child care, and the local café would hire me as a waitress, 35 hours a week, every morning from 7:30 to 10:30 plus three afternoons and an evening. With tips it would cover tuition.

Dr. Jack and his wife had four little children. I slept in a tiny garret room upstairs with a bed like a ship's bunk, and there were three other lodgers in this big lakeside summer house: a couple from the music department, and an older theatre student. When I made dinner, it was for a table of ten.

I still had my heart in music, and I wanted to try out for the concertos concert, so I enrolled for one credit-hour in piano and practiced like crazy. My letters were cheerful.

Oh boy, am I busy! Between work and the children and rehearsing, madly practicing the piano, and sleeping, there isn't much time left over. Which is all right by me. I eat ravenously, go to bed early, sleep like the dead, and get up with the birds.

Besides playing Delia in 'The Old Maid' I am doing lights for the show. Dr. Jack scrounged up some old ceiling fixtures, and we have rewired them and will hang them from cross-beams in Giddings.

I am about to take a stab as making matzoh balls for chicken soup. The fact that I have never made a matzoh ball doesn't faze me; I've never lit a show before either, but that isn't holding me back.

I'd gotten the summer I wanted and the work that would pay for it. I could rightly congratulate myself for independence, but the tone of that letter still sounds like all the others from the Ann Arbor years: terminal cheeriness in an effort to please. It would still be years before I could write an honest letter to my parents.

The Devil's Disciple was cast a week before *The Old Maid* opened, with pretty much the same lead actors in both plays. The male lead in *Disciple* was my fellow lodger. Three summers ago, he had played Claudius in Interlochen's *Hamlet*; I was a high school camper at the time, and my parents saw the production on one of their visits. I was wildly embarassed at my mother's attempt to interrupt with applause after Claudius' prayer scene; he was good, OK, but I was sixteen and parental extravagance was mortifying. Now I was happy to be cast opposite a good actor, grateful for anything that didn't make me look bad. And when *The Old Maid* opened, I was anything but bad:

We opened last night, and we were very, very good. All kinds of audience swarmed around afterward and practically carried me off on their shoulders, as did the cast. We almost had two disasters—missed entrance cues. The first time I just said, "I'd better call Tina in now," went to the door and got her. The second time wasn't so easy, as her entrance was a surprise, so I had to fill with business and pray. But we came through all right—audience not much the wiser.

The drama class, waitressing, rehearsing, performing, intermittent child care, and taking my turns cooking for the family—I still found time for the hours and hours of piano practice on the piece that I hoped would get me into the concertos program: Schumann's *A Minor Piano Concerto*. The audition was memorable. I was confronted with a huge black nine-foot Steinway grand, and it took far more strength than the easy upright I'd been using. As soon as I was under way, I thought "Oh God, I'll never get through this." Mr. Harris had told me I had unusual power and speed for the size of my hands, and I had been proud of that. It wasn't enough. All my concentration was on the burning pain in my forearms as I tried to deliver the goods, and any thought of delicacy and nuance was out the window. I desperately wanted to stand up, slam down the keyboard lid, and yell "Uncle!" Instead, I played to the end, went out, found an empty practice cabin, and collapsed in tears.

I put on a brave face, but it was a blow. Being unable to grasp analytic geometry had rocked my self-image as a math champ, and now all my gold medals from piano contests were right down the toilet along with the square root of minus one. The consolation was that theatre was still there for me, and so were the warm summer nights, the full moon, and something else.

There has been a gorgeous yellow full moon the last two nights. We were so entranced by this and by the warmth and calm of the water that we went night-swimming two nights in a row. It was lovely.

Concealed below those discreet words was the beginning of an affair with Dr. Jack. The toddler Cindy's bedroom was on the third floor with mine, two tiny garret rooms on either side of the steep rickety stairs. One night, Dr. Jack came up to kiss Robin good night and then came into my room. When he leaned down and kissed me, I couldn't believe it. Any scruples vanished. Then we went night-swimming.

Elizabeth: One of Many

~

From today's perspective, given the endless revelations of powerful men taking advantage, it's hard to write this without seeming to excuse his actions, and nothing in my experience negates the pain felt by countless women and girls. But I was very hungry. I'd had a crush on this man since high school. In the fall I would start my year of penance at home. This summer was my last fling, playing two major roles, not to mention being in a place I loved. The idea of living in Dr. Jack's house was foolhardy, but I turned a deaf ear to my own warnings. Part of me wanted the worst to happen, even courted it. Having never developed any ethical structure at all, I didn't register the magnitude of the transgression: he was an older married man and I was his student. I was blind, and I didn't want to see, I only wanted to feel. He was in his thirties and foolish. I was nineteen and foolish.

~

My vodka-soaked accident with the sneaky Belgian had ended the virginity issue, and no matter how I hid that from myself, deep down I knew it had happened. This was my first fully-conscious sex with someone I was hungry for: at night, in the water, with a full moon. It was over in a moment, but it wasn't the last time. It's hard to be furtive in a house with nine other people, four of them children, and private episodes were brief and rare. There must have been suspicions, because toward summer's end when Dr. Jack's parents visited, they staged a confrontation.

They were sitting out on the dock with white wine in the afternoon sun and invited me to sit with them. "You did a wonderful job in *The Devil's Disciple*; you're a good actress." "Thank you, well, I was just following Dr. Jack's directions." "Are you going to continue studying theatre?" "I've applied to Northwestern but I haven't heard back yet." "You know, we've heard some rumor about you and Jack, and it has made us uncomfortable. His good reputation is important." After a startled pause, I took a deep breath and responded as if they were joking. They didn't laugh. I kept it as light as my reeling brain would allow and cobbled together my denials. I don't think they believed me, but they let the interrogation come to an end.

During my childhood what I'd learned was not about right or wrong, it was about not getting caught. Right and wrong weren't on the menu. The process of learning personal responsibility hadn't begun. Drunk with infatuation, presented with a desirous man, and having at last outrun the virginity police, I had taken what was offered and reveled in it. His ardor and praise were lavish, and for that little span of time I was an erotic goddess. While I did care about the man himself, what set me alight was being fully immersed in the white-water rapids of sex, saying yes to every moment.

The last performances of *Devil's Disciple* were a complete success, and I had the heady experience of being recognized and praised in the camp. There were two weeks left: no rehearsals, no performances, just finishing the class, doing final piano work, and trying not to recognize that the summer was almost over. The final symphony concert was August 23rd, and as usual, the whole audience wept as the slow gentle music of Hansen's *Les Preludes* began the final minute of the last night of camp. It ended, the musicians put down their instruments, the conductor ritually snapped his baton in two, and the traditional silence (no applause) was broken only by sniffles. I packed up to begin my year of penance at Valparaiso University, back home in Indiana.

∼

Back Home Again in Indiana was a hit song in 1917 and became a jazz standard; I hated it. I was stuck in my bedroom with its pink walls, ruffled green-and-white checkered gingham curtains, ruffled bedspread, and ruffled dressing-table skirt: a very girly room, and I would have to spend the next year in it. Eight years ago a decorator had been hired for a bedroom make-over.

My mother complained that I was female but not feminine, hence the ruffles. Yards and yards of gingham got cut, stitched and ruffled, and my father rebuilt the west wall: six big drawers topped by cabinets. They bought me a maple study desk with a gooseneck lamp and my very own little Royal portable typewriter. Until I went to Ann Arbor, I lived amid ruffles.

Now I had to focus on the present, make peace with the gingham, and find a life beyond those pink walls. When classes started at Valparaiso University, I was past ready to plunge in. I'd already had two weeks back home remembering how to dodge my mother once the gin hit the coffee cup, and I couldn't afford depression. In Ann Arbor, I'd hide in my dorm room and compulsively oversleep or make myself sick eating the fruitcake and sweet wine sent as gifts from home. I couldn't do that here. I was technically away from my mother while I was at classes, but in my mind I was always skewered by her gaze. I did my best to remember how I got through high school. My lifeline of theatre had been yanked away, and it was too easy to be miserable.

I'd been in a swirl of high-energy performing, surrounded by the crazy people who'd become my tribe; all that was gone. The window beside my bed faced east toward the catalpa tree, the gravel country road, the robin's-egg blue mailbox, and the next farm's cornfields. The sun blared at me as I got ready to drive myself to my 7:30 a.m. Spanish class. My father's commute to Chicago was early too, and I enjoyed making breakfast for both of us; I'd have time for a chat before my mother came downstairs. Somehow being damaged goods made me feel more adult, and it was a relief not to be cowering under a load of lies and secrets. I'd hit bottom, the worst had happened, and I was still breathing. Now I had to prove I could be a student again.

My fall classes were Spanish, English Lit, History of England, Intro to Philosophy, and believe it or not, Calculus. It was my last chance to do hard math without having to dance with imaginary numbers; if I succeeded, I might be able to think of myself as a brain once again. Spring was an even bigger chunk: Spanish, History of Civilization, Modern Drama, Short Story Writing, Theory of Government, and Shakespeare. I even signed up for two credits of piano; I wanted to heal my wounds on that score too.

At Valpo I went to my classes with grim determination, the way I used to swallow my smelly vitamin syrup before the school bus came. All during the fall I behaved myself. Then on January 4th the community theatre had auditions for *The Seven Year Itch*; I went, got cast as The Girl and started rehearsals the week after spring classes began. I was back in my world again and loving it.

~

I hadn't learned a damn thing from my failures. Disaster heard the band playing, asked me to dance, and off I went. My spring classes were uninspiring, and being on stage again was an intoxication. When the show opened, I had just turned twenty, and the paper printed a great review. It was only four performances, but we'd broken all attendance records for the Community Theatre's five years of existence. Then it was over.

My piano teacher nudged me out of my doldrums by convincing me to do a recital. All the rehearsal discipline I'd learned from theatre went into preparing for the piano "show." He selected bravura pieces from my repertoire and even coached me on what to wear and how to do my hair to maximize the image of a petite dainty shepherdess who came out in high heels and her apple-green bridesmaid's dress, sat down at the piano, and walloped the hell out of Brahms. Mission accomplished: I got back in the saddle, played my recital, and quit while I was ahead.

I must have seen what was coming, but I didn't resist. I was alive again.

~

I had a boyfriend. Kenny, five years older, had family in Valparaiso and wrote for the town newspaper; his younger brother was a year behind me in high school. Some of his pals were active in the community theatre; we met at *Seven Year Itch* rehearsals and hit it off. He was smart, funny, had a lot of friends, and was socially adept. Even my mother liked him.

I liked him too, and sex seemed a reasonable extension of our friendship. He had a car, and one of his favorite things on dates was to drive to a bar near the University of Chicago for pitchers of beer. I wasn't of legal drinking age, but Kenny was a regular customer and the bartender didn't pay attention to me. I always hit the ladies' room right before we left, but the drive back took over an hour. When he'd pull the car off into a cornfield and move to the back seat, my appreciation of his endeavors was not as focused as it might have been. I could have just said, "Wait, I need to take a pee" and used the rows of corn as a screen, but my self-assurance wasn't up to it.

Kenny knew people in other area theatres as well, and when the Dunes Summer Theatre was planning a production of *Peter Pan*, he made sure I knew about the auditions. I was cast as Peter, and the little theatre built a bargain-basement version of flying: I hid behind a curtain, clipped my harness to the single rope that went through a ceiling pulley, and jumped off a window bench while a stagehand hauled me up. One matinee, the crew hadn't checked whether the rope and clip were in place behind the window frame. They weren't. It took a while before somebody realized, and meanwhile I was strutting my little-boy self around the Darlings' bedroom touting the power of belief: "Follow me, jump when I jump, and pretty soon we'll all be flying!" I heard a scuffle offstage, jumped back on the window seat, got hooked up, and finally flew.

My hair was tightly bound by a nylon stocking under my green cap, and my flying harness was uncomfortable and itchy. When the show was over, I'd make a beeline to my dressing room to get out of cap and harness. Kids weren't supposed to come backstage, but once a little boy snuck into my dressing room, took one look at my long blonde hair, and burst into tears: "Peter Pan's a girrrrrl!"

Kenny was amiable company through the summer, but I got obsessed with a member of the lighting crew at Dunes, a tall moody Polish guy who already had a girlfriend. After a few glances lasted too long, we began hanging out after hours in his cabin, nipping Scotch from his bottle, listening to his records, and eventually kissing to the point of painful frustration. I wanted more, but didn't get it until all the shows had closed and we had one last date. He was my souvenir from the summer, and I thought about him for years.

There was another summer bright spot. Two years ago I'd done some part-time work for George and Dottie Bowers, local people I knew from gatherings hosted by my parents. They ran an in-home editing business with clients like *Who's Who in America*, and that summer they hired me as a junior editor. After a day's work in their basement office, I always hated to leave. They were people I could talk to, who saw me. I loved them.

They'd even given me a window into a social life. When I was in high school, I got an invitation to go tobogganing—there would be other young people there. I had a wonderful time and even got my first teenage kiss. I was invited again to other parties, and it was my first experience being social with intelligent people who treated me as just another person. It was dazzling. Sure, I had braces and coke-bottle glasses, but that didn't matter; we could all laugh together.

George and Dottie were the first adults with whom I felt kinship. Their house was in the woods not far east of us, up the hill from Highway 6. They were smart, literate, funny, held their liquor well (unlike my mother), and were a bit younger than my folks. They showed me an adult world I could feel part of. I didn't know the word *Bohemian* then, but it's what they were and what I became.

My final day before I left for Northwestern, I thanked them for giving me a job and a refuge, and we had a big hug. It was the last time I ever saw them. In January 1962, there was a ghastly midnight fire that burned George and Dottie's house to the ground—with them in it. Their loss was a kick in the gut.

∼

The real world was a slippery slope. It had taken me seventeen years to set myself up as a brain, rack up honors, and tack myself to the wall. When that identity collapsed, a new one was hard to bring into focus. The piano had been a solace and salvation, and then became a painful litany of guilt and inadequacy. I'd believed that I was gifted, but I wasn't good enough for concertos at summer camp. My acting had gotten me applause and congratulations, but did that mean anything? Could I build a life on that?

My high-octane sex drive would have gotten me into trouble if I hadn't had thick glasses, clunky corrective shoes, short hair and braces. My crushes never connected, but when I turned into a cute blonde with bouncy cleavage, it was a whole new ball game. I scored no home runs. I'd go after this guy and veer off toward that guy, get a few solid hits and then slide into third on my face. I began to suspect I'd never have a long-term relationship. What was the point of being attractive if I didn't hang on to anyone?

I'd gone off to Ann Arbor with an image of myself riding my excellent brain to the finish line of an MD in a white coat. Then theatre ignited a passion deeper than medicine, but I kept faking. I didn't have the guts to stand up and say, "I was wrong, I was scared, and I lied; I need to apologize and work for what I really want." When I told my father I wanted to go to Northwestern, I meant it, but I was also saying what would get me out of a mess. Being functional in the real world was a long way off.

∼

When I started writing this months ago, I realized that I didn't know how I did with my classes at Valpo. Northwestern had accepted me, so I would have needed a transcript. I found a copy among my mother's letters, and the grades were all A's and B's. Was that real or a forgery? I couldn't remember, and that was deeply disturbing. I needed to know, so I sent for my official records. The pandemic had closed down academic offices to a skeleton staff, and it took three months for the transcript to arrive. I sweated every day of those months.

It was devastating. I thought I'd prepared myself for bad news, but it hit hard. I had to sit down, close my eyes, and breathe. Four grades were incompletes that became failures; Spanish, History, and Piano were A's. Those three instructors loved what they were doing, and I did the work gladly. The other four—Short-Story Writing, Theory of Government, Modern Drama, and Shakespeare—were just a cold set of assignments, my heart wasn't in it, and I blew them off.

I don't know what I did with the time. Depression is a strange beast, and it radically affected my memory. I don't remember if my beloved cats were still there. I don't know if I practiced for my recital on my piano at home. I can't remember much about my daily time in the house, or what I did after I drove to campus. Maybe I sat in the car reading science fiction until it was time to go home. Maybe I thought I'd pull off a Hail Mary pass and ace my final exams. I must have known that my grades would sink me.

What's clear is that I sent Northwestern a forged transcript and then wiped my memory. Now I've recovered some images: renting a post office box, inventing a business that requested a transcript for a prospective employee, doing the forgery, sending A's and B's to Northwestern, and then blanking it out for sixty years. Facing the reality of yet another fraud, I felt a sick grief, and at the same time I was grateful. It got me my life-mate.

7.

Well, Let's Do It

In mid-September 1960, heaving a massive sigh of relief, I packed up from my ruffled bedroom and checked into my Northwestern dormitory. It was actually the fourth floor of the North Shore Hotel in Evanston, women only, with curfew hours. It was an old hotel, built in 1919—musty threadbare carpet, heavy dark wood, steam radiators encrusted with multiple coats of cracked paint. Its elevator rattled up to a dorm desk where students took mandatory shifts answering phones and signing girls in and out. It was by no means classy, but it felt friendly, like an old battered shoe. I was assigned to a quad: two rooms connected together, two girls to each room. By pure luck my roommate never showed up, and I wheedled my way into being the sole occupant without extra expense.

Northwestern had a hefty reputation in theatre training. I was going to honor my agreement with my father, take all they could offer and kick ass. My mother had made me agree to get a teaching certificate, but I thought I could do that as well with no sweat. The fall theatre season included *Antigone* and *King Lear*, and auditions were right away. There was an impressive range of talent but one actor's magnificent voice stood out. It was a large auditorium and

I couldn't see his face clearly, but everyone seemed to know him, and I could easily find out his name.

The grand lady of the theatre faculty, Alvina Krause, would be directing *King Lear* and seemed to like my reading of Cordelia; on top of that I was enrolled in two of Miss Krause's acting classes. I also had a required history class and a weird elective: Intro to Astrophysics. The prof was J. Allen Hynek, whose UFO research was being studied by the Air Force and Hollywood, and that was intriguing. But the fifth class turned out to be the icing on the cake: Stage Lighting. I could be a techie again and learn from the ground up how everything worked.

Prof. Ted Fuchs had a Brooklyn accent, a dry humor, and taught the art of survival in a world of crappy lighting equipment: do it yourself and learn to do it right. His jokes cracked me up, but they were so deadpan that only one other person in the class was snorting. The good-looking blond guy across the aisle was as red-faced as I was from the strain of maintaining academic decorum, and soon I realized that he was the one whose voice had stunned me at the auditions. He got cast and I didn't, but it didn't matter; now I knew his name and we were going to spend three months sitting across from each other, laughing at the jokes. By the end of the second month we were lovers.

He was a sophomore and had been in a number of productions, but the top stories were about his coat and his pencil. Even in the coldest weather he often went without a coat, which was odd, but last year he had fallen down icy steps that caused the pencil in his shirt pocket to hit at just the right angle to stab straight in between his ribs. In the hospital, a surgical team was readied in case it had hit an artery or the heart itself, but when the time came they simply pulled the pencil out. They didn't let him keep it.

He was in acting classes, but his real passion was directing. Our first collaboration was one of his directing class projects, the murder scene from *Woyzeck*. He hated the available version, and together we created our own translation from the German. I played Marie, he directed, and a fellow acting student played the soldier who would kill me. It was an odd forest scene, dark and nearly wordless, ending with a brutal knife to the face. High stakes, and it worked. At the end, nobody moved or breathed.

I'd never had a director like this before, one who trusted the power of silence and created focus that made tiny movements speak volumes. I had faith in him, and he saw me as a collaborator, a fellow artist, a human being, and with him I felt the first inklings of a different stake in theatre. I had a partner.

I had no such luck in my acting classes. Miss Krause was brilliant, but only for those who were on her wavelength and could survive her denunciations. I wasn't and couldn't. I never did grasp what was meant by the assignments. We were to study an animal and embody its spirit; we were to visit an art museum, focus on one painting, then recreate its emotional essence; we were to go into memory to generate emotion from something in our past—all valid exercises in context, but I could see no context. I really got savaged for one exercise requiring me to read an imaginary letter sent by a boyfriend jilting me. It was to be a private moment, though there were two other students on stage doing their own thing at the same time. "What is this? You're faking. Sit down."

Miss Krause was too much like my mother—the age and the unpredictable violence—and my spine collapsed. Those who could stand their ground got stronger, but I heard that echo, "You're faking!" and shriveled. Miss Krause loved theatre to the marrow of her bones and demanded that it be practiced by strong, capable artists. Weaklings were to be weeded out.

My confusion was painful. Coming to Northwestern I'd been on a roll as a actress, and I touched something new in the *Woyzeck* scene. In that, I was good and I knew why. In acting class I wasn't good and I didn't know why. What I did know was that I wanted to spend as much time as possible with Conrad Bishop.

Well, Let's Do It

The week after the class performance of *Woyzeck*, we went on our first date to a Sunday matinee movie: *A Lesson in Love*, Ingmar Bergman's early comedy about an unravelling marriage that reknits into something stronger. First date, first Bergman, and I was knocked sideways.

I wrote home: *Bergman uses the camera the way a sculptor would use a chisel. All the extraneous things are cut out, and the structure of the whole work is right there. Today was the kind of beautiful day that makes it almost impossible to stay indoors.* After I got back from the movie, I tried to study, but instead I went outdoors, scuffed around in the dry leaves, and looked at the lake. After supper it was darker, and then I could work.

I had been hit hard. It was difficult to think about anything other than this strange Iowa guy who seemed to be from a planet as alien as mine. The first kiss was a lightning-bolt, like taking an impossible breath and riding it onto a Ferris wheel. I almost wept, and when we released into an embrace, my head fit neatly into his shoulder as if that were its proper home. It's the first time I really sensed that I was small, and it was delightful. I would have crawled into his pocket if I could.

Spending time with this person was at the top of my list, but many weekends I was expected to go back to Valpo, especially during the fall hunting season, to keep tabs on the house while they spent time in Cadillac. They had a new station wagon, so they lent me the old Chrysler New Yorker; I tried to obey the speed limits on the way back to Evanston and Conrad.

We spent hours in a student hangout called The Hut—great hot chocolate, lousy service (unless you just barged up to the kitchen window and yelled for it yourself), and a good jukebox. Edith Piaf singing *Milord* got played so often it's a miracle that the vinyl survived. Some late afternoons we'd find an empty classroom and he'd read poetry to me—Dylan Thomas, cummings, Housman. He became my world.

We went on another Bergman date to see a double feature in Chicago. On the train back, I suddenly found myself shaking, weeping, and gasping for breath. I didn't know why I was having this fit. Poor Conrad just sat with me until I got quiet, and suddenly I knew. *My God, this is the one.* Within the week, we got into the back seat of the Chrysler, parked on a frigid Evanston street with the windows fogged, and sealed our fate. We still celebrate November 13th as our true anniversary; the formal wedding only tied the bow of legality on what had already happened.

～

Now, sixty years later, I still remember thinking, "What the hell was that?" Pitching a fit on the El train felt like stepping into an empty elevator shaft, and I hadn't seen it coming. One quick glimpse through the veil, a long road with whiplash changes—it scared me to death, but this was the one. I barely knew him.

I was confused. He wasn't remotely the kind of guy I'd been attracted to. I had usually courted dark Leos, wild and edgy and good at providing unhappy endings. I didn't feel the same spark with this quiet blond Libra, odd and brilliant, the only child of a single mom who had little money but endless love. Although he was a brilliant director and we clicked erotically, I was baffled at finding myself super-glued to one person.

I'd never known anyone like him. Quiet, intense, determined, with a privately surreal style of writing and drawing, he lost all shyness when directing and was a confident artist. He was gentle, honest, and very strange. The guys I had known were easy to see or easy to see through. He was almost a part of me and yet something I couldn't quite comprehend; but right from the beginning I felt like a different person with him—neither an ornament nor an object to control, I was his peer, and I had to learn to see myself as someone who could be respected. That took a long time.

I was head-over-heels and knew in my gut that this was my life-mate, and at the same time I was terrified of commitment. I had developed a taste for being a huntress dating a string of guys. After finally exploring sex and staking out my territory, I was about to fence myself in and wasn't sure I approved. I simultaneously went full speed and tried to derail the train. One night I sneaked out of the dorm and took the El down to a folk bar where I knew a big sweaty Scotch-drinking singer was holding court. I was in full hunter mode; on the way downtown I saw my face reflected in the train window and couldn't recognize myself. I got to the bar, met the guy, accepted free Scotch, and stayed the night. It wasn't all a script out of the paperbacks; at one point he grumbled, "Ask your girlfriends how to make a guy hard." But in some crazy way it felt necessary. Once this crackpot escapade was over, I knew what I wanted, and I was ready.

∼

Thanksgiving and Christmas breaks felt like months, and Conrad sent wonderfully strange letters, written in pencil and decorated with bizarre drawings. What he wrote sounded like something translated from a foreign language, but it was spoken directly from his heart, and I heard it. The drawings were angular fusions of cartoons and Picasso, not polished art but disturbingly compelling. I began to sense how much I had yet to learn about him.

The logistics of intimacy proved difficult. I was in a women's dorm with curfew hours—no males allowed—and when Evanston is cold it's really cold. It was a measure of our dedication that we often hid in a grove of trees by the lakefront, backed against a tree trunk, generating what heat we could with stand-up necking. The level of frustration was driving us nuts, so Conrad started asking around; eventually a friend lent us the key to his off-campus apartment for some afternoon trysts, with unpredictable interruptions. Once there was pounding at the door and a shout: "I need to check the pork roast!" Sixty years have passed, but we still crack each other up by yelling, "Pork roast!"

My other lust was to get more of the powerful experience I'd had in the scene from *Woyzeck*. Conrad applied to do a spring workshop production of the play. We labored together translating from the German and finished a script after Christmas break. I could hardly wait to play Marie, but it didn't happen. With two other shows on the bill, there weren't enough male actors to cast it, and he switched to Ghelderode's *Women at the Tomb*. Like *Woyzeck*, it was bizarre, fragmentary and surreal, but without the kind of story that had moved me. It's what I could get, though, and as the Layer-Out of the Dead I smeared Vaseline and baby powder in my hair, turned the mugging dial up to eleven, and made do with broad clowning. As an actress, I was on hold, but at least I was working with my lover.

His capacity for work was almost frightening. His goal was to teach theatre at the university level and direct classics: at this time, the professional regional theatre was only in its infancy. By enrolling in summer sessions, he could get his Bachelor's degree early, stay at Northwestern for his Master's, then go elsewhere for a doctorate. He was a sophomore and it would be a long road, but we'd travel it together.

In the department's main season, I wasn't cast at all. Conrad had a heavy rehearsal schedule as the blind Tiresias in *Antigone* in December, then as the pompous Uncle in *The Girl from Maxim's* in January. I should have put my solitary energy into my academic courses, but I didn't. The exception was Stage Lighting; it was fascinating and useful, and I worked my ass off. I still have the notes and diagrams from class that Dr. Fuchs made us bind into our own self-made textbooks. He gave me an A in the fall and winter quarters, and I got an A in Directing in spring. My other grades were incompletes, drops and flunks, and I trotted out my forgery skills.

By the end of first quarter, I was put on academic probation, worked my way out of it in winter quarter, and flopped again in the spring. Conrad had received permission to live off campus, saying he couldn't concentrate in the dorm; the dean didn't have to know that the major distraction was frustrated sex. He found a flat to share with a fellow theatre student, I mustered the courage to go to Planned Parenthood, and at last we were able to spend whole nights together.

Then came the phone call. I'd signed out of my dorm for a weekend tryst, saying I was going home; my mother called the dorm, and the switchboard girl said I was home in Valpo. When I got back to the dorm, I had a message: "You signed out to go home. Where *were* you?" I was too unsettled to fabricate a plausible lie. "I spent the time with Conrad." All hell broke loose: I was now a certified slut. She ended a long screaming bout by declaring: "You're just going to get married before you disgrace me!"

It was a violent phone call, and as I was telling Conrad, I was still snuffling tears. We were walking toward campus alongside a park with a black wrought-iron fence, and I was idly sticking out my hand to whap the bars with my fingers. When I got to that final ultimatum, he stopped and stood there. I rubbed my tingling fingers and waited for him to speak.

"Well, let's do it."

I just looked at him. Ever since the end of the long Christmas separation, we'd known we would marry—sometime in the future. It would be a full two years before he finished at Northwestern, and a PhD would take at least another three years. Here he was, suggesting that we call the bluff, cut to the chase, and learn to survive. Once I started breathing again, we began to discuss practical details, and soon I got grounded enough to realize how funny it was. I was supposed to feel shamed, and instead I was being given what I wanted. I heard Br'er Rabbit pleading, "Oh please don't throw me in the briar patch!" and began to giggle.

We did some fast research on economic survival and it was encouraging. I could get a part-time job as a lighting assistant for the Children's Theatre and earn $1,400. He checked the terms of his scholarship and found that, yes, they'd pay him the $800 that would have covered his dorm and meal plan. The placement office had work in the library for $1.50 an hour. I'd already done some paid music gigs singing folk songs for women's clubs and coffeehouses. After asking some married students what they were paying for rent, it looked as if we could get through a year on $2,500—this being a day when our weekly grocery bill was about $20.

Yes, it could happen. At the beginning of June, Conrad called his mother, told her he was planning to marry, then sent her a long detailed letter about how we could support ourselves. He was not yet twenty years old. It was impressive reasoning, but his mother was terrified that he might abandon his plans, trying to please a girl who had been raised with all the advantages.

She wrote back immediately, affirming her trust, speaking honestly about her fears, then this: *I have no advice now or ever—do not plan to give any. Suggestions yes and encouragement yes, but any decisions to be made are yours—the two of you. I would feel that I was gaining a daughter, which I never had, and will be to her the same as to you.* She said she would visit Evanston in early July, just before the summer shows opened. We set a wedding date for August.

The summer session was short, just six weeks. I enrolled in two classes in the Ed School, gritting my teeth and obeying my mother's orders to get a teaching certificate. We were both cast in the Summer Festival shows, and I got a room in "Krause House," two blocks from Conrad's little third-floor garret. Miss Krause, who regularly rented rooms to theatre students, went away to her summer theatre every year, and the rules for tenants were pretty much like "Don't wreck anything and don't make a mess."

The second-floor kitchen opened onto a roomy open porch; six of us decided to pool our food budgets and eat dinners communally. I'd learned a lot at Interlochen about feeding a bunch of people, and I volunteered to do most of the shopping and cooking. We were all in the summer shows and had only two hours between afternoon and evening rehearsals, so we had to become an effective kitchen team. Juggling diverse personalities, appetites, and skills took some adjustments, but we worked it out: the smell of fresh-baked bread is very persuasive. Hassles were smoothed out, slackers learned to do their share, and everybody enjoyed the result. It proved to be good training for our eventual lurch out of academia into ensemble theatre.

My roommate and I cleaned the grimy kitchen, scraped layers of ancient grease from the oven, found the screens for the porch, and hauled out a table and chairs. We shared a little bedroom that opened onto a living room with hardwood floors and bare walls. When there was time, I could grab a little privacy with Conrad at his place, but most nights I was in my own room. When my roommate's boyfriend spent the night, the two of them sacked out in a sleeping bag on the living room floor. The bare room amplified sound, the lovers were uninhibited, and it was an education. The boyfriend's best line? "You were born to love fucking!"

I was not born to love Ed School. My morning classes were deadly, and I started blowing them off; my mind was on other things. The wedding had been set for August 12th. Theatre rehearsals were all afternoon and evening, and after July 4th we were both performing six nights a week for a month, four plays in rotating repertory, and I was cooking for five other ravenous actors. Somehow amidst all this, I got a wedding dress, registered on Marshall Fields' gift list, got a blood test and marriage license, and snuck into Conrad's bed whenever possible.

Margaret Bishop took the train from Council Bluffs on July 2nd, checked into her hotel room, and came directly to Conrad's apartment—much earlier than expected. The summer heat was intense, and we were still in bed without a stitch on when we heard a knock on the door—not the best way to meet your future mother-in-law. He thought fast. "Hold on, hold on, I'm not dressed. Can I meet you at the hotel? Let's have breakfast there." I controlled my panic, we listened to the footsteps going down the stairs, and when the front door shut, we collapsed in sweaty relief. "Wait five minutes after I leave and then scoot. We'll meet for dinner at Krause House."

That afternoon I gathered a big paper bag full of my favorite greens—lamb's quarters grew profusely in the neighborhood alleys—and was about to put my risen loaves of bread in the oven when Conrad and Margaret arrived. The introduction was perfect; her worried mother's heart was eased by seeing me foraging in the alley and putting together a hearty meal for a bunch of people on a nickel-and-dime budget. This upper-class girl was going to do all right with the hard-scrabble life to come. We were mother and daughter from the first hug.

The summer performances ended on August 2nd, the classes were nearly over, and there was still lots to do. I made a plea to my profs to delay my exams until after the wedding and was granted mercy. Then there was the question: once married, where would we live? We took the advice of some grad student couples to look for rooms in a private home; we soon found a little detached cottage on the grounds of an upscale house in a suburb. In exchange for very low rent, I was expected to do occasional cooking, and we were to keep watch on the grounds. It seemed workable. The previous tenant had left an epic mess, but there wasn't time for more than a quick sweep. Our stuff got hauled and stacked; the rest could wait until after the honeymoon.

Margaret came to Indiana a few days before the wedding and was put up, along with Conrad, at a local motel. Most of the decisions were made by the Davisons, who also paid the expense. Mary had wanted the high drama of an Episcopal service, but since none of us were Episcopalian, the church said no. Plan B was a Unitarian minister and a home garden ceremony, which was beautiful.

Well, Let's Do It

Folding chairs for fifty people were arranged in a semicircle on the huge back lawn, facing a majestic blue spruce tree that served as an altar backdrop. A portable electric organ had been rented, a catering crew set out the reception food and champagne in the screened summer-house, and a four-tiered wedding cake was delivered from Chicago's Palmer House.

Mary's brother was a high-end professional photographer and did the wedding book with all the traditional shots; the finished book was three inches thick. The bride was posed looking into a huge mirror, her mother beaming at her side. The groom put a boutonniere in the lapel of his best man. The maid of honor hiked the bride's ballerina-length skirt to display the lacy garter. The groom, the bride's father, and the minister posed for a solemn conference in the den. It felt like a dress rehearsal, costumes and all, with a hackneyed script, but we performed it.

The little Hammond organ beside the blue spruce was played by Mary's life-long friend Miss Vogt, whose regular job was playing the enormous pipe organ at Wanamaker's in Philadelphia; but she managed fine on this rented pipsqueak. She began the processional music, and bride and father walked solemnly from the back of the house to the spot in front of the tree. I was scared that I'd sink a high heel of my white satin shoes into the grass and fall flat on my face, the groom was anxious he'd drop the ring, and the minister was just plain terrified—he'd never done a wedding before. But everyone smiled in the photos.

The guests were mostly well-heeled people in their sixties, friends of my parents, and I was relieved that I could remember their names. The groom's garret-mate was his best man, the bride's high school friend was her maid of honor, and together with Conrad's mom, this contingent of the wedding party stood out as dissimilar, but all were delighted. Vows, rings, kiss: it was real, and most important, it was legal. The show was about to end and we could hardly wait for the curtain call. I cut the cake, hugged and grinned madly, and finally changed into civilian clothes. After throwing the bouquet and scurrying through the rice, we got into the car and took off. I did the driving.

The performance was done, we were in charge, and the contrast couldn't have been more extreme. We would spend a few days alone at the summer house in Cadillac, but I wanted something all our own for that first night. I had been to Sleeping Bear Sand Dunes on picnics with Interlochen students, and that's where we went. My bridal night was on the lakefront side of a dune with a tent and sleeping bags; our first married breakfast was bacon and eggs and coffee, courtesy of an iron skillet, a battered tin pot, and a campfire—a relief after the extravagant catering. We had a few quiet days at the house, swimming, canoeing, and fishing, then drove back to our suburban cottage and got down to the business of learning to live together.

At Northwestern my sense of identity had been crumbling. Being a brain was no longer a winner, and I didn't yet have a grasp on my next role. Old academic pride made me enroll in Astrophysics, and adding education classes implied a self-confidence that was past its sell-by date. I saw myself as an actress and had come to Northwestern confident in my ability. Then acting class became a ritual of humiliation, and I couldn't get even bit parts except in the summer shows. I was too fragmented to realize that I was making the same mistakes again and again. Flunking and forgery were not going to be sustainable.

Then I discovered a new person to be: one who does things. My summer of being a boarding-house cook had been hugely satisfying. I was qualified for a paying job as a lighting assistant. I would play a key role in being self-supporting. I could be a working woman.

Well, Let's Do It

Mary Stuart, 1960

The Prodigal, 1961

8/12/61

8.

Fraud

I grew up in executive affluence where I never felt I belonged. The garret and the rooming-house were a better fit, but here in the caretaker's cottage I was back in a world of wealth, this time as "the help." The lady of the house was an echo of my mother, rigid and domineering, and whim was law. The Black chauffeur gave me some insight into the quirks of the household, but that didn't strengthen my backbone. I had been too well trained in submission and listening between the lines.

The owners were paranoid about their property. Theoretically, they understood about class schedules, but negotiation was prickly for rehearsals and my part-time work. I wondered what they thought would happen if an actual intruder appeared. My muscles were getting a workout carrying heavy lighting instruments up and down ladders (my crew chief couldn't deal with heights), but I couldn't quite see myself or Conrad delivering a knockout punch to a burglar. Demands increased and tempers frayed. My housekeeping went to hell, push came to shove, and when we were asked to leave, it was a huge relief.

We found a basement apartment that would let us have the cat we'd just adopted. It was close enough to campus to walk if the car didn't start and far enough to curse the blizzard winds when they came screaming off the lake. I still remember walking backwards up to campus, crying with rage at the cold.

I was twenty-one, old enough to vote, and that's what I did. Without realizing it, I took the first steps toward wriggling out of my bonds. When I stopped pursuing Miss Krause's approval, I was walking away from my mother. When I left the wealthy suburban estate, I was walking away from my mother. I'd found someone who felt like my kin, and I was beginning a journey. There was no goal, no map, no way to read the road signs. I clung to the immediate: the next salad, the next show, the next kiss. This strange new comradeship, rooted in love and collaboration, was as unnerving as the worst assaults of my mother. Those at least were familiar to me; now I was on untried ground.

Not having to serve the suburbanites gave me more time, which disappeared instantly into Conrad's next project, a staging of Brecht's *Baal*. I'd been deeply involved in translation from the start, and now that my evenings were free, I could play a role. My immersion into *Woyzeck* had left me dangling when it was scrapped for another play; this was even more of a challenge. There had been no prior English translation—it was Brecht's first play, a seamy and sordid one, and my German classes hadn't included lessons in 1918 obscene Munich slang. Never mind. I dyed my hair flaming red, got comfortable with rumpling Baal's rancid bedsheets as Sophie, and worked on setting Brecht's songs to music. The work was high-voltage, and the two male leads increased the level of sparks. The lead actor was also a folksinger, part of our summer meal group, tall and powerfully good-looking. Baal's lover Ekart had been Conrad's dorm roommate; with his wicked intelligence and ferret-slim build, he was a good match. I got a strong erotic buzz from both of them and hid it fairly well. The four of us created the production together, putting in many hours of rehearsal and more hours as rowdy drinking buddies.

The play was wildly sexual on many levels. Baal is an abusive erotic omnivore, manipulating the men and women who are drawn to his power as poet and singer. Among his trophies are a married woman, a disciple's fiancee (who drowns herself), two sisters (at the same time), the redheaded Sophie whom he gets pregnant and discards, and his composer chum Ekart—not something you'd expect to find on an undergraduate Lab Theatre bill in the early Sixties. It had been tough enough to get the script approved, and X-rated staging wasn't on the menu, but we did what we could and it worked. One prof didn't like the staging because it wasn't filthy enough but said there were scenes he'd remember as long as he worked in theatre. One student—with a bit of a Don Juan reputation—huffed to Conrad, "You can't put that kind of thing on stage." His reply: "Well, we just did." I loved the risk. Being a collaborator was changing me. Making risky choices was in the service of the work, and I was in harness with a creative artist who could hold the vision.

It's lucky that he had the vision, because right after *Baal* closed I lost a contact lens and didn't have a spare. I'd gotten lenses at the end of high school, and it had taken the optometrist a year to get something I could wear. Getting a spare set hadn't occurred to me. Now all I had was an old pair of glasses from high school; every time I looked in the mirror and saw pin-eyes in ugly frames, I wanted to cry, but I was so nearsighted that I had no choice during the weeks it took to get new lenses. Getting the red out of my hair took a long time, and for a while it looked lousy. Conrad was cast as the lead in the January departmental production, *He Who Gets Slapped*, and between his library job, rehearsals and classes, we saw very little of each other until we fell into bed at midnight. The process of *Baal* had been a non-stop high, and now I was plopped alone on my butt, hating the way I looked and feeling very sorry for myself. It didn't help that the old Chrysler wouldn't start and campus was a twenty-minute trek north against the wind.

Fraud

Depression was an unfamiliar term to me but an old companion. I started wearing the same dumpy black clothes every day with no makeup and badly-kept hair, but I chalked it up to being too busy. In addition to my classes and lighting job, I was working part-time on campus for $1.25 an hour, trying to straighten out the membership records of the American Educational Theatre Association. Every three years, the files rotated to a different university, and now it was teetering in piles all over a room of the theatre department. The organization had 5,000 members but no system for keeping track of billing, payments, or mailing newsletters. The prof in charge didn't have a clue. I finally took a stand and said I couldn't make any progress unless I could start a new system from scratch. I got carte blanche and a raise to $1.50. It's always easier to wash dishes in somebody else's kitchen, and I succeeded in cleaning up a mess I hadn't made.

The prof made a crack about how my appearance had changed: "Once a girl gets married, she lets herself go." I kept my mouth shut and took my rage out on the address machine, whacking the heavy arm down with extra-hard bangs on each newsletter. In the coming decades I learned that I had an ally in managing episodes of depression: physical labor. I'd done the right thing.

∽

I've mentioned depression: here are some of the ways it's made itself known to me.

Difficulty getting up in the morning was one. There aren't many people who love getting on with the day, but this was different. I could be wide awake and find it impossible to rise from the bed, as if my limbs had turned to lead. Eventually, anxiety about things I needed to do would win out, but some people experience this so acutely that they've spent most of a day lying there. I used to think I was just lazy, more evidence of being defective, but now I'm intensely grateful that the desire to see the colors of the sunrise wins out.

A variant on this was getting home from the grocery store, parking, then sitting in the car for a long time before being able to open the door. I was looking forward to cooking something tasty, but it could take a long time before being able to let life go on. This doesn't happen often now, but it still shows up.

Trying to concentrate and organize myself is like herding cats. Sometimes I can make a list, and sometimes it's nearly impossible. And if I do get started on the first task, something else will jump into my mind and hijack my attention. There's an inner voice waiting to say, "You can't do this."

Over the years, I've had several ways of blotting things out. Obsessive reading was one, alcohol was another, and a really weird one, still, is getting completely submerged in a task. When it's something I know how to do well, like audio editing or detailed accounting, once I get going it's hard to emerge. It's almost an avoidance of the rest of life.

There are times when I move in slow motion behind a dirty glass wall. Nothing has any color. The longest and worst span of this was the spring of 1985. We were planning a six-week family trip to Europe in the summer; I expected to feel excited and delighted, but I was a lump of mud. I'd just been in our production of *Dark of the Moon*, a play I loved, and then *Macbeth* had a revival run, and performing with Conrad was special. After Europe we were going to pick up our first family dog. Everything was humming and I was mud. I asked CB to throw away the ant poison.

I got out of it by burning the woodpile. We lived out in the country, the previous tenant had left a pile of junk lumber out back, and rats moved into it. When I found a dead rat in the room where the kids watched Saturday morning cartoons, it was too much. I put on my barn jacket and boots, went outside and raked a fire-circle, ringing it with stones. "Need some help?" No, I wanted to do it myself. It took all weekend. It was raining a little, but I didn't care. I kept dragging the ratty wood and nursing the fire, and when it was all ash I could see colors again. The mud had moved on. Intense, focused physical labor is my friend.

~

By early February, Conrad's play was over, I had a handle on the office mess, we'd done huge sacks of laundry, and he read poetry to me while I did three days of ironing. The Chrysler started again. Our little tortoise-shell cat was litter-trained after months of playing dumb, and Conrad's mom had sent us enough green stamps to get a shower curtain. I was running our household on $25 a week with money left over for an occasional beer. I was wearing my new lenses, washing my hair, and putting on makeup again. Time to get our own car.

The VW was getting popular in the US after years of weak sales, and $1,600 would buy one. We did the research, ran the numbers, and made the plunge: a new olive-green Beetle. For my birthday, my mother offered to pay the trucking bill to get my baby grand piano to Evanston, and she insisted on giving us the bonus of an old green Naugahyde couch. I loved having the piano again; the green couch, not so much. It was huge, cold, slithery, and dominated any space it was in. I never learned to like it, though over the next fifteen years we schlepped it cross-country three times. When we moved to Pennsylvania in 1977, I gathered up my courage and advertised it. Somebody paid me and took the damn thing away.

The spring quarter was crazy but exciting. I was stressed about doing practice teaching. I'd never even done babysitting, and my only close contact with kids was the family at Interlochen. How was I going to communicate with these little aliens? I was assigned to a first-grade class, and found that it wasn't much different from working on a scene: watch, listen, respond, build the energy. The kids had made the first steps into reading and arithmetic, and I treated it as a safari into a strange, rich territory. They sat on the floor, I sat on the floor. When they pulled their little chairs into a circle, I made them giggle by sitting on a little chair myself. When they had to do things in small groups, I had each group choose a leader, and they stayed focused whether I was with their group or not. By April, I got a comment from my supervisor that my student teaching was the best that she had ever seen. Damn, I could actually do this. I had a new card in my deck.

The theatre department had a new faculty member with a good reputation as a director. After an acting drought of three months, I got cast in his first production. Conrad was to be Hector in *Tiger at the Gates*; I played his sister Cassandra, cursed to foresee the future and never to be believed. It was a painful role, but it was good to be in rehearsals together again.

I wrote to Margaret: *I have such a sense of well-being with Conrad; he is so steady and loving. The bond between us grows stronger every minute of every day. I bless the day I came to Northwestern, because I can't imagine what life would be without him.*

He was my ideal director, but his intensity as a scholar was almost scary. He wanted to finish his B.S. early and had taken summer classes every year, so he'd graduate at the end of December 1962. Zoom: straight on for an M.A., and by September of 1963 he'd be starting a PhD. The faculty urged him to aim high and recommended Stanford. A reconnaisance trip was planned to follow the summer session.

Margaret had fond memories of California, prompting her to ask if she could go with us and share the cost of gas. In 1929, she and her girlfriend Velma drove from Iowa to Los Angeles and had quite a summer. She was nineteen and girls just didn't do such a thing, but the next summer she did it again. After the third summer she sent word back to her country one-room school: "I'm not coming back. Get my brother to teach."

I loved Margaret. The story of those California adventures astonished me; I couldn't imagine having the spunk to do that.

Once her boy was on his own as a married man, Mom started kicking up her heels. Arthur Murray offered free dance lessons; she not only took the free series, she finagled taking more freebies in different places. She had a good figure to start with, and after trimming up she was hotly pursued by more than a few men. Margaret would be good company.

In the meantime, spring-quarter research papers had Conrad pinned to the wall. Translation, editorial help, shoulder rubs and sympathy: I could do all that and be a vicarious scholar. In a funny way, I enjoyed it because I wasn't the quarterback, I was just on the team. More papers had him strapped to the typewriter all summer, and I escaped by taking banjo classes at the Old Town School of Folk Music. My elegant 5-string White Lady had sat unused in its case for months, and now I buckled down and made it ring. He claimed to enjoy my practicing.

After my student teaching, I started applying for jobs, and by July I was hired to teach kindergarden in Skokie with a salary of $4,850. We'd get back from our California trip on Labor Day, I'd spend the rest of the week at teacher workshops, and my classroom teaching would start the next Monday.

The trip was great. Stanford was unlike anything I'd ever seen. A huge campus, gently rolling hills, palm trees, Mission Revival architecture, lots of rosy stucco, and barefoot students. I got a giggle when we went to the Student Union and saw a sign on the tables: *Please wear at least shirt and shoes.* We had seventeen days and loved the trip. On the way back we saw the Grand Canyon, but what impressed Margaret most was California's clean motels, in which she made discreet efforts to give us marital privacy.

We got home on schedule, the workshops were useful, and a week later I met my kids. I'd wanted first grade, having loved my student teaching at that level, and kindergarten presented new challenges. One little boy came out of the bathroom weeping because he didn't know how to get his pants back on, and a little girl didn't know her name, but they all settled in together, and I began to get everyone tuned into the safari of playing and learning.

Then the roof fell in.

∽

I was a fraud. I wasn't certified, I had bluffed my way into student teaching and hadn't even graduated. I was a walking Ponzi scheme, and after three weeks I got caught. The principal called me in; he was not a happy man. "You're a good teacher, why couldn't you have done this right? But I have to let you go." At least he saw to it that I got paid for a full month.

The two summer courses where I'd requested delayed exams? I drove to campus to do that, but I never showed up to take them. I lied to Conrad. Back in the fall quarter I completed two classes, blew off two completely, and got an A for directing a one-act play. Winter quarter was a loss, and I was officially dismissed on March 23rd. When I'd done my student teaching, I not only hadn't completed the required courses, I wasn't even a student.

I'd entered Northwestern as a fraud, and I finished as a fraud.

Nobody knew, not even me. The part of me that did know was walled off so effectively that I convinced myself I was going to finesse it. I'd gotten away with it at Ann Arbor multiple times—until I didn't. I'd been on such a high for the summer—learning banjo, a week in Cadillac, the road trip to California, and getting hired for an actual teaching job with good money—I couldn't afford to know that the axe was inevitable. When it fell, I was cornered and scared. I could have probably been defined as nuts.

Mornings, I'd get in the VW and head for "school." That meant parking somewhere out of the way, walking to the back entrance of our apartment building, and letting myself into the laundry room. I'd sit in a dark corner on the floor behind the dryer all day, in a kind of trance. Late afternoon I "came home" and took the little wad of toilet paper out of the phone's ringer where I'd crammed it each morning so calls wouldn't be heard.

Then came the afternoon when his face told me that he knew. A dean had informed another dean; they called him in, told him, and recommended that I get help. We wouldn't have my teaching salary. When he got his degree at the end of December, his undergrad scholarship would end and grad school tuition would start. There had been no word yet on scholarship support for his M.A. He told the deans that he would likely have to drop out; they went into damage control mode—he was a star student—and assured him that he'd have a graduate scholarship.

When he said what he'd been told, I straight up denied it. I accused him of not having faith in me, and we both wept. I clung to denial, he stuck with reality. At last he said, "It's happened. However it happened, it's happened. So what are we going to do?"

He said "we." In my shock, I'd been sure he would leave me. How not? I'd deceived him, built our future with rotten timber. How was trust possible now? Exhaustion set in, and when we could bear to touch, we sat in soggy silence holding each other. Then we began to talk with honesty.

I had never known I could have unconditional love. I didn't know it existed for me. I didn't know that was possible. The awful surprise was that it hurt. It hurt worse than all the rage and humiliation and shaming that I knew so well. It meant I had to open and be vulnerable when every fiber in me wanted to roll up like a pill bug and pull my mind into darkness. I would have to begin the deep work of change. He was there for me, but I'd have to do the work myself, now and for the rest of my life.

9.

Music

That crisis was our third wedding. The first was in a freezing, fogged-up car on an Evanston street; the second was an opulent event attended by dressed-up people who wished us well in spite of not quite knowing who we were; and the third was sharing tears on the dingy steps of a basement apartment. The rest of my life? Radical changes, of course, occasional crises, sometimes sheer terror, but now I could indulge in a modest sigh of relief. It would get better.

∼

I went from being a fake working woman to being a real one: I checked the want ads, went to work in a dental office, bought a uniform, and brought home a good honest paycheck every month. That was a start.

Teeth are unromantic; desk-work is even more so. Strangely, it was soothing to be in a world without glamour or competition. Answer the phone, make appointments, open the mail, balance the checking account, all the while hearing the drilling and scraping and muffled yelps. The dentist was in his early fifties, very nice, tall, and good-looking. In an adjoining room, the hygienist did the cleaning and was blunt in saying, "Never let a dentist clean your teeth. They don't have the time, and they sure don't have the touch." After work my uniform smelled like pungent disinfectants—not unpleasant, just businesslike. I grew to like it.

I had no formal training in bookkeeping, but I figured out their system and followed it. The dentist's dad was an accountant, and every month the books would go to him for a day or two. It was my private goal just once to get them back without any change or correction, but that never happened. My math was fine, my writing was elegantly clear, the checkbook always balanced, and keeping ledgers was something I learned easily. Figuring out the reasons for his changes was a first-rate education. I became fluent in Accounts Payable, Accounts Receivable and Petty Cash. Years later, when I had to learn full double-entry bookkeeping, I gave silent thanks to that dentist's dad for my grasp of the basics.

There were no more lies between us, but for what we would tell our parents, we opted for benevolent fiction. Conrad agreed to back me up, and we managed to thread our way through the next nine months without serious challenge, weaseling around my mother's demands to see my nonexistent diploma. I'd write letters with things like this: *Ever try to blow sixty-seven noses? Don't.*

I was heavily involved with Conrad's lab production of Aeschylus' tragedy *Prometheus Bound*, starting with dressing a dozen dolls for preparatory work on staging, then dyeing yards and yards of cotton tobacco cloth in the bathtub, a beautiful gauze in blues and greens that would make flowing robes for the twelve sea-nymphs of the chorus. I'd never tried large-scale fabric dyeing and found that I loved it, even at the cost of blue and green hands for a week. As time went on, I had many challenges playing with fabric color and became skilled at mixing custom hues. It was something that was needed: I learned how to do it, did it, bleached and scrubbed the bathtub, and thought, OK, I did that. I had no idea how many yards of fabric—not to mention sewing, set construction, and electrical wiring—awaited me in the future.

But then the impossible loomed: the play needed music, and he asked me to provide it. Usually a student director or prof used tape recordings dubbed from classical records, but not this student. "You're a musician," he said, "so do our music." I said he was crazy. I'd once taken a course in composition which proved I had absolutely no talent for it. My training was classical piano; composing was something other people did. Besides, the piano or guitar would be all wrong. We went back and forth, and then he said, "How about a different instrument? One you've never used. Maybe a koto?"

We'd been hooked on Japanese movies, and I thought the koto was the most romantic instrument I'd ever seen. The player knelt on the floor behind a long narrow wooden arch; its thirteen silk strings were tuned by moveable ivory bridges shaped like tiny Eiffel Towers. The sound was more pungent than a harp, alien and ancient. Attraction conquered resistance, and I agreed to take the plunge. An exotic San Francisco music store ordered one for me; nobody had one in stock, so it had to be custom made in Japan. We somehow managed the money. March wasn't far away, and I sweated bullets, afraid I'd made an awful mistake, but when the koto arrived and I set to work, it was perfect.

Prometheus Bound took me into a new persona. When the koto arrived and I pried off the lid of the crate, the fragrance of the paulownia wood erased my fear. Its prominent grain gave the koto's curved top the look of a flowing stream, and its scent was like cedar, but sweeter. I arranged the string bridges in a Greek Aeolian mode, then brushed my fingers across the taut silk strings, and something in me blinked open. This was alive. I started plucking strings at random, and everything made musical sense. The instrument was speaking with me.

I took it regularly to rehearsal, set it on the floor in front of the stage, knelt behind it, and listened to the actors' lines. The koto itself spoke back. I didn't have to prove anything, I just had to get out of the way and let the music speak. It was intoxicating. For weeks I interacted with rehearsals, found shapes and themes, and eventually came to performance with music responsive to the moment. There was no going back. I could no longer say I couldn't compose: I created my first score, it was a success, and I was part of the team.

∼

By now I've done scores for more than fifty productions, not to mention music for five radio series. The koto opened the door, and by our third year at Stanford I had enough freedom to try using the piano. In the Northwestern version of *Tiger at the Gates*, with Conrad as Hector and me as Cassandra, the play was an elegant comedy. While at Stanford, we restaged it, and ours had all the elegance of a hot-dog stand. Helen was a spoiled teen temptress, her lover Paris a rich playboy addicted to porn, and our approach reflected our revulsion at the bombing of North Vietnam. What my head came up with for Helen's theme was a crooning sax over a ya-da-da ya-da-da pop piano. I was flabbergasted that I could improvise something like this on the piano: I always thought I hated pop music, but I called the style forth from unknown memory banks. I recruited a sax player and drummer, and we taped not only Helen's theme but some downright rock'n'roll stomping stuff. I didn't know I had it in me or how much fun it would be.

With that score, I surprised myself. There must be a huge warehouse of neurons in my brain where all the music I've ever heard is stored, whether I liked it or not. I grew up studying classical piano and turning up my nose at anything else, so I was more than surprised when this score came straight out of what I thought I hated. The sax crooned and screeched, the drums kicked and stomped, and I banged the keyboard with rock-star energy. I gave myself permission to step out of bounds. The feminine harp-like koto had been a start. Now I could do rowdy.

What followed were seventy catchy ditties for *The Beggar's Opera*, the choral cries from the gut for *Hecuba*, honky-tonk piano for *A Streetcar Named Desire*, acid-rock harpsichord for *The Revenger's Tragedy*, the thunderous electronics of *Tamburlaine*—on and on.

I'd never studied those styles and have no idea how my mind came up with them. I was exhausted and facing deadlines, so I probably did most of this very late at night, possibly drinking red wine as consolation and inspiration. I'm pretty sure I was working in what became a regular approach in later years: start with a bass line, play it again and again till it's automatic, then let the right hand chime in with whatever it feels like doing. Nowadays I can record multiple tracks, play back the foundation track, and concentrate on improvising with it, a form of split-time jazz. Doing that in pre-electronic days took some doing.

In an instant, my whole world of music had changed; instead of learning, practicing, and being judged, it was possible to step into an endless flow that had always been there. I became a channel, responding to the scene to be supported, shaping the music, letting it create itself. The path to lovemaking should be like that.

~

When word came from Stanford, it was good. Conrad was accepted as a PhD candidate and would get a substantial fellowship. The original proposal was $1,500, and when they upped it to $2,000 he didn't object. At last we could know what was coming next. There would be at least three years at Stanford (the minimum for a PhD) with generous financial support; I now had a marketable skill with a good recommendation, so we started to talk about making a baby. It didn't take long to feel certain enough to say a retroactive thank-you to Planned Parenthood and start experiencing a new kind of love-making. I was breathless at the thought of becoming pregnant and naive enough to think it would be that simple. Good thing I didn't hold my breath, because it took nine years and another radical life-shift for that to happen. It did, but that's jumping ahead across nine very eventful years.

All this time our bruises were slowly healing, and life got faster and friskier. In June we went to New York for eight days, found ourselves a walk-up room on West 76th Street, binged on Truffaut films in the Village and saw a bale of theatre: *Who's Afraid of Virginia Woolf*, *Strange Interlude* (which took all day), *The Blacks*, *A Month in the Country*, *The Pinter Plays*, and *The Typist & The Tiger*. We had tickets for the Living Theatre's *The Brig*, but that was the day their theatre was padlocked by the IRS. I cooked our dinners in an electric frypan and shopped every day, there being no fridge. When our time was up, we drove back through Canada, stopped at Stratford, saw *Troilus and Cressida*, got home Sunday, and went to work Monday. Then one Saturday in August, we hopped into the VW at 3 a.m. with our *Baal* actor and his girlfriend and drove nonstop to Minneapolis, where the Guthrie Theatre had begun its amazing life. That day we saw Moliere's *The Miser* and Chekhov's *Three Sisters*, and on Sunday afternoon, a four-hour *Hamlet*. Early Monday morning back in Evanston, I thought, "We just did what?"

Conrad's last exam was mid-August; we finished packing our stuff into the movers' boxes and celebrated by buying a portable tape recorder, a white Wollensak. There was time for a week in Cadillac, canoeing and lazing about, and Conrad's mom joined us. Then we all drove back to Evanston, met the movers, got everything loaded, and kept right on going to Council Bluffs. After ten days with Margaret, the two of us headed off to a new chapter in the West.

∽

Three years earlier, the roller-coaster had finished its slow haul upward and started its wild ride. Off to Northwestern, a high dive into lifetime love, the startlement of collaboration, and a quick sprint into marriage. The discovery that, yes, I could run a household on small change, and yes, I could get a little distance from my mother. Exhaustion and exhilaration in the making of *Baal*, partnership in a theatre team. Heart-stopping twists of descent, all the time suppressing the knowledge that I would land in a nasty swamp. When the crash happened, it was painful, but it didn't destroy us. What I lost was meant to be lost, the self-image of the star student on the outside concealing the amoral cheater on the inside. My skills delayed the reckoning, but when the time came, I gained much more than I lost. I had unconditional love, I could stop lying, and I could work an honest job. I could create music, and eventually I could be an actress again. Survival was possible. And suddenly, California.

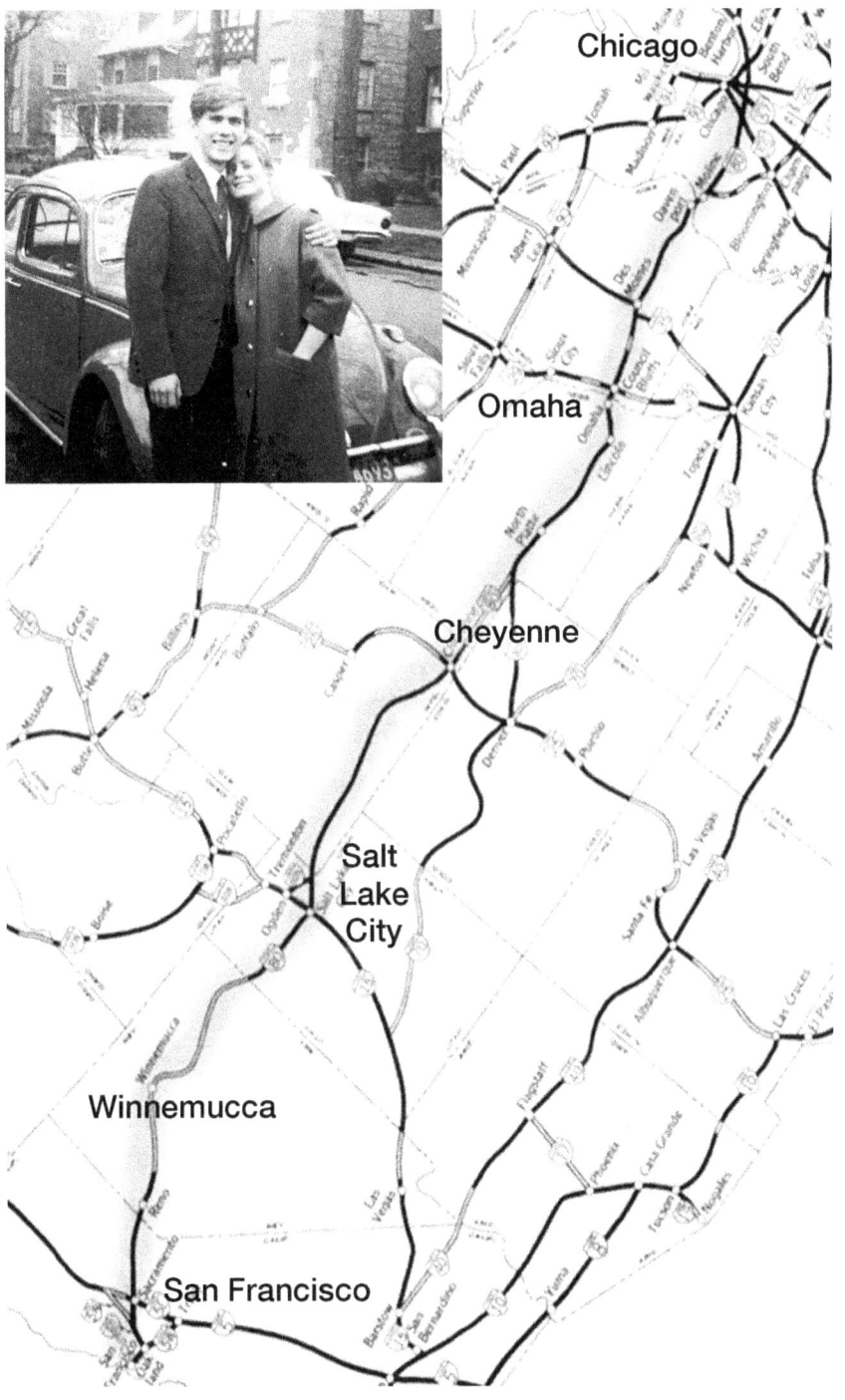

10.
Rehab

At Northwestern I'd survived the equivalent of a car crash, and California was intensive rehab. It was demanding, often exhausting, but over the three years at Stanford there were no disasters, and I could feel a new strength. Conrad was on the final lap toward his goal of teaching university theatre and directing the work that he loved. I was his partner, eager to find what our future would bring.

This chapter is only a road-map of daily life—what I did in my roles of maker and doer. Deeper than that was my growth as an artist. That will be the next chapter.

∼

Something new was beginning. On September 3rd we set out from Council Bluffs at the break of day with suitcases and duffels, a sack of Margaret's sandwiches and a load of boxes, including a metal trunk full of Conrad's essential books. It would be more than 1,700 miles; some stretches of Interstate 80 had been built, but much of the trip was on old US 40. Utah was very hot and the Beetle was heavily loaded, so we kept the speed down. Road construction made Donner Pass a literal cliff-hanger, but we arrived on the fifth day of our odyssey.

Rehab

While looking for a place near Stanford, we stayed with my father's relatives in Berkeley, urbane and gracious hosts. They welcomed the tired sweaty pair on Saturday evening, pointed the way to the shower, and offered cold white wine. Sunday supper featured fresh-caught salmon, sliced thin and eaten raw—a startling, delicious new insight. Their house in the Berkeley hills was a welcome respite each evening after chasing rental listings. By the end of Tuesday we had found an affordable place, and Wednesday morning we said our farewells.

After nearly two years in a basement, I'd almost forgotten what it meant to see the morning sun, but for the $90 per month that we'd paid in Evanston, we got a spacious, sunny one-bedroom, though not as close to Stanford as we'd like. The apartment court was a horseshoe, ten families on two stories, open and full of light. No grass, just gravel, ground ivy, and big-leafed plants. We bought an office chair on rollers to zoom around our new desk, a 6'8" door on wrought-iron legs. Three bucks rented a pair of air mattresses; otherwise, it was bare floor. We waited for our moving van.

Having heard nasty tales about movers, we'd researched companies and settled on Mayflower—not the wisest choice. The day we got our lease, we called, gave our address and asked for delivery. No problem, they told us; we'd get a heads-up call telling us the exact time of delivery and the amount due. We waited. After two weeks, the truck showed up with no warning. The bill was nearly $600—twice the estimate—and we had to pay cash on the spot or the load would go into storage for a hefty added sum.

We had opened a California checking account, but our savings were still in the Evanston bank. Fortunately, Stanford had paid the first installment of Conrad's fellowship, but the balance left us flat broke. I had found a job with a nearby dentist but wouldn't get paid soon enough. The rent was due in five days, so we made a desperate call to Margaret and asked for a quickie loan. The money came in time, we paid the rent, and next day the first paycheck came.

Only students had been eligible for Northwestern's plays, so I expected no acting at Stanford. But at the department's welcoming reception, we were asked if we would audition for *Hamlet*: Hell, yes! I was cast as Ophelia and Conrad would be my brother Laertes. Margaret always said we looked like brother and sister, and someone agreed.

I was elated to have a major role, but rehearsals were distressingly dumpy. The director was a pleasant prof with lots of money (he and his wife were toilet heirs, the union of American Standard and Universal Rundle). He had a huge scholarly library and not the foggiest notion of directing. "Why don't you stand over there, yes?" and "I can't hear you on that passage." I got through it, telling myself, "Don't complain: this will look impressive on your credits," and immediately got cast in a French comedy as a sour old chaperone with the soul of a pickle. Conrad was the Baron, a role he described as a cross between Mrs. Malaprop and Bullwinkle J. Moose. Not substantial, but it was fun to work in comedy together.

Our schedules were merciless. I quit my dental job in Palo Alto after a month: watching that dentist pull every tooth from a young man's head left me with nightmares. I found a better-paying desk job in an orthodontist's office (no blood, just my own painful memories of braces), but it was in San Carlos, half an hour's drive north. I'd have time for a fast lunch, then a rushed dinner before rehearsals. I took pride in making good meals no matter what, learning tricks of preparing ahead and feeling more grounded than I'd ever been. It was two years into the marriage, but making this household felt different. I was a provider, earning more than half our income and putting food on the table. I was an actress again, and California put a new spring in my step. Above all, my mother was 2,200 miles away.

When I longed for a role I could get my teeth into, I had no idea what was about to happen. In high school I had heard Lotte Lenya's songs from *The Threepenny Opera* on the radio and was smitten. I bought my own album and played it over and over. My love affair with German had started in high school, and these songs touched something deep, especially the repressed rage in *The Black Freighter* (*Seeräuber Jenny*). This year, Stanford had enticed Carl Weber, a directing assistant to Bertolt Brecht at the Berliner Ensemble, to come as guest faculty, and now he would do *The Threepenny Opera* at Stanford. His auditions required singing: "It's an opera!" I was petrified but sang the T*he Black Freighter* in German, the way I knew it. I was cast as Jenny.

But February was a difficult span for marital togetherness. I had a full-time job with a half-hour commute, while rehearsing for *Threepenny*, keeping us fed, paying the bills, and doing laundry, while he was directing Strindberg's *Creditors* and of course taking classes. To top it off, our performances were on the same dates, so I could only see his show in rehearsal, taking breaks to slip down to the rehearsal room below the main stage. I liked it, and so did audiences. Conrad was making his mark, and I was doing well as an actress; we survived the rush.

We got the boost of good news. For 1964-65, Conrad was offered the Assistantship in Acting and Directing. He would teach a class, get a tuition waiver and $2,000. We were on a roll but still on separate tracks. As soon as those shows were over, Conrad was playing the suicidal outcast in *The Zoo Story*, and I plunged into the key female role in Ibsen's *Rosmersholm*.

Next, Conrad was cast as a lead in Weber's staging of Shakespeare's *Two Gentlemen of Verona*. His rehearsals would be intense in April and May, and I was looking for anything I could do. A flurry of news featured a new theatre about to open locally. The central force in the enterprise was a tiny Russian lady filled with boundless energy and a gale-force love of theatre. When auditions were held for Chekhov's *Platonov*, I got a good role.

It was downhill from there. Her abilities as a director were confined to "Keep it simple, darling." After a few chaotic rehearsals, I knew I had made a mistake and was facing a month's run. I gritted my teeth and did my best. Like *Hamlet*, it was a case of chalking it up to experience.

◊

I'd thought we had an advantage in our marriage, being in the same career. Some professionals work in different offices, have different challenges and successes, learn the jargon unique to their careers, and then have trouble communicating at home. I'd thought we weren't like that. We were not only passionately invested in the same path but had already done some deep collaborations. It was startling to be on a promising path and find that our progress was beginning to keep us apart. We weren't spending much time together, and the demands of our work were claiming a lot of our energy.

In a way, it was a good thing that this issue reared its head early. We began to find strategies that gave us times of strong togetherness, brief as they might be, and in the years to come they proved invaluable. We'd find ourselves in the same bind again and again, but our repertory of creating wormholes to sweetness kept growing. Whenever I'd drift toward thinking, "I can't live like this," I'd find I didn't need to try. Something would poke its head out of our grab bag and lead us back to intense connection. It wasn't always easy, but it was always possible.

Summer break, I had a full-time job, but it was like a vacation. Neither of us had rehearsals, and Conrad had only one class. On weekends we could spend time at beaches like San Gregorio and Pescadero, and I developed a ritual picnic: a bag of chicken legs in teriyaki marinade, a sack of juicy figs, a chunk of Muenster cheese, and a bottle of semi-dry ruby port.

The narrow road wound around the hills to the coast, and I loved to make the VW dance on the curves. Going south, we'd pick our beach. A short walk beneath the high bluffs usually gave us a place to ourselves among the huge rocks in one of the sheltered coves. We wore swimsuits under our clothes for sunning, but sometimes it was secluded enough to risk getting naked.

Grilling the chicken didn't require constant attention. When sitting at the fire, I could watch the hawks riding the updrafts. Sometimes I counted to a hundred before I saw a wing move. The air smelled of seaweed and salt, the sun was gentle, California hummed through my body, and the orthodontist's office was a million miles away. I hadn't felt so completely alive since my preschool solo wandering in woods and fields. I was in my skin again.

We moved to an apartment in Menlo Park, and that soured quickly. It was closer to campus, but we craved a certain earthiness, and Menlo Park was adamantly Formica. In August we moved again. By now we were experts: rent or borrow a pickup truck, haggle with the piano movers, throw a moving party for friends. We found a place in a downscale neighborhood, a doggy two-story shoebox building bathed in freeway exhaust, but somehow it felt better. As soon as we got settled, we bought a Vespa scooter for Conrad to get to campus, while I drove the car to work.

Fall arrived, the second year at Stanford began, and I felt unsettled, with no roles coming up for me. I'd been sour about having gotten stuck in *Platonov* for weeks while Conrad was acting for Charlie Weber. The orthodontist had given me a raise, but the full-time hours and commute were wearing on me.

And pregnancy wasn't happening. I talked to the lab girl at my office who'd been trying for six years with no luck, and thyroid pills got her pregnant in a month. We had the same doctor, who obliged with a prescription; now every month was a cliff-hanger. It weighed on us, but in retrospect the multiverse knew better.

There was one thing I could do something about: my job. We had a modest cushion of savings, and I got up my courage and talked to the orthodontist: "My schedule is killing me. I like this office and I don't want to quit. Is there any way I could be part-time?" He was startled but cooperative and hired a woman to do phone, reception, and scheduling, so I could just keep the books. I got along fine with Charmeon, a tall pretty lady who was maybe ten years older but didn't mind being trained by a kid. It was a hectic two weeks of doing and teaching, but things got stable. With luck I'd find some pick-up work close to home.

It was complicated having vacations whose dates didn't match. Conrad had a six-week break at the end of the summer session, but my vacation from work was just ten days in mid-September. We'd ordered tickets for *Saint Joan* at the Guthrie as soon as my dates were set, and on my first day off we set out for Minneapolis. It was the only show we had time to see, but a stunning production. The next day we drove to Council Bluffs, and Margaret was overjoyed to have us again. By the time we pointed the VW westward, we'd been stuffed to the gills with soggy Midwestern food. We realized how much a year of California cooking had changed our habits and were relieved to get back to the new normal.

I was about to get serious with a job search when fortune smiled: Stanford hired me to do publicity for their shows. It wasn't much money, but the paychecks kept me from feeling guilty about cutting back my hours. I even had my own office, a key to the building, formal letterhead, and I could set my own schedule.

The theatre faculty had grown. Gerry Hiken had a substantial list of credits as a character actor. Leon Katz was a legendary exponent of literature. Gerry was short and funny and huggable, Leon was a tall leonine force of intellect, and both were brilliant.

Gerry was slated to direct *The Sea Gull*, my first publicity assignment. Stanford had been doing basic press releases and newspaper ads, so there was a template. The usual promo was easy, and I even thought of a quirky cheap angle: the personals.

Kostya loves Nina—signed, Sea Gull
Peter loves everybody—Sea Gull
Tons and tons of love—Sea Gull

The first promo work was easy, but the next production was Anouilh's *Time Remembered*, and the designer came up with a stunning silk-screen design that featured a peacock's gorgeous fanned tail over the whole area. It was up to me to hand-cut a stencil and print the thing—photographic screens existed, but not on our budget. It involved cutting a lacquer film on a wax-paper backing so ink areas could be peeled up, but it was as tricky as finding where to start on a roll of Scotch tape, and there were countless ways to screw up. That damned tail had well over a hundred little tear-drop shapes at the end of the feather vanes. It took five days of work, but the result was gorgeous, and I had a new skill that proved essential for the coming years.

I also got an odd little gig: a weekly task of catering lunch for physicists at SLAC. The Stanford Linear Accelerator was a very big deal. Every week about fifty physicists from the Stanford physics department and from anywhere else in the world would get together to yak about their work. For two years, the departmental secretaries had to drop what they were doing on Wednesdays to cater this lunch, and eventually they said, "Enough."

I was hired with another girl at $2 an hour to drive to the delicatessens to pick up the goods. Trays, utensils, and disposable paper tablecloths were already there. We made nice arrangements, put out the sodas, brewed coffee, and waited for the locusts to descend. We were smiling wallpaper until everyone left, then we ate the leftovers. We were told to bill for a minimum of four hours.

I was processed, got neatly wrapped in red tape, and received a radiation badge. I signed a form that said if I invented anything I couldn't sell the patent without SLAC's permission, and they scheduled me for a prepaid physical. I didn't confess that I actually understood what some of the honchos were saying. I just ate the top-notch salami and threw out the trash.

On the theatrical level the second year included work that changed my inner being profoundly. I'd been hungering for collaboration, and it manifested in productions that shaped our future for years to come. We did a two-person play, *The Fourposter*, at the Russian lady's theatre. Conrad directed a pair of one-acts, *In the Shadow of the Glen* and *Kinuta*; I acted in one and composed a score for the other. Leon cast us both in his adaptation of Dostoyevski's *The Possessed*. We produced Menotti's one-act opera, *The Medium*, for an independent group in Palo Alto, and the same group gave us a late-summer slot for D. H. Lawrence's *David*. It was a high-octane finish to a blazing year.

At the end of the second year, we moved again. The pressure had been building: some tenants had rowdy little kids, then more rowdy kids came over to play, and the last straw was a family who beat their kids. We had a friend with a little house "across the tracks," in the less-white area of East Palo Alto. When we really looked, this part of town was sweet. The population was mainly Asian, a smaller percentage Black, and about 10% white. It felt like Tom Sawyer territory: dirt streets, no traffic, and fruit trees everywhere.

We found a cottage with a huge almond tree in the back yard, branches bending low with a heavy crop of nuts. We learned that green almonds could be eaten whole before the furry outsides hardened into shells—a strange pungent milky flavor with a hint of the nut-to-be. Spring brought apricots, figs, and what we called the fig-bird. It had a long narrow tail that flicked up and down as it stabbed every single fig with its long pointy beak; we got very few to eat for ourselves. There was a low white picket fence with roses, scraggly but blooming, enclosing a scruffy patch of grass. The street was soft powdery dirt, perfect for barefoot walks. At night I could hear dogs barking in the distance, an echo of country childhood.

The cottage was old, a bit shabby, and had a floor furnace. It took a while to get used to looking at the iron grate in the floor, seeing gas flames directly beneath it, and giving thanks we didn't have a cat that could catch on fire. I was startled to find roaches under the fridge, the first ones I'd seen in California. In spite of violent cleaning and spraying, the bugs were there to stay, but so was the clean air and the sunlight.

San Francisco was like a famous next-door neighbor: fascinating but not part of our everyday life. Going to the beach was simple—drive there, park, and bliss out—but the city was a daunting project. Once, we attacked that head-on and asked to borrow a friend's place while she was away. We walked everywhere in North Beach, sat for hours in Caffe Trieste, looked with wild eyes at the books in City Lights, and marveled at how much food you could get at a neighborhood diner for two dollars: a big bowl of thick soup and all the bread and butter you could eat.

Our schedule made trips infrequent, but they were memorable. Carl Weber directed *The Caucasian Chalk Circle* at the Actors Workshop, and we were so blown away that we went for a second time. The San Francisco Mime Troupe created a satire on racism in the form of a blackface minstrel show. At curtain call, they all removed their white gloves and showed their palms, and only then did you know who was Black and who wasn't.

An improvisational comedy group called Pitchell Players was forming, and I remember one of the funniest sketches I've ever seen anywhere. A young man applies for an office job on the basis of his smile: he feels his smile would improve the office. Decades later, we took the essence of that character and created one of our enduring pieces, *The Entrepreneur*.

We went to the city just enough to fall in love with it. When we moved back to California in 1999, we thought about grounding ourselves there, living and making theatre in San Francisco, but we opted for Sebastopol. We still visit Caffe Trieste, City Lights, and Golden Gate Park, and to our delight they are just as wondrous.

Elizabeth: One of Many

Our third year at Stanford, everything felt different. There was now a professional company in residence, with no student productions. Charlie Weber had left after our first year, and now Leon was gone. The department felt like an empty echoing gym. Conrad faced three days of written comps in December, and his dissertation would loom over the rest of the year, but our urge to do theatre was unstoppable. I played Gretchen in *Faust* for a modest little company that performed only on Monday nights, but it ran for eight weeks. Conrad directed *Tiger at the Gates* for another company. I played Helen and composed a score.

I was working a crazy quilt of jobs. I continued keeping books for the orthodontist, did billing work for another dentist, and in January took on a task for my personal physician—a genius diagnostician and a very quirky man. He was six months behind in his billing, and I was hired to get him out of the mess. His back office was crammed with Stonehenge-like stacks of patient files, which no one was allowed to touch. As long as they were exactly in the order in which he'd seen the patients, he could recall the visit, write up their charts, and give them to me for billing. In the final months, the heat was awful, and he suggested that I work in his nearby air-conditioned house. That helped, and I learned a handy housekeeping tip: keep your vodka in the freezer.

Two days after *Tiger* closed, we went east for an intense six weeks of Conrad's dissertation research on 19th century melodramatic acting: a month at Harvard and then two weeks at Lincoln Center in New York. Harvard's Houghton Library was our home from 9 to 5 weekdays, 9 to 1 on Saturdays. The librarian who handled the special collection of theatre materials allowed us access to the basement, where we sorted through the dusty stacks. I'd brought along staff paper, and whenever the promptbooks had music in them, I hand-copied the scores. Later in our rented room I could give Conrad an idea what that music sounded like, and little by little we realized how integral it was.

Mention melodrama and what pops up is the idea of corny over-the-top acting, but melodrama—though scorned by some—was the most popular form of theatre in the 19th century and affected its audiences strongly. Characters are unsubtle but varied, conflict runs high, and the action operates on a logic more musical than behavioral. Some of its style can still be found in opera or in action movies, whose scores use the same logic: when the music starts an ominous growling, bad stuff is coming. Audiences get it.

Later we went to Lincoln Center. Harvard's library had been quiet, organized, efficient, and respectful of the research efforts of scholars. Lincoln Center's fifth floor Special Collections likewise had a priceless array of manuscripts, diaries, playbills and recordings, but viewing them required call slips limited to three at a time. The sullen girl at the counter would take half an hour before coming back with one book, unable to find the others. The entire floor was carpeted and divided by glass walls with steel-framed doors; take three steps across the tomato-red carpet and you were zapped with a hefty spark when you touched the door. No wonder the staff was cranky.

When we got home to our blooming almond tree with our bales of notes, the marathon began. The dissertation had to be completed by August to qualify for the orals, and the final draft had to be in before we could leave for Conrad's first teaching job: University of South Carolina.

The Stanford theatre department was under par at advising grad students how to look for work. By the time he started applications, it had all been picked to the bone. What was left was the Deep South. So be it; he signed a one-year contract. Then he socked into a writing schedule of five pages a day, finished a draft, aced his orals, and the typing marathon began: one month to finish the redraft and type two hundred and sixty-one pages on a rented IBM Selectric: carbon ribbon, original and three copies. We typed in shifts, carefully: corrections had to be made four times.

August went fast. We needed to be in South Carolina by September 14 and had booked the movers for August 31 to avoid another month's rent. I sold the baby grand piano, my life-long companion. Yard sales got rid of the rest, and the movers picked up our boxes. But by move-out day, there was still a lot of typing to do. We were rescued by a saint. A cast member from *The Medium* had a sweet cool airy house in Palo Alto, and he took us in, fed us, and put up with the IBM clacking until all hours. God bless Paul, who also taught me the French way of making omelets.

Our poor Beetle was crammed with too many books when we finally said goodbye to Paul, goodbye to California, and chugged east. On the morning we crossed the state line into South Carolina, we stopped at a diner, ate eggs and watery grits, and I wept.

⁓

The three years of California had a profound effect on multiple facets of who I was becoming. My acting and my music changed, and so did my experience with the world of work. It became more intentional and more satisfying. That wasn't new, but in our life at Stanford I was more conscious of what my options were and how essential my contribution was. Conrad's Stanford financial support was solid, but no way could we have lived on that alone. I was proud of having quit that first dental job when I found it disturbing and of having asked the orthodontist to give me part-time when full-time became unworkable. I did a fancy dance among jobs, balancing paychecks with theatre work, and I had the supreme accolade of having my orthodontist and my physician both begging me to do just a few more days before we took off for South Carolina. I was a good manager. The bills got paid, the checkbook balanced, meals were cooked from scratch, and our clothes were clean. Driving home after work in San Carlos, warming the dinner I'd put together that morning, running to the theatre, and still being on deck afterward for love—I got good at this.

Rehab

I even dared to flirt a bit with the world of learning. I wasn't a student now, but I knew high energy when I saw it. Leon Katz became a light for Conrad through the graduate seminars, but he was also a powerful beacon for me in the realm I'd abandoned after my collegiate fiascos. During *The Possessed*, we began a delicious ritual. After rehearsals we would follow Leon to a cafe and sit with coffee, cherry cheesecake, and intense conversation until the wee hours. Being part of those late-night exchanges, though I was more witness than participant, was significant. Leon was a magnet, and I discovered an almost erotic energy again in pursuit of learning. In the summer of 1965, I signed up for an intensive course in Russian just for the hell of it. I got through the course with flying colors, and when we later traveled through Poland, I found that my Russian vocabulary served me well in grocery stores.

Most of all, I reclaimed my body. The South Bay climate returned me to the embodied life I'd had when I was a little proto-pagan playing in the Indiana woods. The day we moved into our first California apartment, once we got the VW unloaded, I kicked off my shoes and went outdoors. The drive from Evanston had been a long grind, we'd just finished three days of apartment-hunting, and I was frazzled. But it was a sunny September day, and the concrete patio was smooth and warm. As a kid I'd always gone barefoot in summer and wiggled my toes in the sandy beach at Cadillac. Ann Arbor and Evanston sidewalks had locked me into shoes, but this was my home now, and dammit, I wanted my bare feet on the ground. That first moment was like a strong electric shock: the soles of my feet tingled and a current shot up my spine—an intense sensation of belonging, of being welcomed home.

California moved into my being and never left during the thirty-three years that we lived elsewhere. Leaving was hard for both of us, but for me it was a piercing pain. Working for the orthodontist in San Carlos, I'd drive home every day with the intoxicating sunset colors over my right shoulder behind the sharp silhouette of the hills. When I got home, I could walk barefoot in the soft dusty streets of our neighborhood. There were times when my native depressions intruded, but that's what San Gregorio was for. In that last year, I'd discovered the soul-healing practice of taking a picnic to the ocean, grilling teriyaki chicken on a makeshift fire, and eating figs washed down with port wine. As we were about to leave California, a song came to me, only the second I'd ever written. It was my celebration and farewell to that special place.

> *The road is twisty and the summer is hot*
> *Our bags are packed and we're ready to go*
> *There's not much time but we'll take what we've got*
> *When San Gregorio calls we don't say no.*
> *Perfect day, and it's almost over*
> *But there's two more sips of the ruby wine*
> *We can stay for five more minutes*
> *Watching gulls play hopscotch at the water line.*
> *The sun is down, it's past time to go*
> *I'll be back some day but I don't know when*
> *San Gregorio sands will be honey and gold*
> *I'll shed my shoes and be home again.*

Linda as Jenny,
The Threepenny Opera,
1964

Conrad & Linda,
The Fourposter, 1964

Linda as Michal
with Leon Katz,
*David,*1965

11.
Learning the Craft

That first Stanford year, what a roller-coaster. When I was tossed out of the University of Michigan I'd just had a string of acting successes—disgraced but secretly proud. As a performer I showed promise, but that didn't mean I knew what I was doing. I got good response from two roles that summer, pleased audiences during my penitential year in Valparaiso, but I still didn't know my craft and didn't know I didn't know it. At Northwestern, where I was supposed to start the real learning, the only thing that dug deeply was working in *Baal*. Then at Stanford, five roles in one year, my learning curve took off, and my future performing life got its foundation.

By the time we moved to California I hadn't been on stage for a year and a half, and the plays I'd just seen in New York and at the Guthrie had me howling in frustration. The role of dental assistant wasn't thrilling, but now my drought was over. We had no collaborations, but at least we were on stage together for the first two shows. Then I was on my own, with three very different directors. Each role taught me something new.

Hamlet was my first Shakespeare, and I didn't have a clue. The director confined his attention to the acoustics, and the guest actor playing Hamlet provided no juice: his inner angst only looked like a bad head cold. I began to fear that my ability to cry real tears wouldn't get me where I needed to go. Without a creative acting partner or meaningful direction, I was utterly at sea.

A prof was playing Claudius, and on a break, I told him I was floundering. He asked me, "OK, in this scene, what is your objective?" Huh? "What do you want, and what is standing in your way?" Those elementary questions surely came up at Northwestern, but that semester of humiliation was so traumatic that nothing stuck in my mind. Now I made up for lost time. In Ophelia's first scene with Hamlet, she does what her father has told her to do: give back all love-tokens and letters. When she does, Hamlet turns on her viciously. What she wants is to keep his affection, but standing in the way is her father's command and his hidden presence. I'd been focusing on her grief, but her active tasks are to deal with Hamlet's rage, to reclaim his love, to conceal her spying father, and to stop shaking. I only got part way, but at least I had a better notion how to make it work. Ophelia got good reviews for a pretty face, a sweet singing voice, and a tormented mad scene. I was glad when it was done.

No Trifling with Love, a nineteenth-century French comedy, was a welcome break. The director was good, Conrad was hilarious, likewise the rest of the cast. I focused on characterization, and it paid off in audience reaction. Not a heavyweight assignment, but welcome. Real life had enough heavyweights.

In *The Threepenny Opera*, Carl Weber jump-started me. He had his work cut out for him: to do in three weeks' rehearsal with a mixed-level cast what would have been, in his Berlin work, at least a six-month process with the best actors in Germany. He cut to the chase and gave blunt directions: "Do it like this. Watch." Others were offended at having their artistry short-circuited, but I couldn't care less, I was so stoked to be Jenny. I worked with his direction and got used to calling him Charlie.

Elizabeth: One of Many

His genius was in choosing expressive behavior. When he said "Do it like this," he was choosing specific actions that let an audience tune into that character instantly. Walk out here, stand still, cock your hip, look right, look left, then stand still and wait for a customer. It was funny: he was short with a little watermelon belly, but when he demonstrated a streetwalker, he nailed it, and for me it sank in to Jenny's core. Never in my acting experience had I thought about what the audience sees. My big talent had been concentrating on what the character feels and crying on cue. This was a crash course: find the behavior, put it on like a bridesmaid's dress and high heels, and see what it does for you. Physical behavior can create an inner life that grounds the character: I got it and never forgot it.

Jenny isn't in many scenes, so I had time to be involved in other aspects. I was paid $2.20 an hour for rehearsal piano, then I became part of the team—a prof and me and Charlie—who restored the "dirty" lyrics sanitized for Off-Broadway. In the *Tango-Ballad* sung by Jenny and Macheath, Brecht's original title translates as *The Pimp's Ballad*. When Jenny gets pregnant, they cope by having sex with her on top; eventually the "inconvenience" goes down the toilet. Rehearsal would stop, we'd stand in the aisle brainstorming obscenities, then find the rhyme. I loved being one of the guys.

Brecht had been clear that Macheath was not a matinee idol: his brutality and money were what served as sex appeal. So Weber cast the biggest operatic tenor he could find: over 300 pounds and a gorgeous voice. Singing and dancing the *Tango-Ballad*, each time we reversed direction I disappeared behind his belly. And bending backwards, I had to use latex glue to keep my breasts from popping out of my corset. Charlie had been explicit about the whores' corsets: cut low, very low. When he went to check them out in the costume shop, he grabbed a huge pair of shears and cut one down to demonstrate; it didn't win him hearts, but it got the point across. The show was a wild success.

Learning the Craft

Rosmersholm was a slap in the face. My character Rebecca has undermined a marriage, caused a suicide, and is haunted by her history of incest. It was a challenging role with a challenging director, a man of massive intelligence and a very dark streak. He had strong ideas of what he wanted but expressed himself in metaphors. He directed me to be completely instinctual: "as open as a fish." I'd never played a fish. My new skills from Weber were of no use. This director wanted only the soul's barbaric yawp. He was totally controlling, and the rehearsals were turbulent and miserable.

But I made some private choices. Rebecca was an outsider: how could I embody that? I wondered how it would affect the role if she were Finnish, not Norwegian. I darkened my hair, accentuated my slant-eyed fox face, and drew on my childhood of being outside those who called the shots. I recalled the behavior of being an erotic predator and went with that. More than once in rehearsals, I was reduced to ugly tears, but I survived. Eventually it opened, it was done, and I nursed my bruises. It got mixed reviews, but my performance was praised. My parents came to see it as they were passing through en route to LA to visit her brother. No comment: I didn't ask, and they didn't offer. Yet six months later, the director wrote a letter. "*Your best moments in Rosmersholm still haunt me with a clarity very unusual in my experience … Whenever you act in this area, I shall, if at all possible, be there to see you.*" When I read it, I wept.

Then came *Platonov*. I gritted my teeth and did competent work. It was up to me to bring the role to life, but I did have help. Conrad gave me strategic advice, and the review was surprisingly good: "*Beautifully and sensitively played; the candid, pious, eager, and tragic wife strikes the play's deepest note.*" Little by little, I was putting my craft together.

In my short vacation time before the second year started, we went to Minneapolis again and saw *St. Joan* at the Guthrie.

This time it began to dawn on me: they weren't just making plays in a theatre, they were making a theatre. The regional repertory theatre scene was only in its infancy: professional theatre had meant Broadway and its spin-off road shows or summer stock. Now companies, large and small, were sprouting. ACT (American Conservatory Theatre) was brand-new and brought their amazing repertory to Stanford for the summer of 1966. The Actor's Workshop was gaining national notice, and the Mime Troupe's work had a huge following. We paid attention.

In our second Stanford year, the two new faculty, Gerry Hiken and Leon Katz, both opened doors for me. Conrad was Gerry's teaching assistant, and I sat in on an acting class. The first exercise was a revelation. I performed something I loved, Polly Garter's song from Dylan Thomas' *Under Milk Wood*; it always made me cry. Gerry said, "Well, that's good, now let's make it better. Don't try to cry, you should try *not* to cry. Come over here by Ellen and tell it straight to her, just one woman telling another woman about her boyfriends. Got a hairbrush in your bag? OK, brush your hair while you sing. Just tell her."

Ellen and I sat close together on rehearsal cubes. We giggled at the descriptions of Tom, Dick and Harry: "Strong as a bear and two yards long ... big as a barrel and three feet thick ... six feet tall and sweet as a cherry..." and then stopped giggling: "But the one I loved best, awake or asleep, was Little Willie Wee, and he's six feet deep." I had to work desperately to keep from crying. Ellen and I sat looking into each other's eyes, and neither of us moved. A pause, then the whole class exhaled in unison. I wasn't crying, but everyone else was. That was Gerry's point. "Don't demonstrate feeling. Make it real and let the audience feel it."

Gerry didn't cast us in *The Sea Gull*. He apologized privately, saying we were too ideal for the parts and he wanted to cast against type. Yet running lights at every performance, we saw how his casting worked. The moody young playwright who kills himself was played by a tall gawky natural comic—Gerry said that in his experience the funniest men were the ones who took their own lives. I'd always thought of Chekhov's plays as depressing, but Chekhov himself insisted that he wrote comedies. Gerry's direction made it tragic and funny at the same time: it was real. The campus review was a wet blanket, and the personals ads didn't help much for the Monday and Tuesday shows, but once word of mouth took over, the place was packed. Nobody pushed out the emotion; they opened the door for the audience to come in.

About this time I stared getting urgent phone messages from the mad little Russian lady who'd directed *Platonov*. When I finally responded, it was a tempting offer. *The Fourposter*, a sentimental two-character play, ran on Broadway in 1951 with Hume Cronyn and Jessica Tandy, husband and wife in real life. The scenes are all set around their fourposter bed, following the couple from their wedding night to their elder years. "Darlings, you would be so good, everyone would come see you!" The chance to work together was tempting, but the rehearsals would probably be hellish. After several changes of mind, we decided that if we stuck together as a unified team, we could survive. And for the most part, we did; the ulcer I started to develop cleared up once it was done.

Together only four years, we were in our mid-twenties, and we were challenged to embody the span of a couple's whole life together. We had to tell the story of thirty-five years of marriage and make it believable for audiences who had actually lived it. The script is oddly non-dramatic; the authentic bond has to be found in the living presence of the actors. I think an audience gets an extra zing when married characters are played by married actors. "They really go to bed together and deal with the wet spot, just like us!"

In spite of the director, we managed to do an effective exploration of years we hadn't yet experienced. Hiken's wife had been a professional makeup artist, and she showed us how to age ourselves in the two minutes we had between each scene. The stage manager had to do everything: change the props, hook my costumes up the back, and run the lights. It was a tiny theatre and every noise carried; our changes were an exercise in speedy stealth.

The director wore high stiletto heels. During a performance, she'd clack around backstage; it took discipline to ignore it. Eventually, the worst happened. In the last scene, the couple are about to move to a small apartment and are saying farewell to their beloved fourposter; they'll leave a bottle of champagne for the incoming newlyweds. As the scene proceeded, Conrad went off-stage to get the champagne—and didn't come back. I had no idea what was happening, so I filled time with a motherly kerfuffle arranging the bed. Still no Conrad. I began talking endearments to the bed, thanking it, saying goodbye. Suddenly, a staccato burst of high heels, and at last he came in with the champagne. The director had gotten a fit of tidiness and put all the props away, including those that hadn't yet been used.

In the long run, it was good for us. Entirely dependent on our own skills, we felt a new level of teamwork. There were great reviews, good box office, and our audiences let us know they were with us. *"You grow so fond of the couple that their quarrel is as painful as it would be between two people you love—except that audience detachment lets you see how funny it is."* For the first time, we were an acting team. Ten years later, it would evolve into a lifetime of performance for the two of us.

Back at Stanford, Conrad directed a pair of one-acts. I had a major role in one and played koto for the other, an adaptation of a Japanese Noh play. *In the Shadow of the Glen* was minimalist and realistic, and he said we'd begin by improvising. My heart sank. At Northwestern, improv exercises had seemed a test of playing a scene without using the script, and I just didn't get it.

It didn't dawn on me that I'd just done that in *The Fourposter* when the bottle couldn't be found. I had held the stage solo for what felt like an eternity. Agnes hasn't read the play, she only knows that this is her last touch of the marriage bed that's cradled her through thirty-five years. Whatever I did was what she'd do, and being alone meant she was free to be sentimental. It was the heart of improvisation, finding how the next moment comes from the now. When I took my koto into *Prometheus Bound*, I was finding a musical response to the actors. Here I was using that same instinct, responding to my surroundings.

We talked about what this Irish peasant would have in her cottage and found thrift store equivalents. We talked about how she spent her long hours alone in this isolated place, and what was affected by her old husband dying. After setting up her room, he said, "It's your kitchen. Just survive the night. I'll take notes." I had no obligation to be dramatic: I just had to pass the time.

Exploring Nora's reality was like the scene in Gerry's class: the point wasn't to show something, it was only to be in this place and do what was needed. It echoed Charlie's mandate to find the behavior, and suddenly it fell into place. This is my home. I pack a pipe and light it. I put the kettle on and make tea. I peel an onion, put the skillet on the fire. I wasn't performing, I was finding how one moment comes from another. When it came time for lines and scenes, they arose from reality.

After the one-acts, Conrad wanted to start another directing project. His work had been well received, but now the faculty said that he should put focus on his dissertation and forget about directing. This did not sit well: he had put careful thought into his proposal. Undergrads were complaining about too few roles, little of his time was used in his assistantship, and he should be having the experience of directing a full-length piece. The rejection trivialized his objectives, and that infuriated him.

It was becoming the story of my life: a failure becomes a blessing. My Ann Arbor debacle brought me my life-mate. Not becoming pregnant deflected and augmented other creative energies. Stanford shutting the door on this project resulted in more than I'd imagined possible. I was as hungry for collaboration as he was for his own production, so we looked elsewhere. We discovered an odd little theatre in Palo Alto, the Peninsula Religious Drama Guild, that focused on contemporary spiritual drama—Christopher Fry, T.S. Eliot, etc. I had loved Menotti's opera *The Medium* ever since I saw it at the Dunes Summer Theatre. I made my pitch to Conrad, we made our pitch to PRDG, somehow rationalizing its spirituality, and it became our first producing venture outside the nest of academia.

The Medium was strange and compelling. Madame Flora (Baba) supports herself by holding seances in her grubby living room with her teenage daughter assisting in illusions. She's a fraud, but an effective one: her clients depend on her to ease their grief for lost loved ones. When something happens that isn't faked, Baba is terrified. She throws out her clients and drunkenly beats the mute street-boy who lives with them, eventually shooting him. At auditions, remarkable people showed up. The title role needs a gorgeous dark voice and impressive acting talent, and we got both. At that time opera singers usually preferred to stand still while singing an aria, certainly not thrashing around. Willene Gunn had no such reservations. When she beat the mute Toby, she really whaled him. We found a thick bathrobe sash that made a loud whack when used as a whip but didn't hurt. Baba methodically sang the same phrase, "So you won't answer, eh?" with every lash, holding a high G-flat on each "eh" and nailing it every time.

After a childhood immersed in music, I had wrenched myself out of that world, but now I worked steadily to learn the piano accompaniment. I'd done rehearsal piano for *Threepenny*, but with *The Medium* I was challenged to play a whole score. I had known and loved that music for years, but regaining the keyboard skill it demanded was hard. Sometimes I had to fight against getting lost in the magic they made on stage and remember to play the score.

Learning the Craft

Our maiden voyage in independent theatre was launched in a local church hall. Conrad designed the set, a low-rent walk-up apartment, and we built it with help from the cast, using styrofoam insulation panels for walls. With multiple peeling layers of wallpaper, it was a convincing rat trap. Everybody pitched in, and we lived in it for three months. The run was scheduled for a month, and houses were good. When we announced a one-month extension, all but the last two shows sold out immediately, and after that we did two weeks in San Francisco. Years later, one of our friends confided, "I wanted to see this thing objectively, to think about it rationally; I saw it three times and never got my head above water."

It was strong magic, more than a box office success: it had a profound effect on the audience and on us. We had attached like piranhas to a project we were determined to do, found people who felt as strongly as we did, and allowed everyone to own the project. I had to recognize, too, that music was my compelling genie; it might lie low for a while, but it would always come back to claim me.

As might be expected, the PRDG was open to another project. Their summer season was to feature "Old Testament heroes," including D. H. Lawrence's *David*. It was lengthy, verbally dense, required a huge cast, and was immense in conception. It would be a challenge, but we risked it. Late one night over cherry cheesecake, Leon Katz agreed to play the principal character Saul.

I played Saul's daughter Michal, helped with the costumes, and hand-built a little harp for David to play. As an actor, Leon was unique. Vocally and physically he made a magnificent Old Testament king, but neither of us knew fight technique, and when he slapped my face he nearly took my head off. Learning lines was a huge problem for this brilliant man, but his presence was so powerful that he could have read a plumbing invoice aloud and held the stage. This was a very different experience from *The*

Medium, a sprawling outdoor production instead of a tight-knit common effort with the feel of a love affair. It was a hot August, the work was exhausting, but when the prophets appeared over the roof of the church, it was impressive. We had wrangled a huge production and survived it.

∼

Another local company scheduled Goethe's *Faust* and asked me to play Gretchen. We were rehearsing another show, but this would run on Monday nights only, and we could work around it; I also agreed to create incidental music, including melodies for verses Gretchen sings. While working, a song jumped into my head: it wasn't for *Faust*, but it was spurred by Gretchen's pregnancy. I'd never written lyrics before and wanted some response. Lunchtime at the orthodontist's office, I asked Charmeon if she would listen.

Love is the reason you came to be, little one
Love filled my eyes and I could not see, little one
Love made a fool of me then
Love could still fool me again
Love is so strong, my little one.

Charmeon burst into tears. She explained that her only daughter recently had to decide whether to carry a baby to term and whether to arrange for adoption. Mother and daughter wept together, eventually deciding the baby would stay in the family. It was the first song I'd ever written, and it touched something deep.

After *Faust*, I was Helen of Troy in *Tiger at the Gates*, the play Northwestern had done with Conrad as Hector and me as Cassandra, now directed by Conrad and produced by the same group as *The Medium* and *David*. Unlike those, this one was instantly controversial. It had been written in 1935 as World War II was brewing, translated into English in 1955 when the Korean War had just ended, and now we were mired in Vietnam. The original title translates literally as *The Trojan War Will Not Take Place*, and in the play neither Greeks nor Trojans want war. The production,

Learning the Craft

in the accurate though hostile words of the suburban reviewer, was "wildly bohemian," "tacky," and "boisterously vulgar." Audience members called the editor to complain about the "stupid review," then a published letter called it "unsuitable for a religious drama group" and asked if the church approved of "bawdy plays." That prompted more letters of appreciation: great free publicity.

We were never seekers of controversy, but we tasted a strong response, our work connecting with what was happening now, and we didn't forget it. As with much of my life, a seed planted may take years to sprout, but it sprouts.

∽

In the three years of California, I remembered what it was like to be in my body. That carried me across the thirty-three years it would take to return. Leaving our little cottage in East Palo Alto, saying good-bye to its scruffy loveliness, I had no idea what was coming next. Our nose-thumbing productions outside the Stanford capsule made me feel there would be more of this, but I had no idea that it would extend to a lifetime. I knew that my bond to this land was deep, but I didn't yet know how long that bond would have to endure. I'm glad I didn't know.

I was grateful for the lessons of Charlie's visible actions, Gerry's focus on the moment, Leon's intellectual force, Conrad's asking the impossible, and how it came together. What *The Four-poster* gave us—being a tightly collaborative duo that could carry a whole show—would be pure gold in the years to come.

And I'm grateful that the music came back. *Threepenny* and *The Medium* reclaimed my keyboard skills for practical use. The koto I'd used in *Prometheus* came back to life again with our Noh play and later with a commission for a grad student's play. I somehow had never thought of myself as a composer, but now I realized, oh yeah, I'm composing this. And my music got its first-ever review: "*Also contributing mightily is a female player of a koto. She is a fine musician and provides a sensitive counterpart to the spoken word."* It was a lovely instrument, and I still have it. I never composed for it again.

So many farewells, and so much to come.

12.
Grits

We moved from one coast to the other, from what had become my heart's rooted place to a country unknown. It wasn't the first time I'd traded one world for another: my high school dedication to medicine as a career had flipped a one-eighty into theatre and I'd found a lifemate in my new world. I had no idea how to translate my obsession with theatre into a career, and now I didn't need to: my mate was gifted and obsessed with a plan, and now it was our plan. In the Stanford years, our work in tandem had given us lavish returns. He racked up stellar points toward his academic career, and I made significant gains in my acting skills. We grew together, supported each other, and now we jumped together off the high board of the PhD.

Bam. South Carolina meant a secure salary and a defined world of work, but I wasn't a part of either one. For the first time in our life together, I didn't need to earn money, and I wasn't a part of what Conrad was paid to do. I was on my own. Then things changed.

∼

By the time I left South Carolina I'd found myself growing fond of the South and enjoying well-cooked grits, but arriving in the early morning of September 12th, the only thing on my mind was finding someplace to live before the moving truck arrived. In the crummy diner that smelled of old mop, we bought a newspaper and turned to the For Rent section. I stopped crying, ate my egg, and pushed the grits over to Conrad (he'd eat anything). The good news was that rents were cheap; the bad news was that there wasn't much to be had.

When Conrad called the theatre (part of the English Department) and told them we'd arrived, we got a dinner invitation for that evening—a blessing. After finding the office and saying hello, we put the search process into high gear. We made appointments with four realtors and spent the afternoon getting glummer and glummer. Places were far from campus or with rooms that a good-sized dog would have trouble turning around in. One realtor thought he might have something, but he'd lost the listing card, so could we call back tomorrow? Sure, why not?

I was tired, rumpled, and sweaty by the time we arrived for dinner at the theatre chair's house, but his wife's warm welcome and a cold gin and tonic helped a lot. Their children were cute as hell, a four-year-old daughter and twin boys six months old, and the informal evening put my depression on hold. He was the only theatre prof in the English Department and was pleased to have a colleague. I felt we would get along well.

Next morning, we almost didn't call the scatter-brained realtor. When we did, he suggested we drive by and call him if we liked what we saw. We found the address and thought he must have made a mistake. It was five minutes from campus in a quiet tree-lined neighborhood, a big house on the corner, white-painted brick with a screened porch, back yard and barbecue, garage and workroom, and it was $125 a month. That couldn't be right, not even in South Carolina. We called back and he said it was true; he hadn't been able to find the keys, but he'd have them by 1 p.m.

We went and got a sandwich and iced tea. I had been unaware that in the South anything that could possibly have sugar in it would be syrupy beyond belief, and asked for a glass of plain water. The realtor met us at the house but had the wrong keys, so we killed time by driving all over Columbia; by four o'clock the keys worked, and I was stunned: hardwood floors, a million closets, everything newly repainted off white, three big bedrooms, two baths, and a dining room with a butler's pantry on the way to the kitchen. I managed to keep from leaping and chorusing "Yes!" with Conrad, and the deal was done. We got the keys then and there, closed the door, fell into each other's arms, and I cried again—this time with a mixture of joy, disbelief, and exhaustion. I headed for the bathroom and wound up in a closet.

After a night's sleep on the floor in our sleeping bags, we set up a bank account and found an appliance store that swore their used stove and fridge would work. Dr. Bishop started classes the next Monday, we got two Siamese kittens on Tuesday, and the movers brought our stuff on Wednesday with a bill that was $200 below estimate. Classes were Monday, Wednesday, and Friday, and an $8,500 salary meant I didn't need to look for a job. Now I was a faculty wife, and our climb up the stairs of academia had brought us to the first landing. I could sit in on his acting classes and sometimes participate when a student didn't have a partner, but our collaborative work didn't come back to life for a month: in October, I was challenged with writing the music for sixty-nine songs.

∽

Music had gotten a new grip on me in the Stanford years. I ventured beyond the koto and discovered that I had a vast internal library in my brain and could use it to create music in genres I never thought I had liked. When we did *The Medium* in Palo Alto, I got a new grip on the power of music to create theatre. I wasn't just an actress: I was a collaborative musician. I didn't realize what that meant until South Carolina walloped us with a new challenge.

∽

The original plan for Conrad's fall production was to stage Camus' *Caligula*, but it was clear from auditions that no student could carry the title role. Plan B was another Camus play, *State of Siege*, but rights were denied. Plan C was to take everyone who'd been cast and put them in John Gay's *The Beggar's Opera*—the play that was the basis for *The Threepenny Opera*: with seventeen men and twelve women, nobody got left out.

But the show needed dozens of songs. In the original 1728 production, those songs were all popular tunes with new satirical lyrics. Italian opera had just started being performed in London, and some thought it was hysterically funny for actors to burst suddenly into song. John Gay took this to a comic extreme: instead of mythic figures or nobility, his characters were lowlife crooks and whores, and the songs were sassy and short, sometimes only four lines long, many concerning crime and political corruption. We used Gay's lyrics, but we needed new tunes that sounded current. I bought a used upright piano for $400—not first-quality, but it had a good action, great bass tone, and I had to learn to love it. I got to work; I didn't have time to be terrified. It was only three years before that I had composed my first music; now I had to write songs for people to sing, arrange music for a small band, and I would be playing live in the pit. Luckily, our house wasn't close to the neighbors, so we got no complaints about the piano banging away in the wee small hours, though I don't know what the kittens thought. I made it: more than one song a day.

My night-time work habits introduced me to the other residents of our house: roaches. The ones I had dealt with in our Palo Alto cottage turned my stomach, but these were something else entirely. They were huge, and when they'd come up the stairs from the basement I swear I could hear their feet clomping. I hoped the cats would hunt them, but no such luck.

I found I was very good at making catchy tunes. The idioms of English music-hall, Gilbert & Sullivan, and cabaret were all in my ear. These things were instant ear-worms, and if I'd gone into writing commercial jingles, I might have grown wealthy and very unhappy. I wrote for the capabilities of specific voices, taught people the songs, and functioned as music director. I'd never been in charge like that, but survival meant Fake It Till You Make It. I forced myself to own what I'd written and make it work—despite the Music Department, who lodged a formal protest to the Dean that we were doing an "opera" without their collaboration: our intro to academic politics. The objection was overruled—our show could hardly be mistaken for opera—but they forbade their students to attend.

We spent many nights after rehearsals decompressing at a student hangout. It was a small ground-floor diner, but when you lifted a hinged segment of the counter and walked behind, there was a narrow stairway down to a large lumpy basement with stone walls covered in aluminum foil, like being inside a baked potato: the South Carolina version of psychedelia. Those who brought guitars played folk and blues, and everybody joined in, singing along with whatever a guitar brought to mind, as pitchers of beer came and went. I was part of the gang, and they were on my side.

Since I played piano in the band, at least I didn't have to write that all out, but I had to provide sheet music for banjo, trumpet, bass, sax, and drums. I didn't know diddly about arrangements, and it took me too long to get parts written for the first act. Even with help from the other musicians, the second and third acts were pretty thin, mostly piano, bass, and drums. The first act sounded great, though, and Conrad—or Dr. B or CB—insisted that the rest was just fine. That was hard to accept. The years with my mother had honed self-criticism to a fine edge: cut yourself down first and then what others say won't hurt so much. I shrank inside at what I hadn't been able to do, but the cast and the audience taught me something: they laughed and clapped and hugged, and I had to admit that it was pretty damn good. A bonding experience, trial by fire, whatever you want to call it—it was totally new for me to have my music be part of an exuberant group celebration.

∼

And then it was over and done. Back when *The Medium* caught fire, we extended the run and savored the intoxication for many more weeks, but that had been our own independent production. This was a different pattern, one dictated by academic theatre. A college production is a type of commodity, prepared, presented, and predictable. When it's gone, it's gone.

∼

The musical recognition was great, but I was hungry for acting. The community theatre had just hired a new director who'd come in with an assertive attitude and a very off-beat season including Brecht, Max Frisch, Pirandello, Moliere—hardly the normal community theatre fare. Next up would be *Six Characters in Search of an Author* and I auditioned. I was cast.

The Stepdaughter is a flamboyant role, and her major conflict is with the Father. It builds toward a scene in a dress shop, a front for a brothel where she works, and her first customer is the Father. He claims he didn't know her, though he'd been stalking her all through her childhood. Conrad's colleague at USC played the Father, a tense pairing, but we worked together OK.

I missed Conrad's guidance, but I had to trust the director while navigating this wild character. I had to sing a French song cabaret-style and launch into provocative dancing—skills I didn't really have. No way could I do the song in the script, so I substituted Piaf's *Milord* from the Evanston coffee shop. At least it was French, and little Piaf's gallant soul inspired my dancing. The translation felt a bit wooden, and there was little chemistry with the cast, but I was rewarded with a lavish review: *The play would have more than justified its presence here had it done no more than introduce the brilliant talents of Linda Bishop, a young actress of remarkable presence, good looks, and sure technique. She was superb.*

Then came auditions for *A Thousand Clowns*, and I was cast as the social worker who comes to do an evaluation and falls into bed with her client, a role played by the director. It was well-suited to him, brash, funny, and quirky, and he was an attractive man. I'd been the focus of his attention in the previous show, and now we were playing with scripted erotic sparks that became real. He had the dark energy of the guys who'd turned me on before I met CB. Onstage we had a hot scene together; the stage kisses moved to the dressing room, then further.

I had never thought about infidelity, and the word *affair* was an old-fashioned word from novels. My mind didn't go there. Love had nothing to do with it; it was all sex. My old dissociative patterns came back; I hid my guilty secret, felt awful about it, and went right on doing it. I'd thought I was done with lying, but old habits made a last gasp. The rest of that spring, I slogged through a swamp of guilt that outweighed the initial buzz. To complicate things, I really liked his wife, an elfin brunette dancer who cracked sophisticated jokes; all four of us developed a social friendship.

The on-stage sparks fizzled. After *Clowns* came *The Happy Haven*, a sour farce with all the emotional appeal of mildew, and it was a grim experience watching the director flounder as sadly as the actors. Nevertheless, we hung out socially all through the spring, the secret stayed secret, the theatre's board fired him, and they left for New York in June. This closure was a relief, and I looked forward to the doors of summer opening.

Conrad was working separately. The other theatre prof had been pressured to stage Shakespeare and chose *Troilus and Cressida*, thinking it likely that no one had ever seen it. CB and several other faculty were asked to audition, and he was cast as Hector. After the cast was posted, the prof apologized: "I feel terrible about this. I read the play again and didn't realize it was such a small part." The local review offered a diplomatic headline: *Troilus and Cressida Shows Evidence of Much Work*.

Our community theatre friends presented Conrad with an innovative opening-night gift. The young boy in *A Thousand Clowns*, which ran while *Troilus and Cressida* was rehearsing, had asked, "Toilet and what?" Their gift was a junked toilet stuffed with colorful plastic flowers, with a big hand-lettered card: *TOILET INCREDIBLE!* We used it as a telephone chair.

∼

What came next was the spirit of *The Medium* coming in to rescue us, riding the memory of our very first collaboration—*Woyzeck*. It was scheduled as the spring production, and its destiny was to be the academic ritual sacrifice: four weeks of rehearsal, four performances, and sudden death. It didn't work out that way. We grabbed it by the horns and made it into something that began to change our lives.

∼

I started work on the sound score. The murder scene was the first thing we had ever done together, and now we were about to bring the full play to life. When the playwright died of typhus in 1837, he was not yet twenty-four and the play was still in fragments. The gent who'd been hired to do set designs turned out to be an annoying lush, so Conrad took over and designed a startling set that was as fragmentary as the play—platforms slanted downward, others uphill, some nine feet in the air. The backdrop was a twenty-foot-high wall of rusted, corrugated tin with two ragged doors, and a pizza-colored moon. It looked like a bombed-out warehouse; but in a strange way, like the set for *The Medium*, it was home.

The student actors rose to the challenge. *Woyzeck* was a major step in our evolution toward an ensemble process. These wild, fearless young people worked with us as peers and adopted us as part of their tribe. They'd gone along for the ride with the goofball comedy of *The Beggar's Opera* and hung on as the train went roaring through the savagery of *Woyzeck*.

And for me, *Woyzeck* was a jolt into yet another musical idiom. I had gone out on a limb with *The Beggar's Opera*, but it wasn't risky; it was a comfortable, bouncy people-pleaser. *Woyzeck* wasn't a different limb, it was a whole different tree. That dark insanity was something I knew well, but it required its own voice. What would make the sounds?

After some dud ideas, I devised a strange instrument. With a six-foot piece of PVC pipe, I sang a wordless, high-pitched keening into one end, with the tape recorder's mike at the other. My voice, distorted by the pipe's reverberation, gave me the sound I wanted. It was hell on breath control, and isolating the cats was tricky, but it was perfect. A hybrid of processed sounds, some melodic, some percussive, its audio environment added momentum to the impending violence in the play. It was my first excursion into manipulated recording and far from being my last.

When audiences saw *Woyzeck*, they didn't know how to react. The play was fragmented and brutal, the set intimidating, the sound score creepy, and the story line disturbing. One reviewer wrote: *Not everyone will like it. They may even find it repulsive—but they cannot deny that it provides a moving theatrical experience.*

~

It actually did something to the audience. Being part of *The Medium* had been life-changing for me, but it was outside the framework of our career path. John Lennon said: "Life is what happens while you're busy making other plans." Now that I'd tasted the life-buzz of provocative theatre within the bounds of academia, I felt an urge to push harder, and we were willing to try USC for another year. The push came big-time in that second year, bracketed by two surreal stints of doing what amounted to summer stock on a steamy tropical island.

~

From mid-June through the end of August, we lived and worked on Hilton Head Island as part of a new Summer School of the Arts. CB taught two courses and directed two plays; as faculty wife I could do whatever I felt like. The drive from Columbia was three hours one way, and it took us three trips to get settled: one to check our apartment, two more to haul stuff. The first trip, he took the cats in the car and I rode the Vespa. I congratulated myself for doing a long scooter trip and kicked myself for not having worn gloves. Until putting in some beach time, I had dark brown hands and snow-white arms.

The William Hilton Inn was our landlord and the site of the performances. It was a pricey resort, but in 1967 money and golf didn't entirely dominate the island. There hadn't been a bridge to the mainland until 1956, and the first gates enclosing the Sea Pines Plantation, giving privacy to the affluent homeowners, had only just been installed. Many of the people who worked for the Inn were from the Gullah community, descendants of slaves freed by the Union army.

Little prefab fourplexes had been built to house faculty, students, and staff, but construction was still in process. The island's soft white sand made great beaches but lousy roads; paving from the main road back to the apartments was still in process, and we couldn't get the car closer than two blocks away. Everything had to be carried a distance, slogging through ankle-deep sand and then up a flight of stairs. Our rooms were furnished in cheap vinyl dorm style but did have air conditioning and a reasonable fridge and stove. After a week or so, the builders even finished the roof and left us in peace.

The island itself was an out-of-body experience, blue waters and white sand beaches with surreal driftwood as far as the eye could see. I had fallen in love with the Pacific shore, got wrenched away, and had been landlocked for a year. This ocean was a very different creature—long sugar-white beaches instead of ochre bluffs—but it was an ocean, and I was happy beyond measure. Once, on a remote beach, we discovered a young dolphin stranded in a tide pool, picked it up, and carried it to open water. Many small villages still remained on the island, and our scooter got us everywhere outside the gated areas. Once we were exploring a dense tropical forest, riding tandem on the scooter along a narrow path. As we went under a low-hanging branch, a mammoth spider landed on Conrad's helmet; I screeched and bucked, and we both went sprawling sideways. After panicked spasms, we got ourselves together and went on, but more circumspectly.

The army of student actors arrived, we did auditions, and everybody got to work. Nine-hour days: three rehearsals of three hours each, plus meal breaks. No classes yet: those didn't start until after the first two plays had opened. It was a repertory schedule: four plays for a week each, then the same four repeating. Although we were there as an educational program, we were clearly regarded as menials. In revenge, two students hatched a plan to capture an alligator from the moat that defined the wealthy enclave and drop it into the pool of the Inn. Various residents had amused themselves by feeding the alligator ham, so the guys were able to lure the beast, but having gotten its attention, they lost spirit for their cause.

The students paid cut-rate rent and bought discounted meals, but what the Inn fed them was miserable. It wasn't long before I was bringing food down to the beach after shows for everybody to enjoy: fruit salad, veggies, warm fresh bread, even cinnamon rolls. I'd spent seven years feeding the two of us on a dime, and now we could afford to share. The magic of moonlight on a white beach, flickers of firelight, the voices and guitars, our tribe gathering and enjoying what I brought—it washed away all the crud of the day.

Performances were in-the-round in the hotel ballroom. Our first play, an obscure, moving family drama *Time and the Conways*, went well, though audiences were small. *The Madwoman of Chaillot* got more traction; it's magical and funny, a charmingly nasty take on capitalism. The Beatles had just released *Sergeant Pepper*, and we used it as preshow music to set the mood. I did the make-up design and had a wonderful time making characters look like iridescent refugees from modern art. There were good reviews for all the shows, and the university bigwigs were impressed with enrollment. The summer was a strange one, but everyone bonded. When the end came, we knew we would miss it.

Returning to Columbia after the first summer, we found that our dining-room table had grown a crop of inch-thick moss—summers were humid in South Carolina. The theatre chair's wife was pregnant again, and he was tense. But Conrad's contract renewal came with a raise, and when the new scene designer, a red-bearded Texan, arrived with his German-born wife, we became instant friends. We didn't say it in public, but we knew we'd be moving on at the end of the year, and we did what we could to find the bright spots.

Over the summer the Vietnam draft doubled its conscription rate. Conrad's occupational deferment (2-A) had been stable, but the Council Bluffs draft board suddenly reclassified him 1-A. According to Margaret, who checked into this, the local draft-board lady's own son had flunked out and got drafted. Local draft boards had the final say on deferments. I panicked, but when the university wrote letters affirming CB's faculty position, they backed off. He called the local draft board for more information and found that when he turned twenty-six in October, he would automatically be reclassified 5-A; by the time the annual review happened in February, he'd be safe. Job hunting to leave USC could begin.

∽

I had spent the summer immersed in theatre, but only in support, not on stage. Back in Columbia, I stayed away from the community theatre until I could see whether the new director had any pizzazz. He didn't—their board was now leery of pizzazz—but I got a call from another local group asking me to take the female role in Murray Schisgal's *Luv*. A silly light-weight piece, but the two guys were good comic actors, and the director used Mike Nichols' stage directions as printed in the script. Smart choice.

I decided to take some pleasure in having a good income. We bought a 35mm camera and realized that if we were going to take it seriously we'd need a darkroom. We also bought a big office-grade electric typewriter, two large living-room rugs, and a handsome floor lamp. I gave Conrad his first surprise birthday party and refrained from writing *Happy 5-A* on the frosting.

The auditions for CB's December trio of Samuel Beckett plays went well, but my instincts didn't work so well when I agreed to do the photo-ready layout for the Beckett poster. These were the days of Prestype lettering, and Conrad had designed a melodrama-style poster that was all different sizes of lettering in fancy boxes with lots of scrolls and stars and exclamation points. I thought it was hilarious and went to the art store for many sheets of different fancy fonts and the right size of posterboard, and went to work.

I'd underestimated the job. It was a 14x17-inch poster, all lettering, large and small. Each letter had to be positioned exactly and rubbed off onto the posterboard, then followed by the next and the next and the next. Along about midnight, I saw what I was in for, and somewhere around five a.m. I started seeing colors where there weren't any. As I was getting close to the bottom of the thing, I looked back over my work. The top lines of letters were starting to peel up their edges.

I wanted badly to get hysterical and crawl all over the ceiling but settled for dunking my head under the kitchen faucet. The top got smoothed back down, the bottom got finished, and I collapsed. I made it to bed, and the layout made it to the print shop. The printed posters became collectors' items, and I never fulfilled my fantasy of sending a bomb to the Prestype people.

Our cats went into heat, both of them, and the yowling was pretty special. We rented a big Siamese tom; he took one look at the ladies and hid under the bed, though at last it came to him what he was there for. The house got quiet and the cats got big. They were due to have their kittens right at the time for parental Christmas visits, so we boarded them with the vet.

I looked forward to spending time with Margaret but dreaded time with my mother. Margaret did not want to visit Cadillac; Mary had been really nasty to her last year. A diplomatic excuse was written, Margaret came by train to Chicago, and we had our own time there. The flight home was ghastly. Atlanta was fogged in, so we were rerouted to Tampa. The weather was still bad, and we were put on a bus to Jacksonville, then another bus to Columbia. No sleep, awful food, and more than twenty-four hours in travel hell: for once it felt good to be home.

We collected our two cats and their seven kittens and tried to heed the vet's warning: keep the two moms and their litters apart, lest one cat attack the other's kits. The cats hadn't read the textbooks; they insisted on piling everybody in one box and taking turns nursing the bunch. One mom (The Scrag) was classic Siamese: skinny, with crossed eyes and a kink in her tail. The other (The Naz, from Lord Buckley's classic routine) was solid, unkinked, with big blue straight-ahead eyes. When it came time to sell the kittens, I'd have to say which kits came from which mom. At first their tails were hairless, and I dunked one litter's tails in Mercurochrome—the only pink-point Siamese in South Carolina. When the tails haired up, I put dots on their bellies.

The senior prof was rehearsing *West Side Story*, and I played piano for dance rehearsals. The dance director was impressive; she declared martial law and whipped her untrained dancers to a level of discipline they didn't know they had in them. After all those hours of playing piano for workouts, I went along after rehearsals for many beers. By the time the official accompanist replaced me, I was very attached to the show, so when the meltdown came, it was agonizing. The better the rehearsals looked, the weirder the director became. He gave no notes at all for the last three rehearsals and during the run never showed his face. On closing night, the cast searched everywhere to give him a gift, finally caught him in the parking lot, and he refused the gift.

It had become urgent to put a push on getting a new job, and we were getting some signs of interest. But then the draft menace ballooned and took center stage—more older men were being called. We couldn't trust the local draft board to honor his 5-A, so Conrad called off the job search and agreed to stay for a third year. Our refuge was total immersion in our spring production, *Hecuba*. My music for this was far beyond anything I had yet done. It took me deep into my core and brought out an honest and deeply-felt expression of grief and rage. In my progress as a composer, I became an adult.

Reacting to America's entanglement in war, Conrad had written an adaptation of the Euripides play. After a ten-year siege, Troy has fallen to the Greeks, who take Queen Hecuba, her daughter Polyxena, and other Trojan women into the ships as slaves. Mid-voyage, the wind dies, and all are marooned in Thrace, victors and vanquished on the barren rocks. The priests prophesy that the sacrifice of Polyxena will unlock the winds. As she prepares to wash her daughter's dead body, Hecuba sees that it's her one remaining son, killed by the island's king. She takes a terrible revenge, but the winds do rise. As the Greeks sail, she leaps overboard, transformed to a dog with blazing eyes. Like Vietnam, a terrible story.

The score was what amounted to a cantata for the chorus of enslaved women. This was my first long, substantial music as a setting for Conrad's words. The composing I'd had to abandon when *State of Siege* was nixed came back as the bones of *Hecuba*. It verged on the operatic; the chorus never spoke—they sang. No catchy ditties here, this was grief and loss and searing rage in seven choral odes. Like *Woyzeck*, it tapped my dark side, and my mother couldn't yell, "Stop crying!" My ten women were there to make the crying heard.

They were masked, chained to each other by neck collars, and made even more vulnerable by their costumes: dark-red body stockings painted to resemble a flayed nakedness. *"Once we were women; now we are cattle. Line up, keep your places, line up, wait."* They were not all trained singers, but everyone was willing to do what it took to express the awful cost of war. I created driving music for Conrad's lines and molded the chorus to become a strong collective voice.

A channel opened: the music ran through my body and took me to a new level as a composer. The score used trumpets, flutes, sax and percussion, but the core of it was a big muscular piano, and I was at the keyboard live in the pit, ducking backstage to appear in my brief scenes. Rehearsing the female chorus was even stronger because I was part of it, singing as leader while pounding the piano. Their grief was my grief, their rage was mine, and we were bound together. None of us were alone.

The immersion in *Hecuba* was so deep that having it end was disorienting. Mounting the production had been hell on wheels. It required a huge cast, and between those who dropped out after auditions and those who fell apart during rehearsals, we lost sixteen people. The others got up to speed, but I'd begun to think that the South had a corner on nervous breakdowns. About half the cast were as passionate as we were, and that's what kept us alive. Audiences were small but mighty, and at least one person came to all three performances.

We'd agreed to stay a third year, but *Hecuba* pushed us over the edge. I was still terrified of the draft, but Conrad sent telegrams to the universities who'd asked him to interview, saying that he was available. Damn the torpedoes, we'd take our chances. We could get through the rest of the spring and another summer at Hilton Head: the distraught director didn't sabotage anyone else's work, only his own. He accepted Conrad's resignation and said he was sorry, but he didn't like Columbia either, so he understood.

Requests for interviews came from SUNY/Binghamton, Antioch, and the Fine Arts school of UW-Milwaukee. The only one to which I went along was Antioch—the students traditionally interviewed the spouse—and I was involved with rehearsals during other trips. Antioch couldn't have been more of a contrast to USC: politically engaged, intellectually vivid, artistically animated. The students were fully involved in decision-making; we saw some productions, talked to everybody, and they made an offer. Once the fumes of excitement subsided, though, I agreed with Conrad that one of Antioch's greatest strengths would be a drawback for us. Contemporary social relevance was paramount to the students, but theatre history and classic literature weren't of much interest. Having just done a powerful *Hecuba*, we couldn't agree with that viewpoint, though it made for a lively campus. I crossed my fingers for Milwaukee.

An offer came: a three-year contract starting at $11,000, a considerable boost. We threw a big party, our way of saying "thank you" and "farewell." We gave notice to our landlord and arranged with the movers to get our stuff on May 31st and put it in storage. My heart was breaking because I had to give up my beloved cats. Conrad had suddenly developed a severe allergy, got tested, and the results were clear. I couldn't bear to sell them; I had to keep them together, especially since one was about to have another litter. A young couple who had bought a kitten from the first round were happy to take both ladies, and the preggers one would give them a nice little income boost: purebred Siamese are pricey.

Packing for the move was a high-speed carnival ride, including cartons of books we could mail to UW-Milwaukee, which offered to store them for the summer. I didn't know how we'd bought so many books in two years. Meantime, I'd been asked to write and record some New Orleans-style barrel-house piano for a local staging of *A Streetcar Named Desire*. I'd never written or played in that idiom, but I said what the hell and did it anyway. My music was a hit: I'd never gotten such a gush of praise.

That final summer, the university waited until the last minute before deciding to offer the Hilton Head program again, but they made up for the frustration by giving us a two-bedroom apartment and paying our rent. Conrad had chosen *The Importance of Being Earnest* and *The Fantasticks*; the other prof would do *A Thurber Carnival* and *Blithe Spirit*. I would do musical direction and piano for *Fantasticks* and get paid $25 per show to play transitions for *Thurber*.

I drove down to the island while CB followed on the scooter. Five minutes after we started out, it began to rain and never stopped for ten days. As soon as we got unloaded, the management dropped a bomb: this year we would be performing not in the hotel ballroom but in a tent. Heat, humidity, mosquitoes, frogs, and bad acoustics—what fun.

The tent promised to be a grotesque experience, and it was. One of the actresses in *Earnest* had to carry on with the genteel tea-scene lines while ignoring the huge horse-fly that had landed on her cleavage. The rains brought out frogs who swarmed the stage, and one jumped into a front-row lady's lap. But the capper was the rainstorm that collapsed the tent, stage lighting and all. The Inn had paid for the tent's rental, delivery and setup, then ignored the need of daily maintenance. The ropes grew slack, the canvas sagged, and when enough gallons of water accumulated, two poles snapped and down it went. The steel beams holding the lights (above the first three rows of audience) only came down partway, being held at one end four feet above the seats by nothing more than the cables supplying power. Everyone ran like hell and no one was injured.

We had thirty-six hours to modify the set, move it into the ballroom, and revise the staging. The two of us and the entire company were up all night to make it happen, but adrenaline is strong medicine, and we were able to stumble through the next performance. The rest of the season was in the ballroom.

The Fantasticks score was not easy for me; it calls for bass, harp and drums, but the major burden is on the piano, and the original pianist must have had monstrous hands. Octave chords all over the place, and my forearms burned worse than they did when I made my concerto attempt; I developed enough new muscle to crush a beer can one-handed. And I put in hours and hours in the darkroom with CB. Our photography was in demand, and we made enough from prints above expenses to buy a new lens.

The Inn had fed the students badly before, but this summer it was worse. It's hard to rehearse sophisticated comedy when half the cast has the trots. I expanded my contribution of night-time beach dinners. The "mystery meat" was disgusting, and I decided to get an extra treat on my Savannah grocery run: lamb for souvlaki, to be skewered and cooked on the campfire. I took along a gallon of marinade, my small cutting board, and a wicked boning knife. On the way back, when Conrad stopped at the toll booth, the tolltaker saw a strange sight and probably told the story for weeks. "This VW pulls up, I look in, and there's a lady with a bloody board in her lap, sawing away at a big piece of meat. Y'all, I'm not making this up!" The midnight souvlaki was to die for.

It felt as if I ran from piano to kitchen to darkroom and back, the only freedom being the late-night beach dinners. Still, those hours with the pure white sand shining in the moonlight, the bonfire crackling, the guitars—it was worth it.

By August 20th it was over and done. Everything got jammed into the VW, Conrad drove the scooter back, and we stayed overnight with a friend in Columbia before hauling ass for Milwaukee. The moving company had weighed the scooter as part of the load, so all we had to do was turn it over to them and pat its round little butt. The next morning we headed north at a stately pace: the

VW was so heavily laden that it wouldn't go more than fifty miles an hour. It would be a long slow trip, but we took time to stop at the state line, yell and whoop, and make some very rude gestures. Damn, that felt good.

～

I'd been on a roller-coaster ever since we left California. The music I was challenged to create, all of it on tough deadlines, wasn't trivial any more; it was up front and substantial. The threat of the draft was always looming; Conrad had spent seven years obsessively preparing for his profession, and now, just starting his career, it might all go to hell. I'd had four years of earning money essential to our survival, and poof, suddenly I didn't need a job. I did acting, made a big splash, wandered down a short dark alley of guilt, and got back out again.

Above all, these two years in alien territory introduced us to a new sense of tribe. The funky, maddening, wonderful student actors became our co-conspirators. We were a little group in a context that didn't much care what we did, and that gave us the freedom to care about each other. When we left, a number of people followed us to Milwaukee, and one became our lifetime friend and colleague. In an interview, Flora said this:

"It started off with that professor who started the acting class. And that group of actors was serious up to a point, but then you-all came, and it really got serious. So I ... I didn't have a life outside of that. (laughs) Didn't do anything but that."

As it turned out, neither did we.

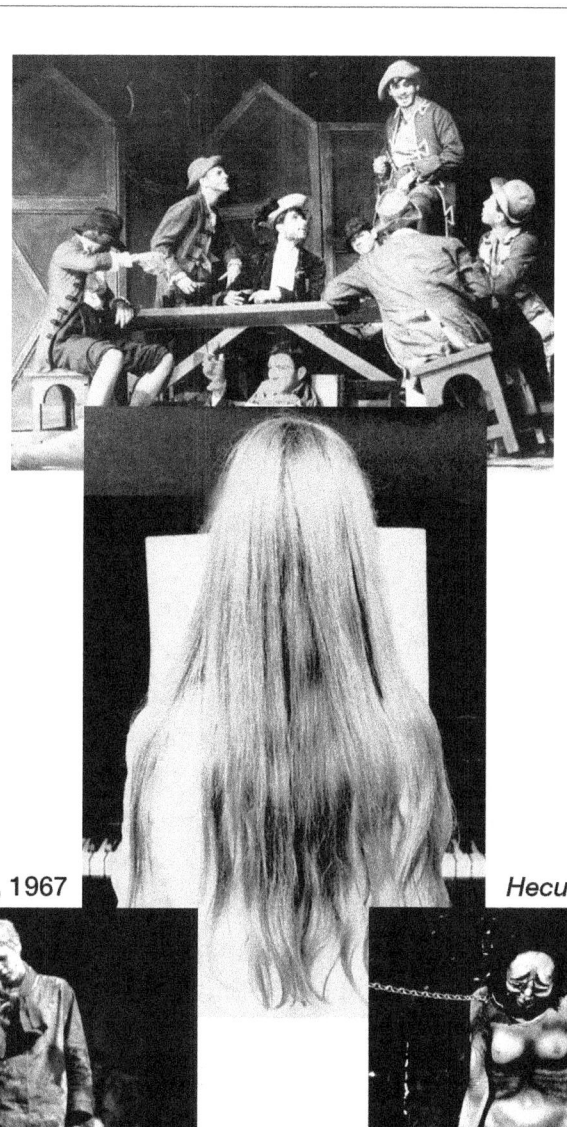

The Beggar's Opera, 1966

Woyzeck, 1967

Hecuba, 1968

13.

Milwaukee

At the stately pace of fifty miles an hour, the first day of driving got us to Knoxville. By dinnertime next day, we were only at the outskirts of Indianapolis. We'd made a late-arrival reservation at the small Milwaukee hotel where Conrad had stayed for his interview, so we decided, what the hell, let's go for it. The next day's house-hunting made it clear that the hordes of incoming students had picked the rentals to the bone, but we found an apartment that would do for a while and grabbed it.

Conrad's description of the campus had been vivid, but I was still knocked flat at the sight of the buildings nestled in the green of Milwaukee's northeast side and downright incredulous when I saw the theatre space. With its wide thrust stage and ample curved seating, it reminded me of the Guthrie Theatre in Minneapolis.

And what knocked me out were the opulent grocery stores. After the South, I was a kid let loose in a candy store. The first time I walked into Sendik's, I nearly fainted: piles of gorgeous tomatoes, red and green and yellow peppers, purple onions, watercress, four kinds of mushrooms, peaches the size of softballs, big sweet strawberries, melons I never knew existed, and then came the meat department. I bought a whole pork tenderloin for 80¢, fed it to us in one go, and went back to buy two more to freeze. But then in early October, rehearsals began and never let up until late May, so dinnertime was usually a rush job. All those wonderful groceries available, little time to devote to cooking, but still a blessing.

And the wine. South Carolina's laws were weird. Since liquor store signs were prohibited from saying *Liquor Store*, they all had a huge red dot for signage, so you could see them for blocks. But the wine was a huge come-down for a Californian. Now I had more money and things worth spending it on. I knew winter would knock me down a peg, but September was lush and lovely. My spirits were high.

～

More than fifty years have passed and I can still feel that bubble of elation. I'd been Conrad's working partner through eight years of single-minded preparation for his career, and now the academic slot machine popped up three cherries and blew goodies all over us. I felt rewarded and cared for. Of course my spirits were high.

What a relief. South Carolina had been a test, and we passed. Now we had a three-year contract, decent money, an interesting city to live in, and the prestige of a fine arts school with magnificent facilities. And best of all, there were more than a hundred drama majors. We could aim high and cast well. It had all been worth it.

～

The first year was a dizzying ride. At the start, I made a wild score for CB's surreal production of *The Revenger's Tragedy*. While that was still in rehearsal, I was commissioned to do a translation and score for Brecht's *A Man's a Man*. I was approached to teach beginning acting in the spring semester, and then the department head asked me to compose music for the season's third show, *A Roaring Good Time*, the play that was the genesis of *Hello, Dolly!* I was in demand and running like hell: translating, composing, and teaching. And at the end of that season, something happened that changed our lives.

The Revenger's Tragedy was a bizarre staging of a dark Jacobean drama. We both acted, he did lights, I did music, and it was obvious that we were a team bent on stretching the conventions of academic theatre. Costumes were built in period line with wide panels of black polyethylene. The lighting was from stark angles in primary colors, and we looked like Times Square after a midnight rain. There was multiple cross-gender casting, and actors' faces had a severely diseased look, textured with liquid latex and cotton. Playing the bastard Spurio, I mimed obscene sex with a male Duchess—from opposite sides of the stage.

The score was a challenge. The walls of our apartment were thick, but I didn't feel easy about working late at night. For better or worse, I don't get into a creative groove until very late, and what was coming to me was really loud. I worked out the themes on the piano but wanted to use a harpsichord for the final tape—suggesting the era of the play while contradicting it with harsh rhythms and dissonances, like our period costumes constructed with reflective plastic.

I didn't have a harpsichord but the music department did, and I sweet-talked them into letting me use it overnight on the little concert stage. They showed me where to turn the light off, locked me in, and left me to jury-rig my "recording studio." I was alone under the one bright worklight that illuminated the polished stage and brought out the warm tones of the harpsichord's wood. The small auditorium was dark, but I could dimly see the curved rows of empty blue seats. Prowling offstage with my flashlight, I found a wooden cube like those used for theatre rehearsals—exactly the right size to slide under the harpsichord and leave head-room for the microphone to lie flat. I needed a pad to prevent rattling; the dressing rooms were unlocked, and I was lucky that someone had left a towel on the counter.

The little Wollensak's mike sat an inch below the soundboard, nearly touching it. Piano strings are hit by padded mallets, but a harpsichord's strings are plucked by individual picks: imagine a banjo on steroids. Its normal concert sound is fairly delicate, but I was gambling that this arrangement would make the notes louder and harsher. Headphones allowed me to preview the sound. Yes! The acid metallic timbre was exactly right. I took a few breaths to center myself, ducked under the keyboard to get the tape rolling, crawled back onto the padded concert stool, and started playing an instrument I'd had my hands on once before in my life.

I spent the night making that sweet little harpsichord sound like a war machine, doing improvisations over and over. This would be my only chance. When I finally hit utter exhaustion and ran out of tape, I hoped I had what I needed. After the cube and the towel were replaced and the extension cord neatly coiled, I picked up my Wollensak, doused the light, and pushed the bar on the exit door. It closed behind me with a hearty thunk, and I was out in the night. After some searching, I found where I'd left the car, got in, and locked the door. I had to sit and breathe the sharp November air to sober up enough to drive home safely: late-night repetitive improvisation puts me into an altered state. In the next days of editing, I knew I had done well. That score still startles me.

Another new faculty member was near us in age and temperament. Ron's first show would be Brecht's *A Man's a Man*; he asked me to do a new translation and write music for the songs. At Stanford I'd collaborated on revised lyrics for *The Threepenny Opera* and got a good feel for finding Brecht's words in English. Now I was both creating the music and crafting words true to the German while trying to make good songs. An example: Widow Begbick advises letting things go—men, houses, names—and the literal translation of the refrain is this: *Don't get hung up on the wave that breaks at your foot; as long as it's in the water, new waves will break on it.* My song, in 3/4 time:

Don't fall in love with a river-wave
That breaks at your feet and then ripples on
If you stand in the water, new waves will keep breaking
Wave after wave they break and are gone.

That very female music was in contrast to the rest of the score, all male military rhythms:

In the night you can fight, there's an enemy, Mama
The bands all play and you get your whiskey
You get to shoot at the enemy, Mama
You can see the sky, it's really there, Mama
And all you can do when you're dead—is stink.

In performance I played piano in the fictional all-girl jazz trio at Widow Begbick's Canteen, wearing a skimpy, spangly costume; the drummer was a cute little guy in drag. Somebody thought of a novel way to advertise the show, and I wore my spangles to play a beat-up piano up and down the campus streets in the back of a pickup truck—in Milwaukee's icy December. I froze, but I wasn't on the sidelines any more. I was right in the midst of the artistic scrum. It worked, I had fun, and I loved the review: *Not only did Bishop perform, she also wrote all the music. Her music was raucous and pleasingly entertaining, almost as though it belonged in a Broadway musical rather than on a college stage.*

As soon as we opened, I launched into creating the score for *A Roaring Good Time*. Once again, lyrics made tunes jump into my head, but I had to deal with a chamber orchestra in the pit: two violins, two flutes, clarinet, bassoon, trombone, cello, bass, and drums. I had done rudimentary arrangements for *The Beggar's Opera* and *Hecuba*; it never sounded the way it did in my head, but at least with those I had a piano to glue it together. Not now. I found myself wishing I'd dug deeper while helping Conrad research melodrama for his dissertation. Orchestral music underscoring stage action was a huge part of that, and if I'd been able to see into the future, I would have copied the arrangements.

I was in way over my head. All I could do was listen carefully to recordings, research the range for each instrument, and remember that the clarinet's sheet music had to be transposed (a written C would come out as B-flat). It was a desperate hail-Mary grind—up all night two nights in a row with a cramping right hand and dry burning eyes—to finish the sheet music. When I heard the results, I was not thrilled. It often sounded thin and the violins were desperately lonely, but it was well-received by the director and the audiences. Now, when I look at my neat musical notation on that old brittle orchestral score, what comes to mind is *What were you thinking?*

The two years in South Carolina had blasted me into a new realm of making music. I didn't think of myself as a composer, and even now, more than fifty years later, I still don't—unless I listen to recordings of what I did. Hearing these old tapes is unsettling. Creating it, I felt like a conduit for sounds from an unknown source; my job was to make it audible and make it work, an artisan doing a job. Now that I hear it as music, my music, I hear it differently: unsettling but pungent.

At Christmas break we had gone to New York, seen a lot of folks visiting from South Carolina, and caught up on what people were doing. Flora had lived in Paris for a while and was now in Ireland. Millie, a stunning six-foot blonde from *Woyzeck* and *Hecuba*, had gotten into NYU. We went to a ton of movies and to the theatre only once. It was The Living Theatre in their adaptation of *Antigone*, and that was the first domino that tipped that year and completely changed our lives.

Neither of us was taken with their interpretation of the play, but seeing their work opened our eyes to a different kind of theatre. Our seats were in the high balcony, and as we were standing up to leave, Conrad looked over the rail, elbowed me, and said, "That's Leon Katz!" We ran down the stairs, shoved rudely through the crowd, and caught him before he left. Leon, our guru from Stanford, had been following The Living Theatre closely since their return from Europe and took us backstage to meet Julian and Judith briefly—"Hello." "Hello."—and had a lot to say about their work. Reverting to past habits, we followed him to a coffee house and talked until 2:30 in the morning. We left, determined to see more of this theatre.

It didn't take long. They toured to Wisconsin, and by mid-January we'd seen two other works, *Frankenstein* and *Paradise Now*. I was knocked out by *Frankenstein*. The performance began with the company sitting in meditation on the floor in front of a massive, three-story steel pipe scaffold, intensely focused on willing a levitation. When that failed—aided by scattered catcalls from the audience—the inevitable fragmentation began, only to coalesce three hours later. At the end they were all in silhouette against a blood-red cyclorama. Slowly they moved within the structure until all the bodies coalesced into the outline of one massive creature, with big battery lights in the arms of two actors providing the glowing eyes. To this day I can still recall the air in that auditorium in Appleton, Wisconsin, fragrant with old wet wood, reminding me of my elementary school. It was daring, visceral, engaged theatre, every action coming from a response to the moment.

The day we got back from New York, I wrote a check that signed us up for a faculty-discount flight to Europe: three summer months in a different world. We needed passports. I had to strong-arm my mother to send me my birth certificate. *Remember that for over eight years we have managed to keep our marriage license, automobile registrations, and insurance matters safe and available, so don't worry.*

∼

In February, I started teaching as an adjunct: Beginning Acting, two classes of twenty students each. It was a required course for majors, and most of the technical theatre students resented it. I was petrified. When my classes began, The Living Theatre was fresh in my mind, and I stepped out into thin air trusting that I could actually map a journey worth taking. Looking back, I have no clue what put me on the right path. Instinct, some books on theatre games, and maybe a sense for responding to students as individuals, but it was dynamite. My approach had nothing to do with learning lines: it was all about response, suspending expectation, and being in the moment with others who were equally vulnerable.

For one session, I brought a stack of paper grocery bags, a pile of kids' scissors, and a bin of markers. They cut out eye-holes, decorated the bags, and then spread out around the big empty studio and put the bags on their heads. I told them they would have five minutes of silence, which would feel like bloody forever, before we started. During that time, they were to do their best to quiet their monkey minds and convince themselves that they didn't know where they were, who they were, or what to expect. And they had no language.

I signaled the start with the gentle ring of a tuning fork. Each person entered the "scene" whenever they wished, and it usually took more than five minutes for everyone to become active. With no script and with limited vision, each encounter with another being was a startling event. Should I freeze? Should I flee? What is that thing anyway? It usually went at least forty-five minutes, no words, and when it was over and they de-bagged, their descriptions of the explorations were amazing. They were at the ground level of acting: see what you see, do what you do because it's a response, not because somebody wrote it. I learned more about acting in my first semester of teaching than I had before or since. I ended the semester eager for the fall to begin.

One indelible memory: I asked them each to prepare a song and share it, whether they thought they could sing or not. A big rangy techie was overwhelmed and sure that she couldn't do it, so we provided her with a setting. We found candles and cushions, turned out the lights, put together the closeness of a late-night party, and asked her to sing: *Leaving on a Jet Plane*. She was radiantly beautiful and left us all in tears.

~

My addiction to being on stage propelled me to audition for the Milwaukee Repertory Theatre's *Marat/Sade*, opening in early March and running for a month, eight performances a week. All major roles were cast within their company, but they wanted a big crowd of anonymous lunatics: the total cast would be forty-two. It was a "cattle-call" audition, just enough time to come in, sing eight bars of something, and leave. Being small and blonde, I figured I could get noticed by singing something low and raucous, so I belted out the beginning of *Pirate Jenny*. The people behind the director's table sat up, whispered, and asked me to sing some more. Then I was asked to use the lyrics as spoken words and improvise with them. That song is a savage revenge fantasy, and I let the rage rip directly at them. I wasn't cast as a nut but as one of the quartet of singing clowns.

It was my first time working with a large professional company—a good experience, more or less. Our quartet of clowns bonded well and put out lots of energy. Much of what we did physically was improvised, with later directorial choices: keep that, expand that, drop that. There was spirit and camaraderie in the rehearsals, but I couldn't help remembering the crazy shows from the South Carolina days. Nobody at USC had professional training, and we certainly didn't have long runs, but there was a kinship, a collective inebriation, a sense of tribe that I deeply missed.

It was a challenge to be doing full rehearsals on an Equity schedule while teaching, finishing and copying a score for UWM, and house-hunting again. We were both running full speed on parallel tracks. We started to prepare for our trip to Europe, which meant a big list of research, stuff to buy, and plans to make. Sure enough, I got sick.

My entry to *Marat/Sade* had been my voice, which was now down to a sad little croak. Fortunately, my clown partner was a long-time pro and knew a remedy. I needed to "coat" my vocal cords, not only to sing but to belt full-voice. An old-time remedy, known to vaudevillians, was tincture of benzoin, an aromatic dark-brown tarry resin. Using it meant pouring boiling water into a basin that could later be thrown away, dropping a big spoonful of tincture in the water, and inhaling the reeking steam. Not easy: it coats your throat, yes, but it can also coat your face and hair. You put vaseline over your face and wrap your head in a towel, leaving a gap for your mouth. You close your eyes and force yourself to take deep breaths of the pungent steam. It was really hard, but it worked. It didn't cure anything, but it got my voice back for the time I needed. I courted sympathy but just got told, "You're responsible for keeping yourself in working order." Tough, but useful.

In the midst of this, keeping daily life going was a weekly challenge. I was grateful that there were laundry machines in the apartment building and that the fridge had a functional freezer. I managed to pay the bills and keep us fed and balance the checking account and do the laundry and still find the energy to make love.

∽

I had cherished one feeling from the South Carolina days, the tribal bonding while doing *Woyzeck* and *Hecuba* in the old derelict auditorium. Making theatre there was an almost transgressive experience. Now we were in high-test academia in a state-of-the-art facility with cushioned seats, where productions were rehearsed, performed, and discarded without leaving a trace in the air. Conrad was directing Strindberg's *Dance of Death*, a big beast of a play with a stunning cast, working for weeks and weeks to bring Strindberg's devastating story to life while accepting the fact that after four performances, it would vanish. That was the norm, of course, but the norm was out of kilter. And other dominoes were lining up.

One night, I dropped in on *Dance of Death* rehearsals, and five of us hung around grousing about the idiocy of throw-away theatre. Impulsively, somebody said, "Let's do something." We set up an improv that we later called "encounters." Line up across from each other. Two people walk toward the center with no planning what happens when they meet. The moment of contact sparks an interaction, it plays itself out, they part, and the next two advance. Our instinct was to be wordless, no plot, but the interactions were compelling. We were completely in the present moment, all senses wide open. Damn, it was exciting, and we planned to start meeting regularly. A dancer friend joined us, and we worked as six in long, sustained, high-energy improvisations.

Three more joined. We became really stretched for time, but the work was truly addictive. We met in classrooms, small rehearsal spaces, in a makeup room, and what manifested were free-form explorations of human interaction, though at times a primal myth resulted in broken chairs or a squashed eggplant.

One of our group posted a note on the department callboard announcing the formation of Theatre X—X as the unknown quantity—and a buzz began among students: what was this weird thing happening? We had already committed to our European trip and others had their own plans, so we would suspend for the summer and then resume. Conrad and I had a deep-seated urge to break the faculty/student, director/actor structure, and work creatively outside the norm, as we had with *The Medium*. We had a gut sense that this might be the channel.

During the spring, our Theatre X work fed into my acting classes. It was my laboratory; I could see the evolution of daring and how it built trust. I was finding a way to transfer what I did in musical composition to what I could do in theatre. Just as one musical phrase begat another, one physical action begat another. There was no uber-God decreeing what would happen; it unfolded from its center.

Now I was on the long ascent of the roller-coaster. There were ongoing improvisational sessions, the intense span of *Marat/Sade*, finishing the score for *A Roaring Good Time*, looking for a new place to live, finding it and moving in, and all the preparations for spending three months in Europe. There, our ticket to flexibility would be camping, traveling on motor scooters that we'd buy in London. It dictated a wild set of challenges. How to cook? How to do laundry? How to find campgrounds? How to know what kind of tent and sleeping bags to get? How to take clothes that dried overnight and would pack into a saddlebag? How to get mail from the States, and how to pay three months of bills from abroad?

We bought *Europe on Five Dollars a Day* and a thick book listing European campgrounds. Some friends agreed to stay in our house and send out the checks we'd written and post-dated for rent and utilities. I went shopping for fabric and made myself a wardrobe that would drip-dry and fold into a packet the size of a shoebox. Some tangerine dacron made a skirt, a long-sleeved coat with a mandarin collar, and a sleeveless skimmer dress. For festive wear, there were two overdresses: a floral print chiffon, and a cream lace swirly thing. Other than that, it was jeans and a pullover. At army surplus and camping stores, we bought nylon duffels, a double sleeping bag, a two-person pup tent with a waterproof floor, a couple of tarps for groundcloths or rain flies, and saddlebags that would sling across the back of a scooter. The best discovery was a little camp stove the size of a small coffee can that burned denatured alcohol and fit inside my two nested cookpots. This was getting real, it was intoxicating, and it planted the seeds of change.

14.
Coping

Our preparations were like winding up a spring-toy, and when we finally boarded the big transatlantic tin can, we popped the trigger. I was sewing right up to the last minute and still hemming on the plane. The buzz from our new theatre gang was high, and I wondered what three months' layoff would do, but suddenly, bam, we were in London. We found a cheap hotel near Russell Square for three nights and got very cozy on a cot-like single bed in the only room available. Jet-lag or no, we rose, shone, ate the vast English breakfast included in the nightly rate, and started our adventure.

That began with a theatre binge. *As You Like It* at the Old Vic, an all-male cast with a young Anthony Hopkins as Audrey and Robert Stephens as Jacques. Next, *Macbeth* in a cut-and-paste version by Charles Marowitz which turned me off but made me anxious to read the play again. And *The Way of the World*, the first time I understood how funny Restoration comedy could be.

That summer was a multi-layered revelation of our ability to deal with the real world. We'd had years of subtle programming that we were eggheads and eggheads couldn't cope. The first test came right away. We thought we'd need two scooters, our budget

Coping

was tight, and after checking ads we found two used machines. Getting to Pride & Clarke in South London was easy, and it was startling to walk up Stockwell Avenue and see block after block of dark-red storefronts, all Pride & Clarke. We bought a used Lambretta, and I rode tandem behind CB to the city center to check on mail at American Express, then northwest to Acton. London streets keep their names for very short shots; after five or six blocks they get a new name. I held the London map, craned around CB's helmet to see street signs, and got us there. We bought an elderly Vespa at Whitby's. CB would ride the Lambretta, I would pilot the Vespa, and we'd meet back at Russell Square.

I quickly discerned that I was riding a lemon. It was half a day in hell, dodging traffic as the scooter died and died and died. The Vespa was heavy and had a bulbous butt; I'm 5'2" with short legs, and the repeated effort of getting the thing to the curb and then stomping the starter had me in tears of fury. The trip took all afternoon and into evening, and cell-phones hadn't been invented. I could only call our hotel where they were holding our luggage and leave messages for Conrad. Like Sisyphus I kept going, abandoned the scooter near Parliament, and took the tube to Russell Square, where CB had waited for hours. After a tearful embrace, we calmed down and got Scotch eggs and beer at the bar of the British Museum. At the hotel we collected our stuff, strapped our bedroll, tent, and saddlebags onto our sole machine, and headed off into the dark for our first campground of the summer. The Lambretta had plenty of pep and we didn't need the Vespa.

The Crystal Palace campground was on the city outskirts, and it was a helluva process getting there. People happily gave directions, but the fireman and bobbie and cabbie all had different advice. Each time we'd find ourselves back at the Elephant & Castle roundabout, shooting off on another tour of industrial London.

After three tries we got it right, but it was pitch dark by then. We pushed the scooter into the murky campground and found a spot, but we had never put up the tent before. After lots of grunting, we said the hell with it and shoved our sleeping bags inside the unpitched tent, crawled in with our heads sticking out the doorflap, and slept. When morning came, our neighbors had a laugh, then trotted over with mugs of steaming tea.

The next morning, I called Whitby's and told them their Vespa was crap, which of course they already knew. I called a scooter mechanic and asked him to join us by the dead beast in front of the House of Lords. Butch arrived with a truck and hauled off the corpse.

That first test gave us a passing grade: we got out of London. We had no real itinerary, the only immediate goal being to visit our former student Flora in Ireland and then a general plan of circling Western Europe. I was exhausted, but I felt like an outlaw: fuckin' terrific.

We headed for the fairy-tale greenery of Wales, and our tailpipe fell off. I picked it up and tied it on top of the tent-roll. The first two camps we tried had no space, but the third was OK, and the owner was a mechanic who reattached our tailpipe. I watched, and when the muffler did the same thing, I wired it back myself. At the ferry port of Fishguard, we celebrated having gotten this far, had a pint at the Farmer's Arms, and fell into contented sleep. A wild night rainstorm taught us that our waterproof tent was not. In the morning, we picked up our sopping sleeping bags and went to the camp store to phone for ferry reservations. We bought food, and the little white-whiskered owner let us spread the bags out to dry. It was a long wait until the 2 p.m. ferry, but at last we made it up the ferry's ramp.

The Irish Channel crossing was rough, and walking took fancy footwork to avoid skidding on other folks' barf. I was amazed that neither of us got seasick, but the smell was a challenge. I found a cafe booth with outside ventilation and distracted myself by writing letters, and by the time we docked at Rosslaer, I'd

Coping

forgotten the stink. Near Dublin we camped overnight in a place full of Roma wagons and the next day found where Flora was staying in Kilcullen. She was housekeeping in a mansion with nearly a hundred rooms, all of them stone empty except for the two downstairs front rooms; the absentee owners had sold the furniture to pay the taxes. Shivering in front of a peat fire, we set up the next domino: "Flora, come make theatre with us in Milwaukee." Six months later, that's exactly what she did.

It was brash, talking to Flora about Theatre X as if it were real, asking her to pick up her life and move it to Milwaukee. I was drunk on being in another country for the first time, and now I was talking to the young woman who'd blown me away with her performance in *Hecuba*. Sitting on cold flagstones in front of sputtering peat, we were outside normal reality, and it became natural to speak of turning a brief theatrical exploration into something that could be life-changing. As we talked, I saw that there was something deeper here than I'd realized, and it felt frightening and exhilarating. This sudden compulsive invitation wasn't just to Flora, it was to all of us.

After we crossed back into Wales, we headed for a camp near Stonehenge. It was almost the summer solstice, and we wanted to see the sun rise over the stones. There was a small campground not too far away, so we sacked out early and set the alarm for 4 a.m. It was cold the next morning, and we had only enough patience for mugs of hot tea: breakfast could wait. Off we went, only to find the site fenced and locked. Anger battled with embarrassment in my sleep-fogged brain: well, of course it would be protected. Why didn't we check in advance?

But I didn't want to come back later. I wanted to see the sun rise over the midsummer stone. As we dithered and shivered, a big limousine pulled up like a shark, and I thought, Omigod, are we gonna get busted for having thought of climbing the fence? No. It was a photographer from the Royal Navy, and he wanted exactly what we did. I showed him my empty pockets (no spray-paint) and Conrad gestured with our camera, no match for his, but decent. After a few minutes the gate opened for the Royal Navy and two grateful civilians.

I can't find words for that sunrise. The massive circle of stones seemed to grow taller as the light began to glow behind their silhouettes, and the pre-dawn breeze was a giant's breath. It took an eternity of grey sky brightening little by little before the first nugget of gold appeared over the heel-stone that rested exactly at the point of touch. The Navy man was there somewhere, but we felt alone in this circle of power. The fiery nugget grew until the whole orb hovered over the stone, and its ascent seemed impossibly fast after the slow prelude. I couldn't begin to comprehend what had been done to bring these giants to the site, stand them on end, and place the lintel stones.

In the years to come, we visited several times and in 1979 brought our little children. The photo of them outside the fences with the stones tiny in the background has been published in the site's centennial celebration book. When I did recent research, I collapsed with giggles when I found that in 1915 a local man bought Stonehenge as a present for his wife. Three years later they gifted it to the nation.

On the ferry from Dover to Calais, I went to the rail, looked back at those white cliffs getting smaller and smaller, and caught my breath. This was a different thing from the trip to Ireland. Now we were leaving the English language and the insane currency I'd managed to understand. In those days, the Brits ignored multiples of ten: it was twelve pence to the shilling, twenty shillings to the pound. I would have to recalculate my spending limits per day and stop being shocked at what looked like insanely high prices: a British pound was $2.40; a French franc was about 20¢.

Coping

After a long haul to Paris, we found the campground. At the back end of the greenery of the Bois de Boulogne, bordering on the Seine, was a huge bare-earth crash pad with tents barely a foot apart. The camp offered an intoxicating stew of languages and other families' cooking, and the ground was so hard that we had to straighten out bent tent-stakes. While cooking supper, I heard something chugging, looked up and saw a barge at eye level moving majestically through the locks—not something I'd ever associated with Paris.

We schmoozed around the city for five days with hints from the guidebooks. There was a fabled little Russian bistro at the top of Rue Mouffetard, the steep market street, and I ordered the most romantic thing I could think of: caviar with blini and icy shots of vodka. It wasn't hard to get used to fresh croissants and aromatic coffee every morning, and I didn't use my little stove for breakfasts much while in France. The subway in New York had impressed me, a great way to get around, but the Paris Metro stations were a revelation—many were real works of art. One had tall glass walls looking out onto what resembled Jurassic plants lit from above by skylights. And the rubber tires on the cars: moving underground at top speed without screeching seemed otherworldly.

When we left Paris, getting around was less elegant. The scooter was a pain in the butt, reliably needing something we couldn't find, a bolt or a belt or a miracle. Still, traveling slowly, hearing and smelling everything, feeling the breeze on our faces, was a world apart from being in a car. I found that I could tell what animals were raised on a nearby farm just by the smell. Sure, I grew up in the country, but I never guessed that my nose could tell sheep from pig from cow. My earth self kicked in and I loved it.

The camping guide was bulky, but it was one of our best investments. France had hundreds of campgrounds ranging from big ones with all amenities to farmer's fields with nothing but a pit toilet, prices ranging from a couple of dollars to free. I cooked and we made daily stops for supplies: the boulangerie for bread, the charcuterie and epicerie for lunch and dinner items, and of course the local wine. The bottles were unlabeled and cost a franc, had three raised stars on the neck, and we turned in empties at the next store. I carried a little net filet that could scrunch up in my pocket and expand to hold a baguette, a bottle of wine, cheese, veggies, fruit, whatever. The alcohol stove held enough fuel to cook for ten minutes, then the hot cup had to be extracted until it was cool enough to refill. I developed a repertory of meals—one-cup, two-cup or three—using one fry-pan, two little pots, a wooden spoon, spatula, and paring knife. We slept on the ground with only our sleeping bag for padding, and our ponchos kept at least some parts of us dry when scootering through rain. Just the basics, and I was having the time of my life.

We meandered south toward Spain through Orleans, Chateauroux and Limoges with a stop to see the prehistoric cave paintings at Lascaux. No luck: it was closed to visitors because the breath of tourists was damaging the paintings. We discovered there was a smaller cave in a pasture nearby where we could pay a farmer for a tour, and that's what we did, on hands and knees looking where the man's flashlight revealed fragments of paintings. "La tete de bison, le dos de bison…" I looked at the sophisticated primitive drawings and found myself looking straight into the eyes of the artist across tens of thousands of years.

On the road south, the scooter shot us a new challenge. We were in the middle of nowhere, and it stopped. Miraculously, a truckload of young French farmers pulled up, saw our problem, and gestured down the road. "Make yourselves at home and wait for us to come back." We pushed the damned scooter a kilometer to their barn and waited. What followed was a shared dinner and a night in the straw. When we asked where the WC was, they made a broad sweeping gesture: "Partout, partout!" Anywhere. The next day, I watched one of the guys take the carburetor apart, fix it, and reassemble it like Heifitz playing the violin. They would accept no payment, but we went into town, bought a bottle of wine, and brought it back. It was a lesson in dropping shame at faulty language, just having fun, and damn the gender of nouns.

We had a camera along, but I found myself almost unable to use it, depending on Conrad to capture things on film, especially once we hit the Dordogne. I got lost in what I was seeing. Sometimes we had to stop in order to use our eyes and not drive off the road in wonder. I remembered what it was like getting glasses at five years old and for the first time seeing the world.

Our route was straight south into Spain, and after Toulouse the Pyrenees were starting to challenge the scooter. It was late in the day as we approached the border. We were always taxed by the shift to a new language and new money. I had studied Spanish intensively in my year at Valparaiso and was good at reading, lousy at speaking, so-so at understanding conversations. Shifting into French hadn't been too traumatic; I could remember some from high school, and most of our interchanges were dealing with campgrounds and grocery stores. But now we were anxious about our laboring scooter, the approach of dusk, and the sudden flump into another country.

The border wasn't bad, but after that we were at sea. Our book showed a campground on our route, but we couldn't find it. Time passed, dusk darkened, and we were getting panicked. About 120 kilometers past the border, we were close to despair when a turn on the steep road revealed a pool of bright light. Saved!

Well, no. We got closer, saw a commercial resort that would clearly be far beyond our budget, but it was dark and we had no choice. At the desk, they asked if we were married, snickered, and proposed a room. We followed the script by asking if we could see it first. Beautiful, spacious, cork floor, bidet, balcony, ouch. We said yes and began to figure how we could scrimp in the future. But it was so good to get off the saddle and stop worrying about falling down the mountain. We got really giddy. I had no food along, so we went to the restaurant, what the hell, and blithely ordered a paella and a bottle of wine: "Put it on the room tab." When we checked out the following morning, the total bill was $2.50. That eased the transition.

Barcelona was next, and we began to see a pattern of campgrounds: they're all next to railroad tracks. This one was hot but had a welcome bamboo canopy over the tent areas. At the campground bar/cafe, we celebrated with a beer. Not far away was a couple enjoying plates of what looked like onion rings. I thought "Oh yes" and pantomimed to the waiter, "Us too." He confirmed, "Calamari!" I didn't know what that was. It arrived, golden and crispy, and I'd crunched a couple of rings before I saw the weeny tentacles. I didn't care. It was the theme of the summer: accept.

It was a long haul to Madrid, and stopping for gas on a secondary road was a trial. We wore big helmets that made us look like bugs and were clearly foreigners. At one stop, the pump was by a farmer's barn and it took a while for him to come ambling down. In the meantime, a wide circle formed around us, about thirty people staring silently. We waved hello: no response. At last the man pumped the crank, the gas rose in the glass cylinder, and we paid and left. My memories of being a four-eyed freak flooded back, and I had a hard time accepting it as "That's interesting."

In Madrid we had a room, not a campground, within walking distance of the Prado. Franco was still in power, and that was impressively clear when we had to wait on the sidewalk for twenty minutes for a parade of tanks to pass. After that, Goya's "Black Paintings" made perfect sense.

The scooter was a growing problem. At one point in Spain we broke down, and our rescuer's driving style in narrow village streets was to take blind corners by leaning on the horn and speeding up. The repair job may have been done with washing-machine parts, but it worked. For a while. More bad luck awaited us along the Riviera: hot, noisy, expensive, and inhospitable to bums like us. We broke down again and were walking toward a town, hoping someone would offer a ride. No angels, and I nearly collapsed with heat exhaustion.

Rounding the corner into Italy, we had the familiar new-language new-money lurch, harder this time because I had no Italian other than guidebook phrases. The first place we stopped for sight-seeing was Taggia's old city. Streets were dark, narrow and twisting, and the upper stories of buildings seemed to lean in toward each other, prevented from falling by arched braces. Once again, my skin crawled with the sensation of being stared at as an alien. It was in the guidebook, so they must have had tourists before, just not tourists who looked like us. When we got back on the road, despite the heat and the traffic I breathed more easily.

Florence was a relief. Our campground was perched high in a hillside olive grove overlooking the Arno. On our first full day, we walked all over the city and were stunned by the magnificent public sculpture, as common as park benches. Our first stop was the Uffizi Gallery, and we came back several times because we'd found bathrooms there and had a hard time finding others. (Our code for needing a pee stop became "Let's go to the Uffizi.") At St. Peter's, the *Pietà* brought me to tears—the weight of this large, beautiful, and very dead man, almost too heavy for Mary to hold. Michelangelo was only twenty-four when he finished this.

The next day was more walking, organized around food instead of art. We grazed our way onward, nibbling at this and that, stopping for an actual lunch of black-pepper squid salad, later getting caffe granita, gelato, and capping it off with huge black figs. By the time we got back to camp, Conrad had turned green. All evening he trudged up and down the hill from tent to toilet while I scrubbed laundry with hard yellow soap and cold water on a metal washboard. The camp was full of trailers with portable TVs, all tuned to the first moon landing. "One small step for man…"

Elizabeth: One of Many

Rome knocked me sideways. Stepping on the ancient stones in the Forum, I was looking inward down a time-tunnel, hearing my blood singing an ancient melody, and realizing I knew that song. In the Coliseum, we were hit with a crashing rainstorm, giving us pause to see the ubiquitous feral cats, perhaps descended from ancient times. And I loved the hilarious mess of a street fair in Trastevere, a working-class area with structures from medieval times. Stands were hawking watermelon slices and oysters in shells; everyone ate with their hands and threw leftovers on the cobblestones.

Florence had been replete with art, Rome was history, and when we got to Venice, we confronted harsh politics. The Lion's Mouth was a stone mailbox for anonymous denunciations, which often led to the Bridge of Sighs and the prison beyond it. I wrote: *What stays with me is that prison. I've never been in one before. As soon as you leave the Council antechambers for the Bridge of Sighs, the polished wood and gilded ceilings change to cold, rough, damp stone. The main prison is four stories high, the lowest at canal level. Most entrances are so low as to force a prisoner to crawl in on his hands and knees. The Council's verdicts were made without the defendant present, no appeal was possible, and the sentence was carried out immediately.*

As we left for Vienna and aimed the scooter toward the pointy Dolomites, a stop sign in a tiny village halted us just alongside a stand where a man was roasting chickens on a spit, basting them with a bottle of fragrant white wine. I didn't even think about the day's budget: "Let's get one!" We stopped at noon in a secluded mountain field and ate most of our chicken, whereupon I had another wild impulse. I took off my clothes, lay back on the grass, and said, "Come make love."

That night's campsite was halfway to Schloss Hochosterwitz, up a dirt path so steep that I had to get off, let Conrad back up the scooter for a roaring start, run after him, and push to get to a flat place. The meadow grass was so thick it was hard to get the tent stakes down to the ground. As I was inside the tent fixing supper, an odd chugging, grinding noise commenced. "If I didn't know better I'd say that's a bus." "Can't be." "Go look." Indeed, it was a huge tourist bus, backing and filling to turn around and go back down. They must have had the same camping guidebook.

We'd had art, history, politics, and Vienna was calories. At a bar open for breakfast, we watched in awe as a big beefy man cracked a raw egg into his liter of beer and downed the whole thing. The next stop was Munich, and on our way a downpour soaked us to the skin. We stopped early at a little country inn equipped with a feather bed and a comfy granny in the kitchen.

Next morning was a trip to the campground just across the River Isar from the Munich zoo. Acres of lawn and trees, café, and laundry facilities with driers—we indulged in the modest luxury. We wandered around the city, a feast for eyes and ears. Paintings and sculpture and puppetry, but the whopper was the Deutsches Museum, the world's largest display of science and technology.

In Munich we took a side trip to Dachau. I could hardly breathe. On the half-hour's train ride back to the Munich campground, I don't think I said a word. Humans did this.

Maybe that psychic shock communicated to the scooter, which never made it out of Munich. It needed to have its clutch re-worked, not a huge job, but it was an Italian Lambretta and the Germans wouldn't deign to have Italian spare parts. We sold it for peanuts and bought train tickets for Frankfurt, Copenhagen, Amsterdam, and London. The previous day, we had splurged on a tiny Olympia portable typewriter, and now our wallets were just about wiped clean. I wrote to Conrad's mom for an emergency loan of $200 and explained how to wire the money to Amsterdam. She figured it out, and we were able to enjoy the end of our trip. The trains were a pleasant experience, but I mourned the loss of the scooter. Trains were like riding in a speedy thermos bottle.

Amsterdam is probably my favorite city on planet Earth, even though our introduction was five days of non-stop rain. The campground was out by the Olympic Stadium on low-lying land, and there wasn't any way to escape being soggy. On the other hand, I discovered a vending machine where the equivalent of a quarter could get either a Coke, a beer, or a bottle of wine. In spite of the rain, I fell in love with the city, wandering its circle of canals, gawking at the houseboats, ducking into tiny bars for a coffee or a genever, the aromatic Dutch gin. Downtown, many stands offered incomparable frites that I devoured with even more enthusiasm than those of Paris. Conrad was more of a museum devotee than I, but Amsterdam made me behave like a drunk heading for the next bar. I tried to be brave about the wet sleeping bags but finally hit the wall. Unable to face packing damp items for the train, we spent the final night in a small hotel before embarking to London.

Ah, London. More theatre, more Guinness, more fish and chips, and afternoons getting on any red double-decker bus, riding wherever it went, getting on another, and finally figuring how to get back. And then it was time to fly home.

～

We brought back dangerous baggage. There was a new momentum to our idea of Theatre X as an actual entity, something that could generate what we'd felt with The Living Theatre. Committing to that was terrifying, but we'd just lived a summer of crisis after crisis and discovered that we had what it took to cope. After the academic corset of Bachelor's, Master's and Doctorate, where every step was pre-planned and by the book, I had just spent three months letting each day be shaped by the day before, trusting that the road would always lead to a sleeping place. It echoed exactly what I'd learned in teaching acting. I could not only survive change, I could take it on the road and love it.

Coping

15.

Theatre X

Home. We'd moved into our newly rented house eight days before leaving for Europe. I was happy to see it again. We'd managed a painting party before we left, and the deep-tone colors of the walls—each room different—were thrilling. The tangerine curtains I'd made cast a lovely warm light, but our boxes were barely unpacked. The three months of summer had been an eye-opening journey, and now I was an explorer in my own house: *Where did I put what?*

The piano downstairs and the bed upstairs were easy to find. I knew what to do in the bed, but after a year of non-stop composing, I had no piano work to do. In one sense it was a relief, in another it felt unsettled.

Then the bed became problematic: I'd gotten a nasty case of bronchitis in London, and now it was deeper. One night I awoke unable to breathe. Not in, not out. I shook Conrad awake and did a desperate pantomime. *Push on my chest, hard.* That got out a miserable little blurt of air, and I managed to get part of an inhale before it blocked again. *Push!* After an endless span—maybe about ten minutes—I could get shallow breaths, but I had to concentrate fiercely on relaxing whatever was on the edge of another spasm. I sat up, CB kept watch, and after a while we felt it was safe to drift off. It happened again the next night, and we didn't get full sleep for the rest of that week. If I took a nap, I had to have him nearby.

Between jet lag and near-asphyxiation, I should have been exhausted, but so much had caught fire that summer the energy still ran high. We had spent more time in the Amsterdam campground and the little London hotel than we had in our new house. "Back home" was another country, and the new Theatre X was another adventure. My head was spinning with images from art museums, street performers, puppetry, mountains, and miles of back roads. We'd survived every near-disaster, and the highs were still reverberating. Once I kicked the bronchitis, I was ready to get into harness.

My schedule was popping. I had two acting classes with a total of forty-two students, teaching two days a week from 10:30 to 2:30 without lunch, and Theatre X was picking up speed. One of the original group had been adamant that we should only improvise, that rehearsal would sully our purity, but she had drifted off to other things. When we got back together, the momentum was huge. Coherent work began, word spread among the theatre students that something new and different was going on, and departmental politics required attention. There was grumbling about the closed group, so we announced three open work sessions, and anyone who came to all was officially in the group. We jumped to eighteen members in a bound.

Unwise, and I didn't have an easy time adjusting. We'd been a little tribe who had built the trust and hyper-awareness essential for deep improvisation. Collaborative leaderless work is productive only when everyone is on the same page, so there were dicey moments. We could sprout good stuff like crabgrass forever, but a consensus emerged that we needed to perform.

The genesis had been from the cast of *Dance of Death*, directed by Conrad. From the start, we wanted the structure to be egalitarian and self-generated, but there was a push-pull between a director's imperative to make things happen and our ideal of collective creation. It was Conrad who finally came right out and said, "Let's do it. Now." We took a deep collective breath, booked the weekend of Oct. 31 in the UWM studio, chose a title, made a poster, and wrote a press release for *X Communication*. We had a little over six weeks to figure out what to perform.

It was the fall of 1969, and ferment was all around us. The Vietnam Moratorium protest on October 15th involved millions of people across the country, and Theatre X took to the streets of Milwaukee with a silent funeral procession, led by an actor in military uniform, wearing an agonized mask and dragging a heavy wooden crucifix—one of our troupe had been a Marine in Vietnam, and most of his platoon had been wiped out. The rest of us followed, carrying large photo posters of Eisenhower, Kennedy, Johnson, and Nixon—the Presidents involved in the war—stopping at intervals for a mock debate on the pros and cons of napalm. That evening we did a performance in the student union of two war-themed pieces. The war pieces weren't simplistic sloganeering; many reflected the costs to those who were actually fighting. Suddenly, we were visible.

Getting to the production had me on deck 24/7, but the energy was always there. Conrad wrote to his mom: *It seems that the busier we are the more energy we have. There are times when suddenly all the gears mesh in exactly the right way and you're endowed with a special strength and magnetism. For us, it has been the theatre group we are organizing, the extraordinary work Linda does in her acting classes, and simply opening the pores and breathing.*

Then *X Communication* opened. It was a wild hodge-podge of short sketches as diverse as the people who created them. We worked barefoot in street clothes with no set and few props. The audience was close up, fully lighted, and the actors who weren't in a sketch sat visibly at the sides. A ref's whistle or a bicycle horn ended each segment. The mugging of a slow-motion football game ("Sculptured Meat in Motion") was followed by a stark evocation of a factory line disrupted by the violent breakdown of two workers. Another piece ("Ceremonies in Concrete") began with a silent man taping out a square on the sidewalk and standing in it. Passers-by challenged his right to that territory, ascribed motives, whipped themselves up to attack and eject him. He walked a short distance away and taped out another square. Some pieces were trivial one-joke affairs; others evoked the war. All of us mingled with the audience before and after. Above all, we achieved a presence.

In our first month we did thirteen events seen by more than a thousand people in seven locations. In a phone call to my mother, I mentioned that we had been working in the Moratorium; her instant response was that we hated America and were traitors to our President. In a letter I responded with uncharacteristic nerve:

If two friends meet on a dark road and commence fighting each other, not knowing who the other is, first they have to see before they can stop fighting. And if there is anything theatre can do, it is to make people see. We seem to be filling a real need, because from our very first performance, we are in demand. People we've never seen before say 'hello' on the street and ask where we're performing next. Not just college people, but everyone from the janitor to the fur-draped clubwoman. At last our work is truly meaning something to us. People sense it, even before the show starts. Many, many have said, 'There's something about all of you, I don't know what, but it's good to be in the same room.'

Exhausting, intoxicating, often maddening, and it felt completely right. A switch had flipped and another map was visible beneath the one we had planned. I hungered for this unpredictable journey with the same appetite I had felt in jouncing through the byways of Europe.

Conrad's mainstage production of *Tamburlaine the Great* began rehearsing at the beginning of January, while Theatre X was already working on Brecht's *The Measures Taken*, another massive undertaking. The first International Brecht Symposium was to take place at UWM in April, and it was logical that one of his plays should be presented. Nobody among the senior faculty liked Brecht, but they suggested that Conrad and Ron (our colleague and collaborator), with their strange new theatre group, might be interested. They proposed *The Measures Taken*, a short play translated by Eric Bentley, who would be attending, and Bentley had access to the full Hanns Eisler musical score. The play required four actors and a chorus who sang all their lines. It was my job to prepare our chorus for what would be the first American performance of the uncut musical version. We had thirteen singers, only four of whom had any vocal training, and the production would be seen by audiences of international scholars. I had my work cut out for me.

But at exactly the same time, I had to compose the sound score for *Tamburlaine*, Marlowe's Elizabethan epic of the futility of conquest, full of violence, warfare, torture—a huge production lasting ten acts, nearly four hours, with a cast of thirty-five, sometimes three stories in the air on the set's immense steel scaffold. Synthesizers were not yet part of my life, so I reached wildly for every sound source that might have the power and strangeness I needed. I wound up recording violin improvisations and playing the tape backwards through a reverb loop, or hitting my piano's strings with kitchen spoons and playing the result half speed to drop the pitch into ominous territory. An accidental gift was discovering that a guitar amp would deliver what sounded like a huge explosion when bumped. It became a massive frightening score with the occasional contrast of Ravel-like piano, as in one scene where two captives spun slowly in a cage suspended from a chain high in the air. By now I have decades of experience with synthesizers and electronic audio effects, but I could not remotely equal that score if I tried.

An invaluable ally arrived mid-chaos. Flora arrived in Milwaukee on February 1st. We had room in our house, so she stayed with us until she found her own place in Apple House, as a gaggle of Theatre X'ers called their group domicile. Its bright apple-green exterior housed many parties, rehearsals, squabbles, and camaraderie. Flora quickly became a mainstay of the company and remained so for the thirty-five years of the ensemble's existence. She still lives in Milwaukee and is still my best friend, but at the time she must have wondered what had possessed her.

After three months of fanatic dedication from cast and crew, *Tamburlaine* had its five performances and was dead, with very mixed response, but I had no time for depression. *The Measures Taken* was coming down the home stretch and flexing its muscles. It was our own theatre doing it, and it could have a life beyond the Symposium. Something had begun to shift profoundly during our summer's journey, and it was starting to make itself known. The stakes were high.

In the play, the five revolutionary agitators in China can only survive and complete their mission if they follow their plan, keep their heads down, and remain incognito. When the Young Comrade repeatedly acts on humane impulse and puts them in mortal jeopardy, he agrees that he must disappear completely. He tries to take his own life and can't pull the trigger. "Do it for me." His body is thrown in a lime-pit. The other four complete their work, return home, and ask the Chorus for judgment.

When the Brecht scholars came to town, I was wound tight. I had worked that Eisler score until I could pulverize the piano, and the Chorus was a solid wall of sound. The four actors had become a seamless teller of their agonizing story, each in turn wearing the mask of the comrade they'd executed to save their mission. The response was explosive.

There were seven Symposium performances, and the discussion after each one often lasted longer than the play. Very little was commentary on the production, except for some scholarly debate about whether a Brecht play should be so moving: its presentational flatness in contrast to the story and the music made it almost unbearable. But political ferment and anti-war protests were on everyone's mind, and more wanted to explore the central question the four agitators had presented to their jury: was there justification for murder in the name of revolutionary goals?

Again I was immersed in using music as a force to empower words. I had provided the lyrical background for *Prometheus Bound*, whose crime was to oppose the tyranny of Zeus, not only rescuing mortals but giving them knowledge of fire, and for this he was condemned to unending bondage and torture. *The Medium* was the tragedy of a woman who lived by her lies and could not endure the possibility that she might possess an actual gift. *Tiger at the Gates* was a full-on assault against the seduction of war. I pitted the seductive slow-dance of Helen's sax against the stomping assault of the troops, and nobody won. Then came *Hecuba*, directly influenced by our Vietnam entanglement, victor and vanquished equally scarred by war. I had lived for months as a channel for the power that those performances generated.

Like *The Medium*, *The Measures Taken* was not my composition, but making it manifest was my job and my passion. Again we had produced something outside the academic structure, though nominally under the roof of the university. It had been anything but easy; for months, the rehearsals had been frustrating and often combative, but commitment and persistence finally made a difference. Like *X Communication*, what was performed was the work of us all. We all had a stake in it, and it would have a future.

When the student strikes happened in May, in the wake of Kent State, word spread that the Milwaukee police were about to move on the students who occupied the Student Union. We'd been invited to perform for the strikers, but they were in the midst of a meeting to determine whether they would stay and be beaten or leave to regroup in the future. One of our actors stood up and said, "We have something to say, and it'll take forty-five minutes." We performed the play for the strikers, and it had never been so raw and real: when the pistol came out, it was electric. The play ended, the debate resumed, but now people were talking in terms of what they'd just seen in the fictional activists' dilemma. That day, we had direct witness to the power of theatre in the real world.

The rest of the semester was an utter dog's breakfast, as the student strikes disrupted classes but not the necessity of filing grades. We did twenty performances with Theatre X around the campus, the city, the state, and a quick trip to Minneapolis — *The Measures Taken*, *X Communication*, and agitprop sketches created for the strike. And the two of us were planning our second European summer.

Then the hammer fell: Conrad's three-year contract would not be renewed. He came home one afternoon after meeting the department head and said it flat out. Their justification, he reported, included doubts about his directorial ability: *Tamburlaine* had strained the department's resources and was regarded by many as a huge "overreach." But foremost was the apparently disruptive presence of Theatre X, for which the senior faculty considered him mainly responsible.

We were utterly blind-sided. We hadn't seen a contract decision forthcoming, and confronted with this reality, we were booted into a new evaluation of our professional goals. We had devoted everything to nurturing an academic career and had thought of Theatre X as something "on the side," though clearly it was vying for center stage. What mattered was what we would do now. The choice was wrenching, and yet the decision was made in an instant. We would not look for another academic post. We would place all our bets on Theatre X.

This dictated a difficult lame-duck year. We had one more year of his salary and my pay as an adjunct, and then we would be on our own. What could we possibly do in a year to make Theatre X pay our bills? Should we cancel our European summer? No. Damn the torpedoes. We would see as much as we could, bring the knowledge home, and put it to work.

When the faculty decision hit, we had already paid for our plane tickets, and I didn't even check on whether or not we could cancel and get a refund. A degree of anger and stubbornness kicked in: they could deliver a kick to our kneecaps, but they damn well weren't going to cripple us. By the time we were packed and ready to go, we knew we were right to take the risk. Our mission for the summer of 1971 was to discover as much as we could about non-traditional theatre and bring it back to Theatre X: three months of pleasure and purpose.

We'd learned our lesson about used scooters and bought a brand-new orange Lambretta, the only color they had. Our rubberized tarp-ponchos being bright yellow, we were highly visible on the road. This time we skipped Ireland and Spain and took more time in Wales, ventured into Scotland, crossed back into France, zipped through Italy into Austria and Germany. Midway through our three months we embarked onto a puppet-fueled new journey that took us behind the Iron Curtain—three weeks in East Germany, Poland and Czechoslovakia—and finished the trip in the Netherlands, Belgium, and London again.

I was glad to have learned the ropes, and familiarity didn't dampen the pleasure. We went to Stonehenge again at dawn, and I sweet-talked the guard into letting us in for five minutes of photography and just being there. In France we tried Lascaux again with no luck, but nearby was the Gouffre de Padirac, a huge hole 100 feet across and 250 feet deep, so massive that by halfway down it generates its own rain, and there are boat trips on the underground river at its base. For centuries, local people were terrified that the Devil lived down there.

Our scooter was well-behaved with minor ailments that were easily nursed until it decided to give us a heart attack by blowing a tire on the autobahn between Munich and Stuttgart. Conrad wrestled it to a stop and got us safely off the road, but what was probably no more than fifteen seconds was an eternity to me as the fenceposts flashed past. It did give us a laugh at the guard post between East Germany and West Berlin, where a big mirror on a low wheeled platform was rolled under the scooter the way they did for cars. I suppressed a snort of laughter at the idea of concealing a refugee under there.

I'd pictured Berlin as a crowded city crammed into walls, so it was a surprise to find it was heavily forested, especially to the west where our campground was. The camp was seven miles from the city center, and the trips back after dark were challenging. So was sleeping: the ground was grassy but very wet. We spread many layers of newspaper under our double sleeping bag and the insulation helped, but it also provided a hiding place for the very large spider that joined us our final night.

The night before the spider, I'd been prepared for an unforgettable theatre experience: we had tickets for *Die Dreigroschenoper* (*The Threepenny Opera*) at the Berliner Ensemble, the legendary company where Carl Weber had been Brecht's assistant. It was indeed unforgettable—the production was listless and stale. As Macheath sang his frantic plea for liberation, the cell door malfunctioned and swung open. The actor pretended not to notice. An institutional theatre can outlive its spark.

The previous night, we'd had a very different experience at the little Forum Theater: Peter Handke's *Publikumsbeschimpfung* (*Offending the Audience*). A one-hour play, it was brilliantly performed at breakneck speed, four actors rattling off a litany of descriptions of the audience and the nature of theatre itself—no plot, no characters, a cross between word-jazz and stand-up, and finally very moving. It had been a sensation and a scandal on the

German stage, and we were lucky to get tickets. Two years later, we staged it in Milwaukee.

My German had almost reached elementary conversational level by then, but once we got into Poland, communication developed potholes. Many people there spoke a little German but were reluctant to do so, given their war experience. Friends advised us to play dumb, speak English, and wait for the other person to offer German. Mime and mugging helped.

On our first night in Poland, once we crossed the border, I hadn't been able to find a food store. In the near-dark, I turned our food sack inside out and found a small heel of bread, an onion, a bit of salt pork, and half an envelope of dry soup mix, and from that I made one of the most satisfying soups of the summer. We still had half a bottle of wine. "God, that was good!" we exclaimed in chorus.

As we crossed major borders, I was aware that we had already crossed our biggest one. The coming year at UWM would be an uncomfortable experience, and when it was over we would be on our own, gambling that our bare-bones, rag-tag ensemble could continue to make new work, build an audience, and somehow succeed. We weren't unique: experimental ensembles were cropping up like flies, but we weren't in New York or Los Angeles. So I was excited about sophisticated, passionate creations I was seeing "in the sticks" that didn't take a back seat to those in Paris, London, or Berlin.

We had used a puppet only once, in a short anti-war piece, but this journey jump-started that interest. We'd become obsessed with puppetry without quite knowing why, saw a few small shows in France and Germany, but the main course was still to come. The art of puppetry in eastern Europe was utterly unlike the US milieu of library story hours. Puppeteers trained first as actors and only then worked to master animating the inanimate. I was bowled over by the design audacity as well; in Poznan we saw a rehearsal with puppets made entirely of straw. Marionettes, hand-and-rod, hand-puppets, big Bunraku-style creatures: each production used a style best suited to the story. Our brains spun with wild possibilities.

The experience of *The Measures Taken* had been my baptism in the political power of theatre. If I'd thought about it, much of our work had strong political content, but that wasn't front and center. Now I was slammed by two stage productions that brought it home. In the huge formal theatre in Warsaw, a production of *Hamlet* began with the audience unable to see the stage: the fire curtain was still down, a big blank wall with the visible outline of a door. We all sat in bourgeois splendor on red velvet seats surrounded by gilded walls until the play began. Bernardo entered in front of the fire curtain, shouted at Francisco backstage, then got his attention by raising an armored fist and delivering a mighty blow to the door. The huge metallic sound was like slamming a heavy door in a warehouse; the audience jumped a foot, then watched as the curtain was slowly cranked up. We could see now that it was a wall of corrugated iron: the action was taking place entirely behind an Iron Curtain.

The staging highlighted the political three-way power struggle between Prince Hamlet, his stepfather Claudius, and the ghost of his dead father—a vigorous and angry ghost, a fighter enlisting his son in a battle against the usurper. When Ophelia came to her mad scene, the huge overhead battens that held the stage lights were lowered nearly to the stage floor. She was not the sweet, sad maiden I had played at Stanford, she was a woman insane with grief, chasing madly through this metallic jungle. I didn't understand Polish, but I already knew every line, and by the end I was in a sweat.

And in Amsterdam we saw *And They Handcuffed the Flowers*, a play that involved the execution of the poet Lorca in 1936, when the Spanish Civil War was only a month old. The little theatre was a few doors away from the Dam, a big open center-city square where young people played guitars and smoked pot. In late August, the normally permissive city banned sleeping overnight, and shortly after we'd got off the tram and made our way to the theatre, the crowd erupted in a riot. Amsterdam police carry wicker shields and nightsticks, and rarely resort to their pistols, but this time they were hit by cobblestones, and three people were wounded by bullets.

The riot was audible inside the theatre, where we sat in safety but on opposite sides of the stage. After we'd purchased our tickets, we were admitted to a small dark room. Actors came in, took each of us firmly by the arm, and led us to scaffold-and-plank seating that left everyone distant from those they'd come in with. I was on my own to experience this play, a work written to express the horrors of political imprisonment. The dreams and visions enacted by the four prisoners were shocking and obscene, no holds barred, and by the time the condemned prisoner was tied into a chair and garrotted from behind, I was shivering.

A solo reed player had been accompanying the performance, blending in with the screaming voices of the riot outside. When the action was done, the musician didn't stop. Tears were streaming down his cheeks as his sax wailed in lament, and I realized that he was playing his own form of kaddish. I was weeping too. When we sensed that he was not going to stop but would go on as long as he could breathe, we began to leave our seats and find each other. Conrad was as shaken as I was, and we went to the theatre's bar and bought shots of genever, the strong old Dutch gin.

We finished the summer in London. We had access to a real bathtub, reveled in our first hot bath since leaving home, then dried off and plunged into an orgy of theatre. Tickets were cheap and we saw seven plays and three movies before getting on the plane for home. I'd crammed myself with Guinness, chips, and pints of bitter, and caught a massive case of bronchitis again. Getting back wasn't easy: there'd been an accident on the New York airfield and we missed our connection, so friends meeting us at the Milwaukee airport had a long wait. We finally got to our house, invited them in, and broke out the wine.

X Communication, Theatre X, 1969

The Measures Taken, Theatre X, 1970

16.

Fits and Starts

I was glad to be back, and more than glad to have the distraction of frantic rehearsals to create Theatre X's new show, which would open in four weeks. This would be our final chapter at UWM, and by now I felt we'd been given a gift: what came next would be of our own making.

It had been exactly ten years since I'd met this odd, brilliant, driven young man and found my life and my limbs intertwined with his. Acting, composing, translating, working, cooking, and loving through the Bachelor's, the Master's, a whale of a thesis and finally a PhD—always sure we knew the path of the career. South Carolina was far from ideal, but what we created onstage was incandescent. Moving to Milwaukee and working with lavish assets was even better—until it wasn't. But I'd always been good at managing money, we had savings, and I could go into high gear as a household Scrooge. There'd be one more year of paychecks, and I was now teaching three classes. We were going to be OK, even though we didn't quite know what would come next. What we did know was that it would be in Milwaukee with Theatre X. After the initial jolt, I'd worked my way around to feeling proud of the coming change.

So I felt sucker-punched when I picked up the college newspaper, five days after CB's 29th birthday, to see the headline: *Theatre Department to Dismiss Instructor*. Dismiss, hell, he hadn't been fired, he just hadn't been renewed. Instructor, my ass, he was an assistant professor. Well, we'd made our choice, but I'd been looking at it from the inside, and this was the cold outside view. I gritted my teeth.

But there wasn't time to grizzle and mope. Theatre X's new show, *What's Left*, was well received, and we'd created some substantial new sketches that would go into our ever-growing touring grab bag. Conrad was directing what would be his final UWM show, a trio of one-acts by Albee, Arrabal, and Mrozek, brashly titled *Three Cheers for Nothing*. And then came the phone call.

It was late, and Margaret was on the line. "Somebody here wants to speak to you." It was his father, whose name was also Conrad, and it was CB's voice exactly except for the Texas accent. Later we learned that he'd called her out of the blue, said, "This is Conrad," then choked up and said nothing. She was panicked, thought her son was calling in grief to tell her that something had happened to me. Instead, it was the man who had deserted her twenty-seven years ago, and he wanted to come to her.

He did, and she told him he needed to go to Milwaukee. He couldn't face meeting his son by himself, so she said they would come together. That's what they did. The man was tall and gaunt, silver-haired, slightly stooped, but his hair was still wavy, and when the smile crept out, you could see that he'd had a killer grin. And around the two of them, mom and dad, was a glow that had not completely extinguished. They stayed two days, I think, but I was too rattled to have a clear memory. The two Conrads spent some private time, and Margaret filled me in on the painful story. I'd known only that she'd been deserted and fought deep poverty as a single mom, and I knew that he'd never wanted children and had said so from the start. Now she told me more.

Fits and Starts

After four years of marriage, she had a baby in October 1941. Once the US joined the war, there were well-paying construction jobs all over the West, and they moved from Denver to Salt Lake City to Colorado Springs, then to Oklahoma, Texas, and Washington. Their marriage dissolved into alcohol, abuse, and his threats to take the kid to the lake and drown him. Margaret stayed with her parents in Iowa when the boy was sick with the measles, but soon her mother got irked and told her to take that kid and leave. She joined her husband in Hanford, Washington, got a job, and lived two months in a bleak trailer, but had to quit when the boy came down with scarlet fever. At that point she bowed to her husband's pressure to go back to Iowa. She got a job at the bomber plant in Omaha, paid the rent her mom demanded, and the last anyone saw of Conrad's dad was just before Christmas in 1944. In 1947, she got a divorce on the grounds of desertion.

Margaret was matter-of-fact while telling me this, and though she'd never said anything to Conrad to make him hate his dad, she'd never hid the truth. I was stunned. This was the man who'd engendered the man I loved. Their voices were nearly identical, they were of similar build and height, and I began noticing other shared traits. This was maybe the first time I ever wondered who engendered me? I'd always known I was adopted and never questioned the fact that I didn't seem to have anything in common with my parents and didn't know anyone who was anything like me. Yet here were two men who could wear each other's shoes. In fact, Conrad's dad forgot to take his good shoes when he left, and we had to send them on.

When she got back home, Margaret wrote: *Needless to say, he couldn't get over how wonderful you both were and how you accepted him. I guess he studied your every expression and grieved about what he had missed in not seeing you grow up. The biggest thrill and shock was when we left and Linda put her arms around his neck. He just couldn't believe that! I'm so proud of you both!!!* Their reunion didn't last: she saw that some things hadn't changed. But we kept in periodic touch with him till his death in 1981.

At UWM, our lame-duck life trudged on, and Theatre X grew progressively more complex. I had forgotten how awful our planning meetings could be. Consensus was a word we used without having learned its meaning. Lots of new theatre groups espoused it, and I don't know how well they did, but we were pretty bad. Ten years later, the two of us began to attend a Friends Meeting and saw what a sophisticated practice the Quakers had developed. At best, it allowed multiple points of view to produce an agreement that could be supported by all. We often achieved that in Theatre X while developing new performance pieces, but in our "business meetings" it sometimes meant nixing ideas until all that was left was the least unacceptable notion.

A new piece needed a title, but a grab-bag of sketches could be anything. It had taken us a full meeting to come up with *What's Left*—not exactly a winner—but once we got a good grip on the show, it hit its stride. We had ten performances in coffee houses in October and November, plus the Wisconsin Thespian Convention.

Among the new sketches was one that stuck with us a long time: *Miss Bleep*. I played a strictly-programmed robot teacher who controlled the restraining bars that kept students in their seats and could zap misbehaving students with "three seconds of electronic correction." She treats the three students as small kids, though they are clearly adults doing their best to endure the situation. The jokes are non-stop until one kid gets zapped mid-cookie and chokes to death. Classic Theatre X: ordinary people coping with lethal surrealism.

In January, we ran a trio of short plays at UWM's Student Union, and one of them was our first full foray into puppetry: *The People vs. The People*. We made sixteen puppets, everything from hand-and-rod puppets to a 10-foot-tall Lady Liberty, and I wrote five very rowdy songs. At the beginning, three defendants are pronounced guilty and sentenced to death, whereupon the Judge orders, "Will the defendants please rise and incriminate themselves?" The Milwaukee Sentinel gave us a huge multi-page feature: we were coming up in the world.

In February, we revived *The Measures Taken*, with a weekend at The Coffee House, which had become a regular venue for us, and then in the UWM Student Union, the same room where we'd performed for the strikers. The Coffee House wanted to host us again in March, but we'd need a new show, so we put together another set of sketches and had another gut-wrenching meeting to come up with a title, *The Zipper Is Stuck*. The title satisfied no one.

In April, we made our first venture into long-haul touring, taking *The Measures Take*n and *X Communication* to Cambridge, MA, where an ex-member was teaching at the Massachusetts College of Art. It was a rough trip in two cars and a van, and we were hit by a blizzard. We had back-to-back performances of *The Measures Taken* in a Cambridge church, and *X Com* played a Brookline high school, Mass Art, and the church again. Financially, it wasn't impressive, but we didn't care. It was a tour: the future.

When we got back, *The Whiteskin Game* was looming. We'd been working steadily, but now we had nine days to get it together. It was a sprawling docudrama staged as a board game on a taped-out thirty-foot US map, with moves determined by a roulette wheel. Audience members got hospital wristbands, either red or white. Whites were seated on folding chairs outside the map to the east, Reds had cushions on the floor inside, and at each move, Whites left the chairs and kicked Reds off their cushions, herding them into chicken-wire "reservations," except for the ones who were moved to the Happy Hunting Grounds. Between moves, we performed sketches based on atrocities drawn from documentary material. It was raggedy and wild, but response was strong.

We had another wild response, a performance of *X Com* at Marshall High School. We were invited by the student committee for the first Earth Day, and though we had no sketches directly related to "clean up your campsite," they said that was no problem. Twelve hundred kids gave us a standing ovation, and then all hell broke loose. Some conservative faculty went steaming into the principal's office and said the performance was filthy and un-American, whereupon the principal got on the PA and told the students to pay no attention to what they'd seen. Other teachers confronted the principal, who had not seen the presentation, whereupon he did another announcement contradicting the first. The next issue of the student paper was filled with Theatre X. It was funny and empowering, until word got around that we'd done something "controversial," and it hurt our bookings.

Milwaukee had inaugurated an annual beer-bash called Summerfest, with big-ticket rock bands in a huge outdoor amphitheatre and other entertainments scattered in colorful tents around the lakeside festival grounds. A Theatre X member had a local rock band, and his agent was booking a mainstage "Fifties Rock Revival." They needed a ten-minute fill between bands as equipment was changed. They offered $300, which was impressive to us in those days. Knowing that this was a huge venue with many drunk patrons, we made something big, brash, and funny—we thought. We built a ten-foot puppet with a guitar, and wrote a broad clown piece, turning him into a rock star. We thought it would work.

But we followed Chuck Berry, and after three encores, patrons were screaming for more. It was time to change the set-up for Little Richard, so the emcee came out, bellowed, "Aaaaand now, here's Theatre X!" and ran like hell. The rocks and beer cans started at once. I was inside the ten-foot puppet, sitting on the shoulders of our six-foot ex-Marine, and we were the only ones who didn't get hit directly. All of us were terrified but mad as hell. It was as if we all had ESP: *They're not gonna push us around, we're gonna do our whole goddamn ten minutes, like it or not!* We finished the sketch and took Ric to the ER for stitches.

Fits and Starts

When it was over, I was in shock. Over the span of two seasons, I'd come to expect that our audiences truly wanted what we had to offer. Our early sketch farragoes were a love-fest, and when we took a hard left turn with *The Measures Taken*, they came right with us. The raucous puppetry of T*he People versus the People* got enthusiastic response. With the Summerfest piece, we had an enraged mob of ten thousand people who wanted our blood. I was inside the big puppet's head and couldn't see a thing. It was ten minutes of wobbly terror in the dark. Welcome to life.

Unwinding in late summer, we took a 7,800-mile road trip west through South Dakota, Montana, Vancouver, and then eight days near San Francisco. Was it a crazy thing to do? Yes, but we needed to get out of Milwaukee for a breather before nailing ourselves to the wall. Doing *The Whiteskin Game* had primed us to see the land that held some of the stories, and CB was curious to revisit the South Dakota town where he'd spent third grade. Above all, I needed to see California again.

Our first stop was in Rapid City to see where Conrad had lived. GPS didn't exist yet, but his memory was good: it was on Silver Street, he remembered, but he couldn't understand why Silver Street ended too soon. Eventually, we realized that the whole neighborhood was gone, bulldozed out of existence for a freeway. The house, the school, the hills where he walked through the snow, all gone. Only memories were left.

My Stanford memories had better luck. We pitched our tent at a hillside campground in a grove of eucalyptus trees near Redwood City, close to our old home turf. Our western trip made me realize how much I loved life on the road: it didn't have to be Europe to be exhilarating. Being in California for eight days again was a homecoming, and my old love got kicked up into high gear. It was hard for me to pack up and head back to Milwaukee and our new life, but the call of that new life was strong. California would be there when the time came.

We ended our four-week road trip on the last Friday in August and came home, set to build a massive puppet adaptation of Lewis Carroll's *Alice* books. In the late-afternoon golden light, I unlocked the front door of our quirky little house on Oakland Avenue, walked in, found everything in good shape, and helped unload the VW. We had a rehearsal at 7:30 at Apple House. I'd left us a pre-cooked meal in the freezer, and after heating, serving, and eating it, I changed clothes, grabbed a jacket, and with CB walked out the front door. We turned south, as we would have done to walk to the UWM theatre, but passed Kenwood Boulevard without turning toward campus. It would be a long seven blocks, but we'd been driving all day, and it felt right to arrive on foot to the first rehearsal of our new life.

17.
New Life

This is a difficult span of time to revisit. After the summer of '71, we were fully committed to making it on our own with Theatre X. Our new life's upward trajectory was impressive. The first season, while we were still with UWM, we did 44 performances, 71 in the second. The third year more than doubled at 154, and the fourth racked up 196. We got state arts council grants to support Wisconsin touring fees. Above all, we built a committed ensemble beyond the initial student group, performers unique and unforgettable. The academic career was history, at least for the present. As it turned out, it was history forever.

I had been on board with all that. The brutal schedule made my head spin, but it was our path toward being a theatre that made new work and paid its actors to perform. Our last teaching paychecks had been in June of 1971. I'd squeezed every nickel and put away a lot during that last fat year, with a wicked thrill like hiding money from an allowance to get set to elope. Now we'd eloped, and I was watching the balance go down and down and down.

Yet it was getting real. Theatre X got its incorporation papers, a bank account, and a post office box. We were all official, even though most of the daily expenses still went through an ad hoc system of petty cash. People bought things with cash or personal check, gave me receipts, and got reimbursed.

We were devoted to the idea of being a collective and operating by consensus, like many groups at that time, but we had little sense what that meant. I was the only one with bookkeeping experience, so it made sense for me to write checks, keep track of withholding when we began to pay, and handle the banking, so that's what I did. And Conrad was the one with a managerial instinct, so that's what he did. His director's bent made him a de facto leader, but he was learning to channel a powerful group effort. The creative work was the core, and that was potent. In our first full-time season we produced *Alice in Wonder*, *Macbeth*, and Beckett's *Endgame*. *X Communication* was a constant, always developing new sketches.

CB wrote an application to the Wisconsin Arts Board requesting support for space rental, and in October they said we'd get $2,000. Good news, but even better was being taken seriously about the future of our collective. Being an Arts Board grantee was an official stamp of approval or at least of hope.

Work on *Alice in Wonder* had been going on since spring, with plans to open at the end of September. Our own adaptation of the Lewis Carroll books, it required a huge number of puppets, and by the opening date, it wasn't remotely ready. Instead, we offered a weekend of improvisations at the Coffee House and rescheduled *Alice* for the East Side Community Center in late October.

Alice was a bear. CB had never directed a puppet show, but then he'd never directed an opera until he did, and at one time he'd never directed a play. He found it, moment by moment. The puppets were a team effort with CB as main designer: 35 puppets in all, major characters plus soldiers, flamingoes, hedgehogs, playing cards, and so on. They were built in our basement by anybody who could pitch in, sculpting in clay, making latex molds, casting in plaster, and thumbing plastic wood into the molds. People came when they could spare some time, and it went on down there from morning through late night. My cooking upped the spice quotient to overcome the reek of the plastic wood's acetone stench.

The set was a bare wall and a live actress in front of it, going through the cardboard boxes of moving. In one, she finds a childhood Alice doll and begins chatting with it. The doll leaps over the top of the wall, and the puppets appear as if from her imagination. These were hand-and-rod puppets, hoisted overhead with one arm operating the head, long rods in the other hand like huge chopsticks to control the puppet's hands. Being the shortest in the cast, I had to build clogs of two-by-fours to get me up to a level with the tallest actor. As a kid I never had ankle strength to be comfortable on skates; this was worse, but I managed.

Plunging headfirst into making the music for *Alice* was another homecoming. I composed the music to Carroll's words and created a score done entirely with human voices recorded on tape, then manipulated. It involved hours with the actors in a living-room circle taping vocal improvisation. Sometimes it was repeated syllables weaving a rhythm; some, as for song accompaniment, were sung. Some takes had to be retaken because we cracked each other up, but nobody minded. I was the composer, but that mostly meant coming up with starter suggestions and then shaping the group's exploration. The hard work came later, taking the raw tape, cutting and editing, adding reverb, pitch-shifting, and layering. The result was endearingly like the puppets: small-scale, weird, and expressive.

I remember that process with great fondness. It was the last spurt of creation in our little multi-colored house, and the memory of our circle sitting on the living-room rug around the tape recorder still makes me smile and cry. After we opened *Alice*, we had to leave that house, and soon afterward my tape recorder was gone. Our new apartment was burgled, and the intruder took my tape deck. It had been my instrument for *Alice*, and I felt violated. I'd bought the TEAC when I was preparing *Tamburlaine*, and I'd bonded with it in the course of that nightmarish score. It was my first experience of being able to do sound-on-sound and reverb on the same machine, and it opened huge doors, but that work was something for which I felt respect, not affection—bombs and torture aren't what's nearest to my heart. But when our circle of co-creators spent hours and hours entrusting their voices to my TEAC, it was love. Insurance enabled me to buy a replacement, but it never felt the same.

The show was incredibly taxing. We could do it because we'd always done challenging physical work. I always remember one trance-inducing exercise we called "circle walk." In a circle, we began to chant and walk in step, mirroring those opposite, then lope in a unified rhythm, allowing each slight change to pass through the circle. Eventually someone broke into the center, exploring a solo physicalization supported by the circle, like a jazz player taking a solo. Then that person would return to the circle, another taking the center. At best, we became a single mind, feeling that we could have levitated the building. Exhaustion was mind-altering.

I was having a hard time integrating all these new levels of existence. The rigid structure of academia was gone. My artistic relation to a sole director was gone, and adapting to a collective wasn't easy. My social skills weren't top-notch. Working within a production was one thing, and becoming a member of a big unruly family was another. In the past, if I had an itchy relationship to a person I could shove that to the background and focus on the director and the work. Now we were all equals, and if I had a toxic response to somebody I had to swallow it or let it out in a wrangle. I was uncomfortable and sometimes downright bitchy.

To top it off, we had to move. Our beautiful little house on Kenwood was too beautiful: the landlord's daughter wanted to live there, and out we went. The week after we opened *Alice*, we moved to a smaller, darker two-flat and mourned the loss of our warmly-glowing walls and ample windows.

New Life

November was fragmented. There were *X Com* gigs in Green Bay and Dubuque between searches for a theatre space, and we even stumbled into making a little extra money. Somebody within the workings of Gimbels department store decided it would be good holiday marketing to do puppet shows in the various Gimbels stores, and we created a short piece with the *Alice* puppets. Basically, though we justified its being an anti-materialist play, we were essentially a lure to get kids into the toy department. Never mind: it made the company nearly five hundred dollars.

∼

A weird bug jumped into my mind, and I proposed that we do Beckett's *Endgame*. I had never directed anything other than classroom work, but there was something in *Endgame* that was profoundly tied to my inner experience, and I wanted to work with Conrad—he was a wonderful Clov, so abrasive and so funny. That play is a sardonic dark look at desolation, my persistent buddy:

"*What's it like?*"
"*Gray. (pause) Gray! (pause) GRRAY!!!*"
"*Gray! Did I hear you say gray?*"
"*Light black.*"

Its bleakness touched me deeply, and I needed to stage it. Back in my collapsing time at Northwestern, one thing that helped me avoid annihilation was reading Camus' *The Myth of Sisyphus* and finding strength in his quiet fuck-you to the gods. It didn't relieve him of his burden, but it made him the master of it. Beckett did that for me. I already knew *Godot*, and *Endgame* was even closer to the edge. I could hear Conrad's voice as Clov, the crippled servant who can't sit down, and another actor had the autocratic temperament of Hamm, the blind tyrant who can't stand up. It went up, it went well, I'm glad I did it, and I never directed again.

∼

Thanks to the Arts Board grant, we could look at potential spaces with the assurance that when one was right, we could grab it. We saw everything from an empty A&P to a strange collection of spaces in a fire-trap, but nothing was right. Then lo and behold, in mid-December we found our theatre: 1247 Water Street, a three-story building snuggled up to an elevated freeway ramp. It had been a hotel, then most recently a toy train factory, and now it was a dirt-and-grease-laden promise of possibilities. It featured a potential performance area—eighteen feet wide, sixty-six feet deep, with a high ceiling—plus ample support space. The owner offered a lease we could afford; we signed and celebrated.

Meantime, UWM's Extension Division had approached us to teach fourteen weeks of puppetry classes starting mid-January and we accepted. I didn't enjoy teaching puppetry, but we needed money any way we could get it, and I did appreciate the irony of being courted by the entity that had kicked us out.

We got the keys to the newly-dubbed Water Street Theatre on New Year's Day, and along with the group I plunged into a month of scraping off layers of grease, hauling out trash, scrubbing and mopping. January was exhausting, but by the beginning of February we'd started to paint and took the risk of scheduling an opening performance of *Alice* for March 3rd.

I was panicked. If an audience actually came, there was nothing for them to sit on. By chance, the same rock musician who'd gotten us the ill-fated Summerfest gig discovered that the mass of wooden folding chairs the mob had later trashed were stored in a warehouse. We could pick through the hundreds or thousands and take anything that was usable for a quarter a chair. That fateful day of facing the mob proved to be our salvation.

Some friends of the theatre threw a fundraising party dubbed "Blue Jeans and Champagne." Champagne was the aspiration, blue jeans the reality. Our tickets had never been more than $1.50. Now there was a lease, utility bills, and a plan to start paying $50 a week to six actors beginning in the spring. Bless the champagne crowd: they brought friends and put money in the hat.

New Life

March 3rd was a grand revival of *Alice*; Theatre X now had its own 99-seat theatre, and every seat was filled. The first night was announced as a benefit, and audience members were encouraged to give whatever they could. After the show, I chatted with a nice doctor who said he wouldn't give money, but he would donate his services to any of our company's women who needed them. He was an ob-gyn.

In our long desire for a child, a string of doctors had advised me that my works were in order, that all I had to do was kick back and stop doing so much stuff. The multiverse knew better. As soon as *Endgame* opened, we'd begun reviving *Alice* for our grand opening, while scraping and scrubbing and painting to make the new space habitable. I was frazzled, exhausted, and stretched to the limit.

The next day we had a matinee and evening show, then we had Sunday free. We celebrated by going to see a movie: *Klute*. I'd always had a mad crush on Donald Sutherland; seeing that film raised my erotic temperature, and our lovemaking that night was epic. That's when I got pregnant. Nine months later I redeemed the doctor's pledge and thanked him profusely.

I had accepted that our new path in theatre was at odds with parenthood and made peace with that. When we had made the final declaration of commitment to this journey, claiming our own performing space, there was no going back. That's when the gates opened. We opened the theatre and I conceived.

It took me a while to know what had happened. Like every female I've known, I kept track of my cycles on a calendar, but on the first missed day I was teaching a puppetry class, the next day *Macbeth* went into rehearsal, and then came the final *Alice*. The next week was two puppetry classes, solid *Macbeth* rehearsals, and five touring gigs. Amid these distractions, my mind started to pay attention to my body, and I got scared. After another week, I called for an appointment with the generous ob-gyn and sweated through the five days before I went to his office. I hadn't said a word to Conrad, and my feelings were all over the map. After years of wanting a baby, there had come a time of letting go, and at last a sense of gratitude. When we had to decide between the academic career and the unknown future, we were free to do it. The two of us were a team and we could survive. And now? I hid my pain that this might make it impossible.

The appointment came, I told Conrad I had to run some errands, and off I went to the doctor's office. He did his exam, took a sample for the lab, then said: "We won't know till the results come back, but I'm pretty sure you're six weeks pregnant."

Time stopped. My frantic brain was overwhelmed by my body's tsunami of joy. I grinned like a lunatic, said "Holy shit!" and went back to the theatre. I put in an afternoon of work with CB in the second-floor office, and when we were leaving for dinner break, I stopped him in the middle of the steep stairs, took a deep breath, and said, "I'm pregnant."

His entire response? "Oh. Good." We went home to dinner.

~

That was weird. He didn't say "Oh God, no!" or let out a groan, and his answer meant acceptance, but I needed more. My own dark feelings had troubled me, then transformed instantly into pure joy. That had been only three hours ago, and I was still wobbly, craving a response. I did get it after a little time had passed. We finally embraced in tears and laughter, doing a mad little stagger in the kitchen, and I knew everything would be fine. Even though I tend to be *allegro furioso* and he is staunchly *andante*, we do make the music work.

~

When did we tell everyone? I have no idea. Life went on as usual. Ten days later we toured *Endgame* to UW-Madison and two weeks after that we opened *Macbeth*. My private knowledge that I was pregnant made the role of Lady Macbeth very personal. In an early scene the Lady says, "I have given suck, and know how tender 'tis to love the babe that milks me," while Macduff says, "He has no children." Now my sense of her loss was knife-sharp.

By mid-May when we toured *Macbeth* to Ann Arbor, we'd told the company. In early June we visited my parents in Cadillac, and on the ferry across Lake Michigan I felt the quickening. God, what a strange sensation! At first I thought it was the lurching ferry. No, it was the lurching baby. So strange, a little goldfish-wiggle: *somebody's in there*. My mother's reaction was cloudy, verging on discomfort, but then I went upstairs, knelt beside my dad's bed, and told him. He was unabashedly joyous, and that was enough to make me happy. It was the last time I saw him. He died June 23rd.

My grief was a long time coming: I was numb. His health had been in a long decline, accelerated by a congestive heart condition. Whenever I'd gone to Cadillac for a visit, my fraught relation with my mother and her overpowering presence made it hard to focus. At the funeral I shriveled. My belly was evident, my clothing was inappropriate, and I hardly knew anybody who was there. A normal daughter would have embraced her normal mother and shared tears and pain, but nothing in our family was normal.

I went home and plunged back into the usual schedule, trying not to think about Michigan. Two weeks later, my mother flew to Los Angeles to stay with her brother for a month, and five days after she got back, we left for five weeks in Europe. As soon as possible after our return, we made a weekend trip to visit, and I hunkered down and tried to let the angry torrents roll off without being either defensive or apologetic. I'd already written a long letter to her and to my brother, so by the time we were all together, I tried to concentrate on making peace. Only a start.

∼

Alice had raised strong interest in puppetry, and I had a hunch that it would be a factor in our future work. When Conrad broached going to the September international puppetry festival in France, I realized he also thought it might be a big deal. He proposed making a short duo piece and performing it at one of the fringe events. I checked with my doctor, who said no problem, and the company said, "Go for it," since the heavy bookings for the grant-supported tour wouldn't kick in until after our return. I booked our plane tickets, found a car-rental agent in Amsterdam (since I wouldn't fit on a scooter), and started making clothes.

CB wrote a short absurdist script, made hand-puppets, and worked with me on making a cassette-tape sound track drawn from sound loops of TV commercials. I tried my best but never got my head wrapped around this piece, what it meant, and how we could rehearse it. Instead I distracted myself with making a wash-and-wear sport jacket for Conrad so he could look dignified at the festival. I joked that the pattern was so complicated that I wouldn't have been surprised to find I'd made a lawnmower. I finished my sewing in London.

When we left Milwaukee, it was 85° and muggy as hell. I was sticky and exhausted from the last-minute tasks, and getting my belly and baggage to O'Hare Airport left me limp and cranky. Boarding the plane took care of that: the big air-conditioned 747 was only about 20% full, and after supper I pulled up armrests and stretched out full length to nap. Anxiety about the unfinished puppets and nagging worries about the cost faded into the delicious collapse of sleep, and by morning London was there for me. After a week-long binge of theatre and Guinness, we took a train and a six-hour ferry ride to Amsterdam and our little rental car.

Trying to rehearse with the puppets was insanely frustrating, with space and focus hard to come by. In London we'd had a room, but now we had a tent and a teeny car. In Hamburg, this came to a boil as we tried to rehearse in a park, and I lost it, cussing and moaning about this project that was infecting every day with its misery. We put our puppets down on the park bench, looked at each other, and breathed. Conrad took the plunge: "Let's just not

New Life

do it." I was so happy I started to cry, hugging him and trying not to get snot on his jacket. My suppressed sobs turned into hiccups, both of us cracked up laughing, and we were as giddy as if we'd won a prize. The park was suddenly beautiful, and the sunshine blessed our mini-revolt. We'd gotten ourselves into a pickle of our own making and at last remembered that we could say "No." A lesson I never forgot.

That evening in Hamburg we saw Kroetz' play *Stallerhof*. The play is simple, brutal, with few words, and the staging was hyper-realistic. Set on a hardscrabble farm, there were hay bales, rough planks, and bright light. Nothing was explained or stylized; these rough-hewn farmers were unshielded and raw in their "is-ness." The retarded daughter gets pregnant by the farmhand, and the mother prepares the only available abortion she knows, a basin of caustic lye soap solution, then orders the girl to strip, and clears the kitchen table. When she turns with the basin in her hands and sees her naked daughter standing there mute, the two look at each other for an eternity, female to female. The mother snaps, "Get your clothes on," and slops the basin's contents onto the floor. The theatrical choices were so starkly simple: let these people be seen, explain nothing. I remembered Charlie Weber's focus: it's what you do, not what you say or what you feel. Here, it was manifest. It still shines in my actor's mind.

We did a responsible job of following up every theatrical contact we'd been given, and people were unfailingly nice. Berlin, Munich, Zurich, Paris—artists who opened their doors and gave us time. In Paris we made an appointment to see Ariane Mnouchkine and got tickets for her staging of *1793* at the Cartoucherie. She was a legend for creating a collective company and producing powerful work. When we came to the Cartoucherie, a huge building that had been a munitions factory, there was nobody visible except the cleaning lady mopping the lobby. The cleaning lady was Mnouchkine. After grousing that her staff hadn't told her of our appointment, she asked us to wait until she had finished. "It's my turn." That struck home to me: this high-powered artist leading a huge ensemble in making significant work was still taking her turn on the menial level. Do what needs doing.

In Berlin we learned a painful lesson. We went again to see *Offending the Audience*. We'd seen it two years ago, were deeply moved, and had scheduled the play on our season for December. It was still a big hit in Berlin—and a disaster. Audiences came in full *Rocky Horror* mode prepared to heckle and chant, and it had become a hollow piece of kitsch. The audience laughed and clapped, but the play itself was a zombie. Speaking afterward to the director, he apologized for what it had become but said he couldn't close it: they needed the money. I recalled this later when *X Com* had become a money-maker performed for college students who drank beer and waited for the silly parts.

The UNIMA festival itself was a puppet version of the Edinburgh Fringe, a wild collection of everything imaginable, from superb to embarrassing, and it was great fun to see it all. When it was over, we stopped in Brussels for three days before catching the plane home, and my indelible memory is of eating *steak au poivre* in a little bistro and sensing how a modest cut of meat can become a ticket to paradise.

∽

In the summer, Conrad had sent for his Stanford transcript and signed up with the Milwaukee Public Schools as a substitute teacher. He registered as a temp, got sent to Harley-Davidson to do inventory, and sold programs at the state fair. I taught acting and puppetry classes in Theatre X's new summer program, an added perk of having a building. It didn't add up to a lot, but it soothed the itch of guilt about paying for Europe again. When we returned in the fall, Conrad started taking a Theatre X salary of $50/week.

Our consensus on salaries was simple: money went where it could make the most difference, to those at the core who could drop some part-time work and put those hours into the theatre. We'd still had savings to draw on, so others had been higher on the list, but our time had come.

    The fall schedule was intense. Our grant had made bookings easier to get, and *X Com* hopped all over Wisconsin in October and November. As my due date grew close, others covered my roles for gigs that were more than an hour away, but I was on stage right down to the wire. One of our key sketches was *Miss Bleep*, and the fact that the robot teacher was very pregnant only made it funnier. I worried that the baby's kicking was visible, but nobody mentioned it.

    I had settled into the gritty routine of office work and was glad when I started drawing my own salary. I'd been doing the work anyway, but now I felt authorized to establish more orderly systems. I needed order. The calendar was marching along to the end of November, and I had to juggle teaching, taking childbirth classes, setting up a diaper service, getting a portable washing machine, and shopping for baby clothes. I had a lot on my mind, including what was happening with my father's will.

    I had to carve out time for a weekend visit to my mother, this time via a local airline, lest I go into labor on the ferryboat. The visit would be only twenty-four hours, and I was mostly successful in keeping it pleasant. The terms of Homer's will were part of the conversation. He had put everything in a living trust for his Mary, stipulating that when she passed, the estate would be divided equally between Chris and me. The lawyers were advising her to sell the southern Illinois farmland, a sizeable parcel Homer had inherited from his dad.

    He had a simple tenant agreement with the family who did the farming: crop costs and sales were split fifty-fifty. They had been good farmers and friends for decades, and had built their own house there. I knew that my dad cared a lot about the people who did the work. Now the Cadillac lawyers were muddying the waters, urging how much simpler it would be to put the farm on the market. I tried my best to get everybody to honor my father's wishes, stressing that before he died he asked if I'd be willing to take the financial reins, writing checks and monitoring crop sales. It took six months of steady lobbying, but by the end of the probate year the farm remained in the trust.

I wrote the checks and kept the partnership records through 1984, when my mother died. When my brother and I met with the lawyers, I made a proposal. Instead of liquidating the assets and splitting the cash between us, I said that I wanted nothing but the farm, and Chris should get everything else. Yes, I was aware that he would come out with a lot more, and that was OK with me. They thought I was nuts, but I had Conrad's backing and I stood firm. My farm friends are still my friends, and they still live on their land.

∽

Except for bumping into the kitchen sink and not being able to pick up stuff from the floor, I was carrying high and well. I took Lamaze classes and visited my chosen hospital, one where I could have the baby in the room with me. I really wanted to nurse and mail-ordered some very strange underwear that theoretically would enable me to save leaked milk for "relief bottles." The baby's favorite actions alternated between pushing so hard against my sternum that it actually bent upward, and then turning the other way and kicking me in the bladder. I only gained 18 pounds, of which 8 lb. 12 oz. was all baby. He proved to be big, 21 inches, and had inherited CB's grand leonine skull. Lamaze wasn't going to help a lot.

Conrad was a strong, loving labor coach, but after thirty-three hours, we were both exhausted and scared. When it was discovered that the doc had never done pelvic measurements, I was sent to X-ray. They conferred, then prepped me for a Caesarian. I had been so sure I was going to have a glorious natural delivery, and the old feeling of failure took hold. It wasn't until the next day, when I got to touch and hold this amazing creature, that I knew without question that I had done well. So strange, to look at that sturdy little foot and think, "Oh, that's what was kicking!" At first it was tricky getting the milk going, since nobody had told me how much water "a lot of water" was, but once the night nurse straightened me out, the milk came in big-time. I'd had CB bring me our cassette player and some music to keep me sane, and I found that that the baby nursed in time to Mozart.

From earliest childhood I'd felt like an other, not really a human being. All the IQ tests and awards and prizes proved me to be a high-quality specimen of whatever I was, but there was no belonging. When I found my lifemate, we bonded completely, but as a duo we were hardly in the mainstream. Now, nursing our son, I was a human woman from hair to toenails, and to top it off, I was a successful mammal. Basics are powerful.

We went home, Conrad and Linda and Eli, and began to discover the shape of our new life together. Our baby carriage was in two parts, a little padded box atop the wheel unit, and that box was pretty much like what Eli had slept in by my hospital bed. When he woke in the night, all I had to do was roll over, pick him up, and nestle him to my breast. Tired as I was, I trusted myself to stay awake until he was back in his bed. Nipples are not equipped with meters, and my only way to know if I had enough milk was how fast he grew. Two pounds in the first month, two and a half the next: he was on his way. The first bath with a slippery baby was an occasion for panic, but everything went well. We all learned fast.

∼

This was the first Theatre X baby, and everyone came to visit. Conrad's mom flew out on the twelfth day, and her joy was luminous. As soon as she left, my mother came, and I managed to ignore how disgusted she was with the process of nursing. Then the all-clear sounded, and *Offending the Audience* opened, returning me to my world of work. I wasn't in the cast, of course, but I was part of what was going on, and very shortly I was back performing *X Com*. I had a little navy-blue corduroy front-pack called a Snugli and could take Eli everywhere, though the bitter Milwaukee winter was a challenge. A normal coat wouldn't cover both me and the baby, so I made myself a double-thick fleece poncho that opened down the front and could wrap around us both. It was also a great hideaway for nursing. I called it "The Woolly" and for years it was my favorite outer garment, with or without baby.

The Vietnam War was still a long-running hit, and Theatre X was asked to do a benefit for a draft-counseling center. In the final piece, I sat center stage in a chair, the six-week-old Eli snuggled in my arms. The group sang "Happy Birthday" quietly in the background as gifts were brought for the baby on each repetition, one by one: baby clothes, older toys, teen stuff, a diploma, a draft notice, and at last a cardboard box. The baby was nestled into the box, a flag was draped over it, and the song ended. People were shocked and chilled. Even I, knowing what would happen, had to work hard to suppress the tears. We could have done the piece with a big plastic baby doll, but only the breath-taking presence of a real life could express what we felt. It's so easy to ignore the fact that every death begins with a birth.

A few weeks later we had a performance at Waupun State Prison, a men's maximum security institution. A baby was deemed contraband, so a sitter kept him in the visitor's lobby while we performed for a very appreciative captive audience surrounded by machine guns. Later that month we also performed at Taycheedah, the women's prison, where he was definitely not contraband. After the performance, as we talked informally with the women, he was the star, passed from embrace to embrace. In the midst of all the cuddling and cooing, I nearly burst into tears. Most of these women were mothers, and for these few minutes, he was their child.

Performing was different for me now. Until Eli was four months old, I was only in *X Com* and the shows were either in Milwaukee or a short drive away. I had to trust that he was going to be safe with a babysitter during a performance, and things usually went well. The only scare we had didn't involve child care. We had a daytime school workshop and I was heading toward the building with the baby in the Snugli. Kids were throwing a baseball, and suddenly there was a thunk right under my chin. After a moment, Eli started to howl, and to my horror I realized he'd been hit in the head. I was terrified. We ran into the school, located the teacher in charge of the event, who agreed that we needed to get medical help. Protocol was protocol, and I was not permitted to ride in the ambulance with my baby. After a ghastly wait in the hospital, we received him back with a verdict: "No problem."

∼

The baseball episode was traumatic, and I am stupefied that I'd forgotten it. What brought it back was a review of our check register from that year (yes, I keep all that stuff) and finding an entry for Milwaukee Children's Hospital, noted as *Eli accident*. After a blip of non-comprehension, it came blaring back. I wrote a paragraph, then told Conrad what I'd dug up and asked him what he remembered. He didn't recall anything about an ambulance and thought it wasn't with Theatre X, since there were only the two of us there. Well, yes, but that check is from April 1973, and Eli was clearly an infant. Memory is amazing. We had both been shaken to the core, but forty-eight years later, each of us had a different recollection, and both had put it in the closet of the past.

∼

The Wisconsin Arts Council had given grants to Theatre X, but now we were personally the recipients of a commission. The tiny town of Mineral Point had an energetic community theatre that wanted to produce a musical about their local history. The idea was quirky and more than a little daunting, but our research was intriguing. Southwestern Wisconsin had its first white settlers in 1827, and shortly thereafter rich lead deposits were found. Mining became a boom, more sophisticated techniques arrived with a wave of experienced miners from Cornwall, and by 1845 half the town had Cornish ancestry. Then the Gold Rush happened and people went west. Today, the town is half the size of its boom years.

I was fascinated by this story of people leaving everything to find a better living across the ocean, forming a community, then being abandoned by their grown children for a new adventure. We took a reconnaissance trip and fell in love with Mineral Point. Everybody knew everybody's little kids, and there was no way to get lost. Many of the original stone houses are still occupied, Cornish pasties and figgyhobbin can be found on menus, and there is strong appreciation of their heritage. Music started singing in my mind, the process was set in motion, and a little over a year later, July of 1974, Shakerag Players opened *Songs of Passersby*.

Writing a musical was a gig on the side. Theatre X created *Queenside* and *Comedying*, one being three surreal one-acts, the other being a script CB wrote based on old *commedia dell'arte* plots and extensive cast improvisations. I performed in both. *Queenside* had its first performances in a tent at Summerfest, a less hazardous setting than our ill-fated rock concert, though we had to suspend one performance temporarily as a parade of elephants passed the tent. One playlet featured *Macbeth*'s three witches in modern dress crooning and dancing in a laundromat. I remember putting on my low-cut summer dress, checking myself in the mirror, and wailing, "Eli just ate my cleavage!" People liked it anyway.

Comedying, with its clowning, magic spells, and cross-dressed lovers befuddled by their attraction was a hit with our regular audiences. At the curtain call, a big trash can filled with ice and bottles of beer got dragged onstage for free sharing. The baby was consuming a lot of milk, and I was delighted to be able to down a beer each night without gaining weight.

That summer we all went to the far northwestern corner of Wisconsin for a two-week residency at a college in Ashland. It was memorable: hard work and a lot of fun. One day we were hosted by a family whose home included an old-fashioned Finnish cedar sauna and a little lake to jump into afterward. Another day we all took a picnic to Copper Falls. We had a rocky cascade and large river pool to ourselves, stripped bare as fish, and spent the day in a green watery paradise. It was a new bliss, being a naked nursing mother on a big sunny rock in the river, among our whole ensemble of wet, splashing artists.

It started to go downhill from there.

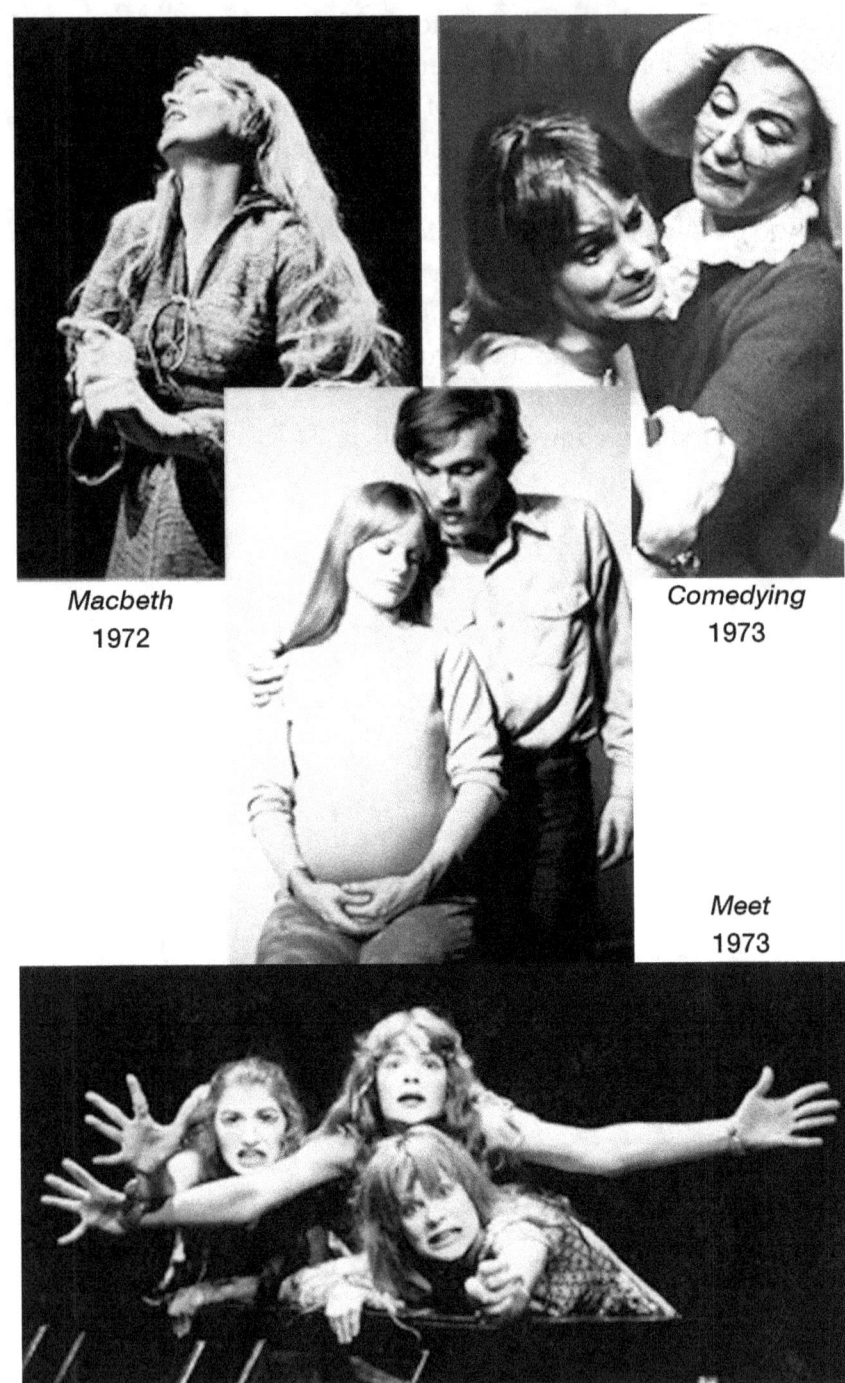

Macbeth
1972

Comedying
1973

Meet
1973

18.

Sink or Swim

We entered a push-pull between the dynamic core of our work and the iron pinch of money. As a twosome, we were grabbing whatever paying gigs we could get, from writing a historical musical to selling programs at the state fair. Theatre X finally had a home where we could make and present our work, and that meant rent, utilities, insurance, and an annual theatre license, plus the small salaries we'd begun to pay. We had a growing audience, but tickets at a top of $2 weren't going to pay the bills. We needed touring gigs, a lot of them. We had a grant that could boost our touring, and we paid to showcase at some college booking conferences and went after block bookings. We got what we asked for, and starting in the fall of '73 we spent a lot of time on the road, touring our ever-expanding repertory of *X Com* pieces.

It was hard to find time and focus to create new work. *Comedying* had been our last full-length original creation. The next thing we did was nominally Theatre X, but mostly the two of us, a commission from a Wisconsin state agency to take over a project that was in trouble: a stage documentary developed with five ex-felons, raising issues of community-based rehabilitation. The original director was good at grant-writing but couldn't get traction on the human stories that were the core of what, in our hands, became *Halfway to Somewhere*. For a couple of months the Water Street Theatre housed ongoing improvisations and rehearsals while fending off an ex-boyfriend of one of the women involved. With them, we created a strong piece, and it went on to perform in nearly a hundred communities. It was a bizarre contrast to the children's play the theatre was running in December, but contrasts, for us, were a way of life.

Our children's pieces were not our prime bandwidth, but we created two shows in December, getting good box office for *Mugnog* (a German play by the Leftist theatre GRIPS) and a repeated sponsorship from Gimbels for *Mr. Punch*. In January of 1974, the grant-supported touring kicked in, and we got onto a non-stop merry-go-round of playing our standard show. *Comedying* and *Queenside* were still in the repertory, but only for local performance.

A couple of years ago we'd seen *Terminal*, an ensemble production by the Open Theatre, and it was a kick in the gut. It was so much the kind of theatre we wanted to be doing, and it was exciting to see others tuned into that wave-length. We had made substantial work—*Offending the Audience, Comedying, Endgame, Macbeth, Alice*—but none of it was practical for long-haul touring. We toured *X Com* heavily because it was sellable, needed only lighting for visibility, and it made us respectable money. We spent most of January, February, and March on the road, thirty-one shows in seven states, with seven actors and a little kid crammed into a van, sleeping in college dorm rooms, eating fast food.

We'd begun our ensemble experience on a high of intense connection with our audiences. Now, our performances weren't fresh, not after sketchy sleep in dorm bunks and a day's drive. Circumstances were sometimes weird. On one campus we had a tiny audience; the booker could get the block price for that date, but they were on spring break.

Sink or Swim

I'd loved being on the road, but not the way it was happening now. Our binding force of creative work was on hold, our schedule shoved us from town to town without seeing much other than college campuses and strip malls, and our tempers were getting frayed from being cooped up. I was so glad when April Fool's Day came around and we were back home, revved up with making a new, darker *X Communication*. Aside from the Gimbels puppet show, it was our first new original piece in a year, and we had a good place to play it.

We'd booked it at The Body Politic on Chicago's Near North Side, where we'd scored with *Comedying*—finally, a chance to take risks on new work. The first act involved our tried-and-true pieces, and the second act was new, including the nightmarish *Pinky the Clown* and *Slappers*. *Pinky* was a demonic version of a TV kids' clown going psycho, counseling kids in classic marketing terms how to kill their families, while *Slappers* pitted two diplomats standing toe-to-toe exchanging a litany of epithets punctuated by real slaps to the chops. It was strong confrontational stuff.

Still, we were nagged by chronic frustrations. As a duo, we felt we had heavy responsibilities, but our communal ideal rejected authority except when pushed to the wall. Our shaky grasp of consensus made decisions a prolonged, frustrating process. We had a two-level company: the seven-person paid core who made the touring bucks that supported it all, and those whose commitments made them occasional performers near home. Trying to blend these in meetings was insane. How could we pay salaries if we didn't tour, and how could we create new work when constantly on the road?

For the two of us, parenthood had brought new obligations, and more were coming. During the run of the new *X Com* in Chicago, I got the stomach flu. After a night spent in the bathroom, the vomiting and diarrhea quit by morning, and I assumed I'd be OK for the afternoon show. It was hot as hell. In the midst of a piece, I started seeing gold sparkles and hearing a buzz, and the next thing I knew I was flat on the floor. I was carried back to a cot in the dressing room, the cast went into a huddle and redistributed roles, and the show went on. Later, I heard that an audience member asked, "Is she pregnant?" I was. I just didn't know it.

On the eastern tour I had figured it would be a good time to start weaning Eli, since the stress was affecting my milk supply. As long as I was nursing I wasn't having cycles, and we wanted another baby. I didn't think we had a lot of time to waste, since it took nine years to get the first. Surprise: it took about five minutes. Somewhere in West Virginia, the weaning had got far enough and I was pregnant again. It was as if Eli dialed the phone and his sister answered. She was due in December.

A new jolt happened as we were preparing for our Body Politic run, and like the pregnancy, it didn't let up. We needed a disturbing clown mask for *Pinky*. Conrad was making it with celastic, a plastic-infused fabric that could be softened with acetone, sculpted into shape and dried to a rigid lightweight form. After years of working with silk-screens and making puppets with plastic wood, we knew the hazards of acetone. Rubber gloves and ample ventilation were required for safe handling, but CB hadn't been careful enough. Mid-rehearsal he began to hallucinate and went into a frantic seizure, suddenly upending chairs, running into walls, roaring with laughter. We were astonished and terrified.

He was impossible to restrain: at last he went bounding down the steep stairs to the street and fell flat in a puddle of mud. He finally got pinned down, wrestled into a car, and off we went to the nearest hospital's ER. I mentioned the possibility of acetone poisoning, and they drew blood from his femoral artery to test for dissolved gases. In the process, gouts of blood sprayed over the white cloth curtains of the cubicle. Seeing that from the other side was a nightmare, and hearing him cursing and shouting made it worse. This was not the man I knew.

Eventually the lab said, "Nope, no toxins." The tired, frustrated physician said, "You're an actor, so you're acting out. Go home." Most likely, he thought it was drugs. My friend Tim bedded us down on the floor in his little apartment, keeping watch in case Conrad got dangerous. Eli had been running a fever for a couple of days, so I had a sleepless night checking the two of them. In the morning Conrad was tired but coherent, and the pediatrician diagnosed Eli with pneumonia that could be kicked with antibiotics. For the moment, we were going to be OK.

I assumed that the acetone had been the problem, but one morning I couldn't wake him for breakfast. He just lay there with incomprehensible mumbles and a goofy smile. When I put my head close, I smelled acetone on his breath. Impossible: he hadn't been working with it this time. Then my old days of reading medical texts kicked in, and the word *ketosis* popped into my mind. When the body has low blood sugar and burns fat instead, one symptom is acetone on the breath. I ran to the kitchen, stirred some honey into orange juice, and carefully dribbled it into his mouth. I managed to avoid choking him and eventually got enough of it down him to bring him around. It was terrifying. I was pregnant and caring for a toddler, and my man's body was messing with his mind. But right now there was work to do.

Three weeks after we opened at The Body Politic, we were enjoying a warm sunny walk before performing, and two things happened: Eli started to wheeze badly and Conrad was seeing people's faces covered with feathers. Columbus Hospital was nearby, and Eli got a shot that cleared up an asthma attack, but I didn't know about the feathers till later. Eventually I raised enough hell with his doctors to start metabolic testing that revealed a serious problem of too little blood sugar. The first diagnosis? "Chronic. Learn to live with it." One doc had a hunch, though, and referred us to a specialist. It would be nearly a year until the drastic surgery that removed a pancreatic tumor. One helluva year.

Elizabeth: One of Many

∼

I was shaken by the chain of events. The big tour ended April 1st, Conrad's first hypoglycemic seizure was May 1st, my pregnancy test was positive on June 7th, and the musical we'd worked on for a year would open in Mineral Point on July 5th.

It was a huge project with a large cast and a little amateur orchestra. In the three weeks before it opened, I was still wrestling with the arrangements, and we had to put a lock on the back room so I could hunker down at the piano and leave the toddler with CB. I loved the characters, I loved the plot, and Conrad's lyrics practically dictated their own tunes, but orchestration was still my weak point. I survived, and it opened well. Theatre X had a good run in Chicago, closed on June 17, and went on summer break. The question was, "Now what?"

Conrad and I sat down for a serious talk about our future. We needed a stable income to support two kids. Our major skills were in creating and performing original theatre, we loved being on the road, and we loved Theatre X, but that future looked chaotic and bleak. Touring had been the major source of income, but the intense spring tour had rankled the actors and killed our joy. The two of us had major administrative responsibility, but group decision-making was always turbulent, and we couldn't make our own choices. The answer was obvious and painful: we had to leave and start over. I think we both wept; I know I did.

We announced it smack in the middle of the run at The Body Politic. I felt in my gut that it was the choice we had to make, but my heart told me we were doing it badly. When I feel I'm wrong I get defensive: that wasn't helpful. When CB is in a bind, he becomes hyper-rational: that wasn't helpful either. We arrived at the decision without consulting our friends, then struggled through the run with the people we loved and were leaving. Conrad wrote a letter detailing our reasons, then we started the process of incorporating our new two-person company and creating our own duo show.

Sink or Swim

It all happened so fast, and yet it felt like our slow-motion blow-out on the autobahn. We ripped out our savings, bought a Dodge Maxivan for touring, and looked for an apartment in Chicago to avoid local competition with Theatre X. In the frenzy of setting this up and the pain of broken relationships, there was still a shining bubble of elation. We were making our own choices, and we two would be responsible for the outcome, sink or swim.

We swam.

∼

Nearly fifty years between then and now—quite a swim. In my wake were the child prodigy, the trapped teen, the delusional college dropout, and the bride. I'd become more or less coherent, a good team worker toward Conrad's career. Abruptly jumping ship from that career, I held my breath and took the leap. Now I was a mother and a partner in our new expedition, dog-paddling toward the vision of our own independent theatre.

I had become all these things without ever having a clear sense of my core identity, but I did discover one thing: I existed. I was real. The years of Theatre X were sweat and laughter, triumph and disappointment, close friendships and abrasive clashes, and when the time came to leave, the grief was sharp and deep. Strangely, so was the gratitude. Those years helped make me real. When I was on stage, my connection with the audience was close and unfiltered. I'd learned a lot of craft in the Stanford years, and this theatre put it into new service. It had purpose, and so did I.

Memoirs typically focus on a crisis or a turning point—achieving fame or overcoming a trauma, finding an authentic self or a mission. For me, I've had so many turning points and new-found challenges that I could almost write a memoir for each of my "seven sisters." One expects that after many changes, life would be more predictable, and that hasn't happened yet.

During my first day of life in 1940 my mother named me Elizabeth. That name was hidden for 38 years in a Brooklyn adoption file, and I became officially Linda Ellin Davison. In 1961 a terrified young Unitarian minister performing his very first wedding ceremony decreed that I was now a wife: Mrs. Conrad Bishop, Linda D. Bishop. In 1978 a friend searched for my name in the 1940 Brooklyn birth registry and called me: "Your name is Elizabeth Fuller." In 1996 I hired a lawyer and changed my name—56 years to complete the circle. It took all those years for me to become Elizabeth Fuller, and she's still evolving.

In the years since 1974? The two of us made good work and it prospered. Theatre X survived and soon gained international respect; we went back for a few joint projects and healed our bruises. Our path had lots of potholes, hairpin turns, and changes, changes, changes. We spent decades on the road, raising the kids in the back of the Dodge van, taking our work into every nook and cranny of society. Like Theatre X, we played for churches, prisons, colleges, high schools, community centers, arts fairs—you name it—and could still rationalize doing a show in a department store.

But the heart of our work always embraced the connection with our audiences and with one another, what we could give and the responses that kept us going. One of our pieces played hundreds of times over the years and changed many lives. In essence, we are storytellers, and we believe that humanity's stories matter.

We're still swimming.

∼